Rob Carless

Foreword by Brian Little

UNDER THE
FLOODLIGHTS

The Story of the English Football League Cup
1960–2024

First published by Pitch Publishing, 2024

Pitch Publishing
9 Donnington Park,
85 Birdham Road,
Chichester,
West Sussex,
PO20 7AJ
www.pitchpublishing.co.uk
info@pitchpublishing.co.uk

ISBN 978 1 80150 740 0

Typesetting and origination by Pitch Publishing
Printed and bound in India by Thomson Press

Contents

This book is dedicated to Bethany and Emily.

I love you both so much and I am in awe of you.

Dad

x

Foreword by Brian Little

Former Leicester City and
Aston Villa manager

When I look back at my career, my participation in the League Cup will be as high as it can be. There are not many who have won it as a player and as a manager, and I am extremely proud to be in illustrious company such as Martin O'Neill (Nottingham Forest and Leicester City) and Tony Book (Manchester City). Furthermore, I have scored the winning goal in one of the finals as well. Not bad for a one-club man!

I could not shake a stick between the fantastic feelings I experienced scoring the winning goal for Aston Villa in that mammoth final of 1977 and managing the club in 1996.

It is a massive trophy to win for the players and the fans alike – and, of course, offers a place in Europe.

I cannot believe it is turning 65 next season. The time for the trophy has just flown; I can remember its early days.

There are times when its stock has been low, but it has always bounced back and the story continues, which can only be a great thing for English football. Just look at the last decade where the likes of Birmingham City,

Cardiff City, Swansea City, Bradford City, Sunderland and Southampton have all been to the finals as well as the so-called 'elite' clubs in England. Or, in other words, the 'usual suspects'.

Here is to the next 65 years.

Inception

The English Football League Cup comes from the strangest of lands.

Originally conceived as part of a new structure to change the number of teams and leagues in England, the competition was always destined to take its place on the 'Bronze' podium. It has never portrayed itself as anything different and it certainly knows its place in the hierarchy of elite trophy-winning in England. It has always known it cannot compete with the Premier League (previously the First Division) or FA Cup; it is, and always has been, the poor relation in terms of prestige and commercial aspects – and, indeed, history.

The League Cup is comfortable in its standing and knows where it belongs. The golden age of football being shown live on terrestrial TV has favoured the FA Cup greatly over the years. The 1970s and the 1980s saw both ITV and BBC show the FA Cup Final live and the build-up to it was hours before on both channels. However, the League Cup Final was generally shown in highlight form for many years.

It also suffers with its timing in the football calendar; it is generally played the last week of February or the first week in March. It does not hold the season's curtain closer like the FA Cup has generally done. After all, May is the month of winners.

Yet, it is important and strong at the same time.

It wasn't always the case as was witnessed in the early part of the 1960s. It took time for it to grow and, based on this, it is no different to any new competition in its genesis.

Did the first World Cup in 1930 or the subsequent ones have the same impact Qatar in 2022 did, or the ones before it? Of course, it didn't. Notwithstanding the issues of the day such as intercontinental travel and war, it simply did not catch the imagination of the football fan.

As was the case with the European Championship (originally known as European Nations' Cup). It made its debut in 1960. The same year that we had the inaugural League Cup, incidentally.

For the first 16 years, the finals only consisted of four countries. In 1980, this was doubled to eight, and it doubled again in 1996. It wasn't of interest to those countries that did not qualify in the early years of the competition. England qualified for the finals for the first time in 1968 alongside Italy, Yugoslavia and the Soviet Union. Italy were paired with the Soviet Union and England with Yugoslavia, who beat the Three Lions 1-0, and amazingly Italy won their game on a coin toss after a goalless draw, and extra time. England faced the Soviet Union in the third-place play-off and won the game 2-0. Italy ended up as champions, beating Yugoslavia 2-0 in a replay in the Stadio Olimpico in Rome. The original match had seen both countries square at 1-1 after extra time. No coin toss on that one!

That all happened just two years after England had been crowned world champions in 1966. There is a simple pub quiz question that perhaps highlights just how much interest new competitions do not capture the public's imagination in their infancy and the football world in general. I would wager that if a quiz host posed the question, 'Who did England beat in the 1966 World Cup Final?' I'd bet 99.9 per cent of the contestants would put down West Germany and the scribe would be immediate.

Now, if the said quiz host had read out the following, 'Who did England beat in the third play-off in the 1968 European Championship?', there would be a significant drop in the percentage of correct answers being the Soviet Union or at the very least long contemplation, in which the quiz host would be firmly asking for the paper to be handed in for marking.

There are many other examples but highlighting both the issues faced by the World Cup and the European Championship at the start puts the League Cup in fine company.

The League Cup is also a competition that has allowed lower league clubs to prosper, with all roads leading to the final. To date, the FA Cup Final has not featured a team from the lower two leagues in England. However, it is prudent to note that Tottenham Hotspur won the competition as a non-league team in 1901.

The giant-killing aspect of the FA Cup is generally done in the rounds leading up to the quarter-finals and semi-finals. However, that is not the case with the League Cup. It has spawned many cup upsets leading to the finals, but some teams have gone all the way. Two teams from the lowest tier in professional football have reached the final – and not just in the early days. While Rochdale were on the receiving end of a two-legged final defeat against Norwich City (they were playing in the Second Division themselves) in the 1961/62 season, Bradford City had earned the right to a final berth in 2012/13 before being beaten comprehensively by Swansea City.

There have been three teams who have represented the third tier in the final as well. Swindon Town and Queens Park Rangers were victorious against top-tier opposition in the form of Arsenal and West Bromwich Albion respectively.

Tottenham Hotspur broke the Third Division hearts of Aston Villa in the 1970/71 season to stop the momentum of Goliath against the David of top-flight football.

It has hosted all-Second Division finals as well, featuring teams from the top flight that were both relegated at the end of the season. It is the most unpredictable of cup competitions and by virtue of this, it sets it apart and is unique.

This book features chapters on all finals in the 20th and 21st centuries (up to and including 2024) and takes a look at how the competition was threatened at the start of the new millennium.

The League Cup has spawned the unlikeliest of heroes on centre stage in front of 100,000 fans at Wembley, when normally it was in front of a couple of thousand where no TV cameras were present in order to capture that moment for prosperity and not just painted from memory.

It has been sponsored by a drink you put into tea, coffee, shakes and breakfast cereals, and by fizzy and energy drinks – and something that little bit stronger. It's been sponsored by betting companies and the Pools, notwithstanding electrical retailers.

It has stood on its own as well.

There is a saying that goes: 'Unless your team dines on the very top tables of football, then football for the rest is one per cent joy and 99 per cent sorrow and disappointment.' After all, it is the hope that destroys, but it's that one per cent we remember. It may be a once-in-a-lifetime feeling, but it is felt nonetheless.

In all, 23 teams have experienced the feeling of winning the League Cup in the 64 years of the competition. Some have won it just once and some have won it significantly more.

The League Cup has provided its fair share of one per cent adulation and reverence to the teams with less expectation, and also continued success with those who possess more of it.

From the players, managers and the supporters, this is the story of the League Cup.

* * *

It is widely accepted in England's rich football history that the very first match to be played under a form of floodlighting was held at Bramall Lane in Sheffield on 14 October 1878. It was an exhibition match between 'The Blues' and 'The Reds', made up of the finest players from Sheffield's Football Association at the time. The advert for the game stated that electric lights were to be used for the illumination of the ground and would be equal to using 2,000 standard candles. The admission was sixpence. Around 12,000 people paid to watch this match under the lights, but the attendance was much higher as a result of people sneaking into the ground. *The Independent* reported, 'The roads to Bramall Lane were completely besieged,' and further added, 'There seemed no end to the ever-coming stream.' The paper went on to say that the experiment had been a success, 'Everybody seemed highly pleased with the result of the experiment, the light being most brilliant and effective.'

The Times offered an alternative view, especially regarding matters on the pitch, 'The brilliance of the light dazzled the players and sometimes caused strange blunders.'

Ten years after this event, the Football League was formed, but it took several decades before the idea of introducing floodlit matches was to become commonplace, other than the odd friendly or exhibition. There were multiple factors that were attributable to this, including First and Second World Wars, the cost and safety aspects, and the Football League rejecting the idea of midweek matches as it kept working men away from the family home.

It wasn't until the 1930s that some clubs started to question this decision not to allow lighting into the stadium architecture. Arsenal had noted that lighting was being used in parts of Europe, and indeed sports like greyhound racing had introduced track lighting, which added to the excitement.

Football was in danger of being left behind.

However, it wasn't until the 1950s that the Football League started to allow lighting to be used in competitive matches, especially in the early formation of various European ties. These games were held midweek, and there was now an opportunity for English teams to play each other during those times in the league, and the opportunity for cup matches to be played midweek, whereas FA Cup fixtures were played mostly on a Saturday at 3pm. That was not going to change and therefore it was ripe for a new competition to be created.

The original idea for a new competition was initially put forward by Stanley Rous. He had played football as a goalkeeper in the lower leagues before turning his attention to becoming a referee. The highlight of his second career was taking charge of the 1934 FA Cup Final between Manchester City and Portsmouth. Four years later he had rewritten 'The Laws of the Game' to make it easier to understand, and his work was greeted positively by the Football Association and overseas. Rous was to subsequently serve the Football Association, UEFA and also FIFA (where he became president) with distinction for many years and was well respected in the game.

However, the actual implementation was carried out by the Football League secretary at the time, Alan Hardaker. Hardaker had accepted the post in 1951 after the retirement of his predecessor, Fred Haworth. It took a further five years before it became official as it appeared that Haworth was reluctant to actually take the plunge and retire. Hardaker took on junior roles on less pay as he played the waiting game. In his autobiography, Hardaker felt that he had been 'badly let down' by the Football League president, Arthur Drewry, at the time. Nonetheless, Hardaker kept his eyes firmly on the prize and took it upon himself to read and study every archived document relating to the Football League since 1888, therefore making himself absolutely indispensable when he did officially become secretary.

He was soon to get down to business.

In 1957, Hardaker was instrumental in what was famously known as 'The Pattern of Football'. The proposal put forward was in two parts. Firstly, it looked at the league structure. Hardaker proposed that the 92 clubs, spread over four divisions in the Football League, become 100 clubs across five divisions. The rationale behind this was to reduce the number of weeks in the football season, allowing for less fixture congestion.

The proposal was defeated after a vote by the member clubs. However, the second part was to introduce a new cup competition called the Football League Cup. With the advent of floodlights, this meant that ties could be accommodated in midweek. This part of the proposal was not defeated by the member clubs, except for a small number. The press also frequently poured scorn over the proposal – Hardaker was not popular on Fleet Street.

Hardaker had taken the idea originally from Stanley Rous and made some changes. Rous had originally suggested that teams knocked out in the early stages of the FA Cup enter the new competition. Hardaker was never shy of telling people that the original idea was from Rous, but firmly believed that it should be a complete standalone competition from the FA Cup and therefore it was accepted that way. Hardaker soon coined a phrase that perfectly described why it needed to be standalone, and the differences between them both: 'The FA Cup is football's Ascot; the League Cup its equivalent of Derby Day at Epsom.'

The Football League Cup was born, and associated clubs competed for this new trophy at the start of the 1960/61 season.

It was time to let the runners and the riders out of their paddocks.

1

The 1960s

Season 1960/61

The Final

First leg: 22 August 1961
Rotherham United 2 (Webster, Kirkman) Aston Villa 0
Millmoor, Rotherham
Attendance: 12,226
Referee: K.A. Collinge

Second leg: 5 September 1961
Aston Villa 3 (O'Neill, Burrows, McParland) Rotherham
United 0 (after extra time)
Villa Park, Birmingham
Attendance: 31,201
Referee: C.W. Kingston
Aston Villa won 3-2 on aggregate

The format for the inaugural Football League Cup from the first round to the quarter-finals was a knockout tournament with replays if there was a stalemate and further ones until there was an actual winner. The semi-finals and the final were two-legged affairs with clubs playing each other home and away. The very first League Cup ties took place on Monday,

26 September 1960 when Second Division Bristol Rovers beat First Division Fulham 2-1 in front of over 20,000 supporters and West Ham United giving back parity to the First Division teams when they defeated second-tier Charlton Athletic 3-1. The very first scorer in the competition was Fulham's centre-forward Maurice Cook, who put his team in the lead after just nine minutes.

If the League Cup had begun slowly with just a couple of games in September, then the following month saw the complete opposite with ties coming thick and fast. Not all teams entered the first round but participated from the second round onwards, and the fixture dictators had deemed it necessary to play both the first and second rounds in the same month, and this did not take into consideration any replays.

The biggest shock of the first round occurred at Layer Road, home of Third Division Colchester United, who embarrassed First Division Newcastle United, beating the Magpies convincingly 4-1.

The shocks continued in the second round with Bradford City from the Third Division beating the might of Manchester United 2-1 and Fourth Division Darlington knocking out West Ham 4-1. Aston Villa and Rotherham both entered in the second round.

First Division Villa eased into the third round with a 4-1 victory over Huddersfield Town, a level below the Midlands giants, and Second Division Rotherham beating Leicester City, one division above them, 2-1 away from home.

Rotherham's reward for taking out the Foxes was a third-round home draw against Bristol Rovers.

Villa's route into the fourth round was not as straightforward. Drawn away to First Division rivals Preston North End, the game ended in a thrilling 3-3 draw which could have gone either way. The replay back at Villa Park saw the home team progress 3-1.

As in the second round, Rotherham were drawn away to a First Division club, swapping the Foxes of Leicester with the Trotters from Bolton Wanderers and once again coming away with a victory, this time 2-0. For Aston Villa, it was a similar situation to the third round, once more sharing a six-goal thriller, but this time at home to Plymouth Argyle. The replay was very much 'after the Lord Mayor's Show' with both teams not able to put the ball into the net. The second replay saw Plymouth once again hosting Villa, and this time it was a goal-fest with no fewer than eight scored; five to Villa and three to the home side.

Both teams were drawn at home in the quarter-finals, and both had comfortable victories by the same scoreline of 3-0, Villa against Wrexham and Rotherham over Portsmouth.

The semi-final draw was made in February 1961 after the conclusion of the quarter-finals. Unlike the rounds up to that point, the semi-finals were played over two legs, with each team playing one leg at home. The matches were played in March, April and May 1961. Aston Villa were drawn away to Burnley in the first leg and Rotherham were drawn at home to Third Division

Shrewsbury Town in the other. The first ever League Cup semi-finals had two teams from the top tier and one each from the second and third.

Rotherham had reached the semi-final without having to endure any replays. It had taken Villa three replays to make the stage, and they made it four to reach the final. The first leg at Turf Moor had finished 1-1, and the return leg at Villa Park ended up 2-2. Penalty shoot-outs were a firm thing in the future so it was to be another replay, which once again saw Villa through, winning 2-1 at Old Trafford.

Rotherham had beaten Shrewsbury 3-2 at Millmoor before a 1-1 draw at Gay Meadow, ensuring that the first ever League Cup Final was contested between the Second Division Millers and Aston Villa of the First Division.

However, it did not take place in the 1960/61 season, but at the start of the following one.

The first leg of the final was played on 22 August 1961 at Millmoor, with just over 12,000 in attendance. After a cagey opening half, the game sprung into life in the 51st minute when Barry Webster opened the scoring for the home team, and then the lead was doubled just four minutes later via Alan Kirkman. Rotherham managed to keep Villa at bay for the remaining 35 minutes and took a 2-0 lead into the second leg.

The return leg took place at Villa Park on 5 September with just shy of 31,500 fans in the stadium, and just like at Millmoor, the first half was goalless, putting enormous pressure on the home team who needed to score at least three goals to win the match with potentially just 45 minutes to play.

The Villa terraces were nervous as were the players on the pitch, but on 68 minutes they were calmed somewhat when Alan O'Neill pulled a goal back. A minute later, Harry Burrows converted to level the tie. Villa Park was rocking. There were no more goals in regulation time and so it was to extra time, something that was alien to Rotherham during the campaign in the cup, but certainly not to Villa. Would there be another replay for them? This was answered in the 112th minute when Villa legend Peter McParland put the ball into the net and for the first time in both games in the final, Villa were ahead. It was to be the final goal of the tournament and made Aston Villa the winners of the inaugural Football League Cup. McParland had been the hero for Villa in 1957 when his two goals against Manchester United in the FA Cup Final had been enough to give his side the victory. Now just four years later he was doing the same in the League Cup.

So, what had started on 26 September 1960 had ended almost 12 months later on 5 September 1961, spanning two seasons.

It was chaotic at times. The competition was derided by the press and failed to capture the imagination of football followers all over the country, except for a few matches where attendances were decent.

Stanley Rous's suggestion and Alan Hardaker's implementation had completed the League Cup's first cycle. It was by no means polished and was very much an uncut gem. There was room for improvement, perhaps a lot more than Hardaker had envisaged.

The questions in his mind started with how was the cup formula going to improve and how would the teams who had not competed be enticed to do so? Could he retain the interest of those teams that had competed as well?

And, more importantly, would the cup survive?

Season 1961/62

The Final

First leg: 26 April 1962
Rochdale 0 Norwich City 3 (Lythgoe 2, Punton)
Spotland, Rochdale
Attendance: 11,123
Referee: A. Holland

Second leg: 1 May 1962
Norwich City 1 (Hill) Rochdale 0
Carrow Road, Norwich City
Attendance: 19,800
Referee: R.H. Mann
Norwich City won 4-0 on aggregate

Alan Hardaker was a man on a mission as the League Cup entered its second season. There were immediate changes made, byes allocated to certain teams with some clubs not joining in the second round, and still a small number of clubs abstained. But it was TV money, just like it is today, that helped maintain the vision for the cup. This contract was agreed for the 1961/62 season and ensured participation from the clubs that had abstained to start to compete.

The immediate changes made were to ensure that the competition was completed in the season it started in, and also to eradicate the fixture pile-up that had seen first- and second-round matches being played at the same time.

Holders Aston Villa had got off to a winning start by beating Bradford City 4-3 away. Runners-up Rotherham United also won on their travels, 1-0 at Darlington. There were no real big cup upsets in the first round, except for perhaps Rochdale, who as a Fourth Division team had drawn away at Second Division Southampton, before finishing the job off with a 2-1 win at Spotland in the replay. Both Leicester City and Swansea Town were given byes into the second round.

Just like in its first season, the eventual winner of the cup didn't enter until the second round, Second Division Norwich City beating Lincoln City from the Third Division at Carrow Road. Rochdale had beaten fellow Fourth Division club Doncaster Rovers, with a comfortable 4-0 victory.

Both Aston Villa and Rotherham continued their quest for another final berth and a possible rematch. Villa won 3-1 at West Ham and Rotherham experienced their first replay after a goalless draw at Kenilworth Road, the home of Luton Town. They won the replay at Millmoor.

There was to be no more defending the cup in the third round for Aston Villa as they slumped to a 3-2 defeat at home to Ipswich Town. The chance for Rotherham to redeem themselves and go one better continued after once again going through after a replay. Drawing 0-0 at Preston North End, they swept their opponents aside 3-0 at Millmoor. Norwich defeated Middlesbrough 3-2 and Rochdale disposed of Second Division Charlton Athletic by a single goal. The big upset in this round occurred at Bournemouth & Boscombe Athletic when the Third Division outfit beat Cardiff City 3-0. Cardiff were plying their trade in the top tier. Leeds United were afforded a bye into the fourth round.

Leeds were to become the latest victims for Rotherham, who experienced their third replay on the trot. Drawing 1-1 at Millmoor, Rotherham came away with a 2-1 victory in the replay at Elland Road.

There were only two other matches in the fourth round, with Blackburn Rovers thrashing Ipswich Town 4-1 and York City edging past Bournemouth 1-0.

The quarter-finals saw the end of Rotherham's remarkable run and ensured that two new teams would contest the final when they were defeated 1-0 at home to Blackburn. Rochdale beat York 2-1 at home and Norwich sailed through to the semi-final with a convincing 4-1 victory at Sunderland. Joining them were Blackpool, after winning 2-1 away at Sheffield United in a replay at Bramall Lane following a 0-0 draw at home.

The semi-final draw saw Rochdale play Blackburn and Norwich against Blackpool, and both were convincing home wins: 3-1 to Rochdale and 4-1 to Norwich. Blackburn and Blackpool exacted revenge by winning their second legs at home, but not with the correct margin to go through to the final, so Norwich and Rochdale both went through 4-3 on aggregate.

The first leg of the final was held at Spotland, Rochdale's ground, on 26 April 1962, and the second leg was held at Carrow Road on 1 May. Norwich dominated the first leg and came away with a 3-0 victory, almost making the second leg a formality, and they followed this up with a 1-0 win to make the aggregate score 4-0. Derrick Lythgoe scored a brace in the first 20 minutes in the first leg and Rochdale never really recovered. Bill Punton added the third on 84 minutes and it was Jimmy Hill who settled matters with the only goal at Carrow Road in the second leg.

It was perhaps a step too far for Rochdale who enthralled fans during all the campaign and were a credit to the bottom tier of English professional football. The *Rochdale Observer* was full of praise for the team's heroics but recognised that the damage was done in the first leg with its headline that read, 'Stale Rochdale Beaten by Norwich Snap'.

Season 1962/63

The Final

First leg: 23 May 1963
Birmingham City 3 (Leek 2, Bloomfield) Aston
Villa 1 (Thomson)
St Andrew's, Birmingham
Attendance: 31,902
Referee: E. Crawford
Second leg: 27 May 1963
Aston Villa 0 Birmingham City 0
Villa Park, Birmingham
Attendance: 37,949
Referee: A.W. Sparling
Birmingham City won 3-1 on aggregate

The city of Birmingham had played its part in the first couple of seasons in the League Cup. Aston Villa had won the first one in 1961 and once again they participated in the final – and their opponents were their local rivals, Birmingham City. It was a real local affair with just over three miles separating Villa Park from St Andrew's. Both legs saw crowds in excess of 30,000 and this really did capture the imagination of both sets of supporters. The League Cup was, at last, starting to make its mark.

The competition was still not running at capacity and the first round was made up of teams primarily from the lower divisions. The most noticeable tie concerned Rochdale, who had made it to the final the previous season. There was to be no Fourth Division fairy tale this year, though, going out after drawing 0-0 away at

Southport, and while it was expected that Rochdale would complete the job at Spotland, they lost 2-1.

Norwich City started the defence of the cup they had won the previous season in style by thrashing Bolton Wanderers 4-0 at Carrow Road on 26 September. There were some high-scoring games in the second round with Leicester City and Charlton Athletic sharing eight goals to take the game to a replay. Elsewhere, Sunderland beat Oldham Athletic 7-1 at Roker Park. West Ham were blowing bubbles and scoring goals for fun when they welcomed Plymouth Argyle and promptly scored six without reply, and Portsmouth put five past south coast rivals Brighton & Hove Albion.

Similar patterns were witnessed at Villa's and Birmingham's opening games in the competition. Villa kicked off their campaign at home on the 24 September with a resounding 6-1 win over Peterborough, and not to be outdone at St Andrew's just two days later were Birmingham, who put five past Doncaster Rovers without reply.

The goal-fest continued as the competition reached the third round. The biggest win came at Brisbane Road, the home of Leyton Orient, with the O's putting nine past a hapless Chester. Damage limitation occurred with the away team netting two themselves.

Aston Villa saw off the challenge of a spirited Stoke City at Villa Park, winning 3-1 and putting themselves into the hat for the next round. Birmingham's route was a little harder, with a 1-1 draw away to Barrow, before sailing past their opponents 5-1 at St Andrew's in the replay – the second time on the trot that the Blues had scored five goals. Norwich had a very similar time to Birmingham themselves, drawing 1-1 at Carlisle United before winning the replay 5-0 in front of their own fans.

It was Aston Villa's turn to be the hotshots in the fourth round at Villa Park, by trouncing Preston North End 6-2. Birmingham and Norwich also found themselves drawn at home – the Blues winning 3-2 against Notts County and Norwich scoring the only goal against Fulham.

The footballing gods had decreed that the draw for the quarter-finals were the winners of year one against the winners of year two in the third season of the competition, on 3 December 1962, when Aston Villa played host to Norwich.

Joe Mercer's Villa eased through to the semi-final for the second time in three seasons with one goal apiece from Derek Dougan and Jimmy McEwan, and a brace from Bobby Thomson to win 4-1. Birmingham could also use phrases like 'eased through' themselves as they progressed to the semi-final by thrashing Manchester City 6-0. The other clubs making it through to join the Birmingham teams were Bury, who beat Leyton Orient away, and Sunderland who defeated Blackburn Rovers 3-2 at home.

The semi-final draw paired Birmingham at home in the first leg and Sunderland at home to Aston Villa.

Villa put themselves almost in the final with a 3-1 victory at Roker Park and Birmingham saw off Bury 3-2 at St Andrew's. Both second legs ended in draws – no goals at Villa Park and 1-1 at Bury, so the third final was an all-Birmingham affair.

The first leg was at St Andrew's on 23 May 1963 with the second leg at Villa Park just four days later.

The build-up to the ties was immense in the Birmingham area and the surrounding West Midlands and both sets of supporters had seen excitement levels rise from the moment that the teams had reached the final and this was generated into ticket sales and through the turnstiles as well, nearly 32,000 attending the match at Birmingham, while nearly 38,000 were present at Villa Park. This afforded Alan Hardaker a smile or two.

It also brought a smile to the face of Birmingham fan Keith Rowbottom and he was firmly in the excited camp, especially as he was able to get a ticket for both games. He recalls, 'I was 15 at the time and a big Birmingham City fan. I lived in a place called Sheldon which was only a couple of miles away from St Andrew's. On a nice day, we were able to walk there and back – and on not so nice days as well. After all, this was the '60s! I couldn't wait to tell my mates that I was going to BOTH legs. I got some jealous stares from a few of them. I couldn't sleep thinking about what would happen with these games. All I knew is that I wanted us to get a good start on the Villa in the home tie.'

This is how the *Birmingham Evening Mail* recalled events in the first leg, 'Referee Ernie Crawford had his hands full right from the opening minutes when Bobby Thomson clattered Johnny Schofield and Ken Leek left an impression on the ankles of Vic Crowe.'

There was no quarter given between the players as the newspaper continued, 'The game was hard-fought to the point of roughness on occasions.

'It was Blues who threaded some incision through the roughhouse. On 14 minutes, Malcolm Beard, Terry Hennessey (who before kick-off was presented with the *Evening Mail and Dispatch* Player of the Year trophy) and Harris worked the ball out to Bertie Auld whose cross was netted by Leek to make it 1-0. Thomson levelled for Villa against the run of play but two goals in 14 minutes just after the break put Blues in charge. Harris and Auld again combined to set up Leek. Then a Harris cross reached Jimmy Bloomfield who tricked two defenders before slotting home a sweet finish. The game ended 3-1 and Blues had one hand on the cup.

'Trailing by two goals, Villa badly needed more firepower for the second leg but [Joe] Mercer still declined to pick the transfer-listed Derek Dougan who admitted he was "bitterly disappointed". It proved a costly stance by the manager. Villa had been here before. Two years earlier they reached the final of the inaugural League Cup and lifted the trophy after turning round a 2-0 first-leg deficit to Rotherham.'

However, it was not to be a repeat from 1961 as both teams played out a 0-0 draw. In truth the second leg never really got going. Villa just could not breach the blue wall and Birmingham became the third winners of the League Cup.

Keith Rowbottom's prediction had come true. Birmingham had taken a strong lead into the game at Villa

Park. After coming back from the second leg, he had to explain to his parents why his clothes were in such a mess.

Keith once again takes up the story, 'For the Villa Park game I made myself a little handheld banner out of an old bed sheet and a couple of pieces of doweling. Villa Park in those days had a running track which was made with that orange-coloured shale. On the night of the game the shale was wet. I grabbed my banner, jumped on to the track, and ran around the whole pitch holding up my banner.

By the time I got back to my place I was covered in the stuff and had little cuts all over me, my jacket was ruined. It was all well worth it as we held on to our 3-1 lead from the first leg.'

Season 1963/64

The Final
First leg: 15 April 1964
Stoke City 1 (Bebbington) Leicester City 1 (Gibson)
Victoria Ground, Stoke-on-Trent
Attendance: 22,369
Referee: W. Clements

Second leg: 22 April 1964
Leicester City 3 (Stringfellow, Gibson, Riley) Stoke City 2 (Viollet, Kinnell)
Filbert Street, Leicester
Attendance: 25,372
Referee: A. Jobling
Leicester City won 4-3 on aggregate

It was a second consecutive all-Midlands final, but this time the teams weren't from the same city or indeed the West Midlands. They came from the eastern and northern tips of the region.

Just like the previous season, the first round consisted of the lower-division clubs and the biggest score was 7-3 in favour of Bradford Park Avenue at home against Bradford City.

Birmingham City's defence of the cup was a weak one in the second round, as they were defeated 2-0 by Norwich City at Carrow Road. Leicester City started their cup campaign with a solid 2-0 victory over Aldershot. Stoke City shared four goals away to Scunthorpe United and then six goals in the first replay before recording a 1-0 victory in the second replay at Hillsborough. The biggest win of the round came at Blackpool as the home team put seven past Charlton Athletic, who managed to score one themselves.

The third round saw Aston Villa soundly beaten 2-0 at home by West Ham United. An early pattern was emerging with the Villa. They had reached two finals and crashed out in the third round twice with both being at home.

Stoke were victorious on home soil and without having to go through two replays, when they beat Bolton Wanderers 3-0. Leicester City came away from a difficult tie with Tranmere Rovers with a 2-1 victory.

Norwich were not goal-shy in the fourth round as they went to Halifax Town and won 7-1. Rotherham also had their shooting boots laced properly when they defeated Millwall 5-2 at Millmoor. Leicester and Stoke also enjoyed home advantage, with the Foxes beating Gillingham 3-1 and Stoke progressing courtesy of a 2-1 victory over Bournemouth & Boscombe Athletic.

Norwich played Leicester in the last League Cup game of 1963, a 1-1 draw on 18 December. The two teams contested the first match of the competition in 1964 with Leicester knocking out the Canaries 2-1 on 15 January. This was to be the only replay in the quarter-finals. Manchester City beat Notts County away by a single goal and Stoke took care of Rotherham at home, winning 3-2. West Ham recorded the biggest victory of the round with a comprehensive 6-0 scoreline against Workington.

The semi-final draw saw Stoke take on Manchester City at home in the first leg and Leicester entertained West Ham in theirs. Stoke took a 2-0 advantage up to Manchester, and Leicester overcame West Ham in a seven-goal thriller, 4-3. Despite valiant efforts from Manchester City, they could only secure a 1-0 victory, but went out 2-1 on aggregate. However, Leicester experienced an easier time at West Ham, winning 2-0 to make it 6-3 on aggregate.

Stoke were the home team in the first leg with the game at Filbert Street set for the return. There was a new team to win the competition and the guarantee of another Midlands team holding up the cup and putting it in the trophy cabinet.

The first leg of the final ended 1-1, which meant that it was all to play at Filbert Street, with Keith Bebbington scoring the goal for Stoke and Dave Gibson doing the same for Leicester. Gibson was on the score sheet in the return leg as well, sandwiched between goals scored by his team-mates Mike Stringfellow and Howard Riley. Stoke most certainly played their part in an enthralling second leg with two goals themselves, scored by Dennis Viollet and George Kinnell. However, it was not enough, and Leicester took the honours to join Villa, Norwich and Birmingham as the cup winners so far. While the attendances in this final were not as much as they were the previous year for the other Midlands cup final derby, the gates were still very significant with crowds of 22,369 and 25,372 respectively.

Leicester had enjoyed their run to win the fourth League Cup Final, and were worthy winners, and now they set their sights on going all the way again and becoming the first team to reach two consecutive finals. The question was – could they do it?

Season 1964/65

The Final
First leg: 15 March 1965
Chelsea 3 (Tambling, Venables, McCreadie) Leicester
City 2 (Appleton, Goodfellow)
Stamford Bridge, London
Attendance: 20,690
Referee: J. Finney

Second leg: 5 April 1965
Leicester City 0 Chelsea 0

Filbert Street, Leicester
Attendance: 26,947
Referee: K. Howley
Chelsea won 3-2 on aggregate

Now in its fifth season, the League Cup was notable for two things. Firstly, it was the first time that a team had got to consecutive finals, with Leicester City being the holders, and it was to be the first time that a team from London had made the final.

Leicester's defence of the cup saw them take on Peterborough United at home. Not many fans would have predicted a replay in this tie, but this is exactly what they got, with the game ending 0-0. Parity was restored at London Road as the Foxes sailed through 2-0. The biggest shock of the round came at Maine Road where Manchester City were beaten 5-3 by Mansfield Town. Chester won a thrilling match when they beat Derby County 5-4 at home and Blackburn Rovers were enjoying their travels, securing a 5-1 win at Burnden Park, home of Bolton Wanderers.

A replay was most certainly not required by Leicester in the third round as they trounced Grimsby Town 5-0 away. Chelsea were also sound winners when they entertained Notts County at Stamford Bridge, winning 4-0. Workington enjoyed another game where they scored goals freely, although it took a replay. The team that had scored nine in the first round, against Barrow, were held to a goalless draw at home to Blackburn. Workington soon found themselves in the goals again as they thrashed Rovers 5-1 at Ewood Park. Aston Villa, no strangers to the final, won a thrilling game at Elland Road, beating Leeds United 3-2.

Villa were back to winning ways in the fourth round and dreaming of final appearance number three as they saw off the challenge of Reading, 3-1 at Villa Park on 4 November 1964. The same night saw Leicester held to a goalless draw at home against Crystal Palace. The replay took place a week later at Selhurst Park with Leicester winning 2-1. Chelsea were at home the same night and played Swansea City just a few miles away, winning 3-2.

The quarter-finals saw both Aston Villa and Leicester trying to emulate Workington in the first round, but just falling short of scoring nine goals with Villa beating Bradford City 7-1 at Villa Park and Leicester beating Coventry City 8-1 at Highfield Road. Braces from Mike Stringfellow, Billy Hodgson and Richie Norman with goals scored by David Gibson and an own goal from George Curtis inflicted the damage for the Foxes in what is now known as the M69 derby. Plymouth beat Northampton Town 1-0 at home, and Workington and Chelsea shared four goals before going to a replay at Stamford Bridge a week before Christmas, the Londoners going through 2-0.

The semi-finals paired Villa and Chelsea together with the first leg at Villa Park, and Leicester entertained Plymouth. Both first legs ended 3-2, with Chelsea winning against Villa and Leicester victorious at Filbert Street. Chelsea and Villa then played out a 1-1 draw in the second leg and Leicester beat Plymouth 1-0 away, Chelsea winning 4-3 on aggregate and Leicester going through 4-2.

Would Leicester taste cup success once more or would there be new winners in the shape of Chelsea? The first leg of the final was held at Stamford Bridge and played on 15 March 1965. A thrilling game saw Chelsea winning 3-2 as they had in the first leg of the semi-final against Villa, with Bobby Tambling giving them the lead just after the half-hour mark. However, just a minute into the second half, Colin Appleton equalised for the Foxes. Shortly after, Terry Venables restored Chelsea's lead from the penalty spot, but again Leicester would level, this time through Jimmy Goodfellow. The cup holders were not letting go of their grip on a second win so easily.

However, with only nine minutes remaining, Eddie McCreadie, normally a left-back but filling in as centre-forward, scored a magnificent goal to make it 3-2. McCreadie had started a mazy run well inside his own half before he ran the near length of the pitch and slotted past Gordon Banks. This time there was no Leicester comeback and Chelsea held on to take a slender lead into the second leg which was played on 5 April 1965. Perhaps the occasion had got to the holders as Leicester simply could not breach the Chelsea defence, and as the night drew to a close with no goals being scored, it meant that the League Cup had a fifth new name engraved with Chelsea winning 3-2 on aggregate. Once again the final had enjoyed healthy attendances with almost 21,000 in West London and just under 27,000 in the East Midlands.

Season 1965/66

The Final

First leg: 9 March 1966
West Ham United 2 (Moore, Byrne) West Bromwich
Albion 1 (Astle)
Upton Park, London
Attendance: 28,558
Referee: D.W. Smith
Second leg: 23 March 1966
West Bromwich Albion 4 (Kaye, Brown, Clark,
Williams) West Ham United 1 (Peters)
The Hawthorns, West Bromwich
Attendance: 31,688
Referee: J. Mitchell
West Bromwich Albion won 5-3 on aggregate

West Bromwich Albion made their debut in the League
Cup in the second round on 22 September 1965. The
draw saw the Baggies at home against local rivals
Walsall. It turned out to be a very good welcome for
Albion as they ran out 3-1 winners at The Hawthorns,
a Stan Bennett own goal and two from Tony Brown
opening their account in the competition. Leicester
City's hope of a third consecutive final was dashed in
the second round, after losing 3-1 to Manchester City
at Maine Road. There were defeats for other previous
winners as well: Norwich City were beaten 2-1 at Stoke
City and Birmingham City were defeated by the same
score at Mansfield Town. The only previous winners to
go through to the third round were Aston Villa who got
a 3-2 victory at Swansea Town. What had happened to

the defending holders – Chelsea? They had elected not to enter the competition, as a third-place finish in the First Division meant that they entered the Inter-Cities Fairs Cup and their manager, Tommy Docherty, and the board had prioritised Europe.

The two biggest wins of the third round were in London. Chelsea's nearest neighbours, Fulham, marched into the fourth round with a convincing 5-0 win at home to Northampton Town, and West Ham United were in the mood down the river in east London, soundly beating Mansfield 4-0. West Brom made it two wins in their debut season with a 4-2 victory at Elland Road against Leeds United.

West Brom were once again drawn against a fellow West Midlands side in Coventry City at Highfield Road. Albion experienced their first replay in the competition after drawing 1-1, but they were soon back to winning ways when they thrashed Coventry 6-1 at The Hawthorns. The goals were scored by Tony Brown, two from Doug Fraser and the match ball was taken home by Jeff Astle who got the other three. West Ham continued their run to the final with a 2-1 victory at Rotherham United. There were also victories for the other teams in claret and blue when Burnley and Aston Villa went through after replays.

The West Midlands pairing theme continued once more for West Brom as they were drawn at home to Aston Villa in the quarter-finals and came out on top courtesy of a 3-1 win at The Hawthorns. West Ham were held at Grimsby Town and there were wins for

Peterborough, who again hit the back of the net four times against Burnley at home without reply. Cardiff City beat Ipswich Town 2-1, West Ham won their replay 1-0 and were the last team standing in claret and blue.

The semi-finals saw both the eventual participants in the final play at home in the first legs, with West Brom taking a 2-1 advantage on 1 December 1965 against Peterborough and then thrashing them 4-2 in the second leg just two weeks later with Tony Brown netting three goals this time around. West Brom had made the final in their first season, a mere six years after the competition started, with the aggregate score being 6-3. There was only a two-week gap between the first and second legs, so it was settled very quickly. The same could not be said about West Ham's semi-final. The first game at West Ham took place on 20 December 1965, five days after West Brom had secured a final berth. The scoreline reflected the Hammers' dominance as they trounced Cardiff 5-2. There was a lengthy delay in the second leg, which took place on 2 February 1966. This time the lead and aggregate score were increased as West Ham beat Cardiff 5-1, thus making it the biggest aggregate score to date in the competition's limited history, which meant the Hammers progressed 10-3.

West Brom played the waiting game and now they knew they faced West Ham in the final. The first leg was played on 9 March 1966 with West Ham being the home team in front of nearly 29,000 fans, coming out on top 2-1 with Bobby Moore and Johnny Byrne scoring.

Albion had taken the lead through Jeff Astle, so it was all to play for in the return leg.

West Ham had won the FA Cup in 1964, and the European Cup Winners' Cup in 1965. They were looking good to make it three consecutive seasons in finals and wins in three different competitions. One could argue that West Ham had simply run out of steam by the time of the second leg as they had endured another great run in the European Cup Winners' Cup during the 1965/66 season before falling at the semi-final hurdle against German team Borussia Dortmund. They had been competitive on four fronts (although their exit in the FA Cup had been in the fourth round after a replay) and it had taken its toll.

However, nothing can be taken away from West Brom as they took the second leg to West Ham from the kick-off in front of a bumper crowd of nearly 32,000 at The Hawthorns, coming out 4-1 winners and hence winning the final on aggregate 5-3, with John Kaye, Tony 'Bomber' Brown, Clive Clark and Graham Williams scoring for the jubilant Throstles with Martin Peters netting for West Ham.

West Ham United had to settle for winning the World Cup instead in 1966.

Season 1966/67

The Final

4 March 1967
Queens Park Rangers 3 (Morgan, Marsh, Lazarus) West
Bromwich Albion 2 (Clark 2)
Wembley Stadium, London
Attendance: 97,952
Referee: W. Crossley

History was made as this was the first season that the final was a showpiece match at Wembley, as had been the case with the FA Cup Final for the past 43 years. The previous season's FA Cup Final witnessed one of its greatest comebacks when Sheffield Wednesday found themselves 2-0 up against Everton with just over 30 minutes remaining. However, it was Everton who won 3-2 by scoring three late goals. The first ever League Cup Final at Wembley witnessed a similar comeback, the difference being that it was accomplished by a team in the Third Division and not from the top flight.

Queens Park Rangers, with Alec Stock at the helm, had played in the Third Division (since the amalgamation of teams from the north and south equivalents) for eight consecutive seasons when they were drawn at home against Colchester United in the first round. It turned out to be a great day for the Loftus Road faithful, tearing apart their opponents 5-0. There was a four-star performance from Rodney Marsh with Mark Lazarus scoring the other. The other major score occurred at Gay Meadow where Shrewsbury Town beat Wrexham

6-1. There were ten first-round replays, which broke the previous season's tally of nine, again showing the competitive nature of the lower divisions.

Chelsea was back in the competition following a 12-month hiatus after winning it in 1965 and promptly took care of business at the Bridge, defeating Charlton Athletic 5-2 in the second round. QPR were slowly making waves and slipping under the radar, drawing 1-1 at Aldershot before winning 2-0 at home in the replay. A Jimmy Langley penalty and another goal for Marsh separated the teams.

West Bromwich Albion continued their fine goalscoring run with a 4-2 home win against Manchester City in the third round. Leicester City matched Fulham's 5-0 home victory against Wolves as they beat Lincoln City at Filbert Street. Chelsea's run had come to an end as well, drawing 1-1 at Blackpool before succumbing to a 3-1 defeat in the replay. Blackpool's scalps had been considerable with the blue of Chelsea joining the red of Manchester United.

In terms of the biggest wins in the fourth round, then it was West Ham United and Northampton Town who took the honours. The Hammers put seven past Leeds United without reply – and at the first time of asking. Northampton went one better and won 8-0 in a replay at home against Brighton & Hove Albion after drawing 1-1 at the Goldstone Ground. Holders West Brom continued their quest for consecutive finals when they beat Swindon Town away. QPR had started to make football folk sit up and take notice as they dispatched previous winners Leicester 4-2. Birmingham City and Blackpool also won their games 4-2 as well, the Blues at Grimsby Town and the Tangerines at home to Fulham.

All quarter-finals were played on 7 December and there were early Christmas presents for Birmingham who beat Sheffield United 3-2 away, and West Bromwich Albion who also won away, 3-1 at Northampton. Third Division QPR defeated Carlisle United 2-1 and finally the resolve of Blackpool faltered at home to West Ham – the Hammers winning 3-1.

The first semi-final paired Birmingham at home to QPR, the surprise package, and West Brom played at home to West Ham in the second semi-final – a repeat of the previous year's final. Both semis produced emphatic scores to practically make the second legs just a formality. QPR were rampant against a shell-shocked Birmingham, winning 4-1. Goals from Marsh (who else), Roger Morgan, Mark Lazarus and a Les Allen goal hit the home team with a second-half blitz. West Ham also felt dazed and confused at The Hawthorns, with Albion ripping them apart 4-0.

It was major advantages to QPR and West Brom that took them down Wembley Way, Rangers beating Birmingham 3-1 in the second leg to go through 7-2 on aggregate and West Ham and West Brom sharing four goals with the Baggies going through 6-2.

Alan Hudson was a 15-year-old Chelsea apprentice and had followed QPR's route to the final. He recalls, 'I played for Chelsea but had been a Fulham supporter growing up. The reason why I followed Rangers in the League Cup that season was that I really liked the way that Rodney Marsh played. I went to every single match after the first couple of rounds, including the semi-final at Birmingham City. It was the first time that I had been to a ground outside London, and we travelled by coach with my dad. It was just a brilliant time following them.

'I was gutted to miss the final, though. After we had played a youth game for Chelsea we would all have to report back to Stamford Bridge, otherwise we were out. I had a little transistor radio with me so at least I could listen to the match. What a comeback it was. I used to keep a scrapbook with all my match reports and, years later, I showed the League Cup run to Rodney Marsh who turned his nose up at it. Let's just say that I loved him as a player and leave it at that!'

So, First Division West Bromwich Albion were playing Third Division Queens Park Rangers at Wembley in front of a near-capacity crowd on 4 March 1967. West Brom were clear favourites to successfully defend their cup and become the first team to win it consecutively – or was there a major cup final upset for the first time?

By the half-time whistle, it had gone to plan for 'Goliath'. Albion took the lead in the first half when Clive Clark scored in the seventh minute. Clark was back on the score sheet once more to give them a 2-0 lead at half-time, and after an hour the score was still 2-0 in the favour of West Midlanders. The League Cup engraver on the day could be forgiven if they wanted to start to scribe 'West Bromwich Albion' on to the trophy. However, football did what it does brilliantly in cup matches – it allowed 'David' to get back into it. QPR reduced the deficit in the 63rd minute when Roger Morgan scored, and then Rodney Marsh sent the fans from London wild when he equalised 11 minutes later. Then Mark Lazarus scored a third goal for QPR in the 80th minute to cap the finest of comebacks. The unbelievable had happened.

The modest team from Loftus Road and members of the Third Division had come back and won against the odds.

Season 1967/68
The Final
2 March 1968
Leeds United 1 (Cooper) Arsenal 0
Wembley Stadium, London
Attendance: 97,887
Referee: L.J. Hamer

Leeds United had been elected to the Second Division in the 1920/21 season. Four years later they were celebrating promotion to the First Division as champions. Three seasons later they were back in the division that they had started in. The pattern of being promoted and relegated became a theme until 1965. This was soon to change, though, with Don Revie in charge of the team. Revie had enjoyed a successful playing career, initially in the Second Division with Leicester City and Hull City before signing for Manchester City in 1951. It was at Maine Road that the centre-forward first experienced top-flight football and appeared in the 1955 FA Cup Final for the club. A shorter spell with Sunderland was then followed up with the final team he represented, Leeds, in 1958. Three years later, Revie was made player-manager while Leeds were still a Second Division outfit. They were promoted once more to the First Division at the end of the 1963/64 season. The impact that Revie and his team made in England's top division was instant as they were runners-up. Leeds had never won a major trophy outside of the Second Division.

In the third round, Queens Park Rangers marched on with a 5-1 victory over Oxford United. Leeds sealed a 3-0 victory at home over Bury and Arsenal beat Reading by a solitary goal at Highbury.

But there was no more romance for QPR in the next round as they were beaten 2-1 at home to Burnley on 31 October 1967. Arsenal defeated Blackburn Rovers 2-1 at Highbury and Leeds got through a tricky away game at Sunderland to win 2-0, Jimmy Greenhoff netting both goals. Fulham and Manchester City served up a feast of great football when they met up at Craven Cottage, the home side taking it 3-2.

The quarter-finals saw two victories and two draws that meant replays before a team could take its place in the semi-finals, and just two games away from Wembley.

The victors without going into a replay were Leeds who again won 2-0, this time at home to Stoke City with Billy Bremner and Peter Lorimer settling matters in the first 15 minutes. Derby County also went through at the Baseball Ground after beating Darlington 5-4 in a thrilling end-to-end match. Arsenal were also involved in a high-scoring tie but shared the six goals scored at Turf Moor with Burnley, though they won the replay 2-1 on home turf. Fulham and Huddersfield drew 1-1 at Craven Cottage, before the Terriers booked their place in the semi-final with a 2-1 victory at home in the replay.

The first leg of the semi-finals both took place on 17 January 1968, with Arsenal beating Huddersfield 3-2 at Highbury and Leeds taking a 1-0 victory at Derby. Arsenal and Leeds both won their second legs as well, the Gunners triumphing 3-1 at Huddersfield which meant a 6-3 aggregate win while Leeds completed the job at home to Derby with a 3-2 scoreline, going through to the final 4-2 on aggregate. This meant an all-First Division final once more after the heroics of Queens Park Rangers at Wembley the season before. If the 1967 final had captured the romance of the underdog winning against all odds and epitomised the beautiful game, the 1968 final did the opposite. It was a dour event and was very much a case of the teams not losing as opposed to winning, and after a series of gruelling tackles from both teams.

The 1968 League Cup was the first trophy Billy Bremner was to lift for Leeds, as well as having Don Revie at the helm – there was much more to come. It wasn't a game for the purists but those hooked on the tactical battles on the football pitch were kept busy. Leeds in previous competitions had been termed as 'unlucky losers' and maybe just winning at all costs was heavy on Revie's mind – even if it meant not entertaining the troops. They'd finished their first season after promotion in 1964 in second place to Manchester United on goal average and were runners-up in the FA Cup Final, losing out to Liverpool after extra time. The game was settled, and at least allowed for something for the hacks to write in the national and local newspapers, in the 20th minute courtesy of a goal scored by their young left-back, Terry Cooper, after a corner was cleared by the Gunners' defence. This would be the start of an amazing period in Leeds' history as they followed the League Cup triumph with league championships, the FA Cup, and the Inter-Cities Fairs Cup on two separate occasions over the next six seasons. The spiral of decline returned in 1974 when Revie left to take the England job. Leeds would not get back to former glories until the 1991/92 season when they claimed their third First Division trophy in their history, the very last team to finish top of the table before it became the Premier League.

Season 1968/69

The Final
15 March 1969
Swindon Town 3 (Smart, Rogers 2) Arsenal 1 (Gould)
after extra-time
Wembley Stadium, London
Attendance: 98,189
Referee: W.G. Handley

The Wiltshire town of Swindon was mentioned in the Domesday book of 1086. It was referred to as 'Suindune'.

The name was derived from the Old English words 'swine' and 'dun'. The meaning of this was 'pig hill' or possibly 'Sweyn's hill', where Sweyn is a personal name. The latter belonged to Scandinavia and was likened to Sven and English swain, meaning a young man. One such young man in 1968 was Don Rogers who had played for Swindon Town since turning professional in 1962. Rogers had joined the club the year before when he had signed on as a youth player. Swindon had been members of the Football League since 1920 when they were elected to it. Nicknamed 'the Robins', they had played in the Western and Southern Leagues prior to this. They were elected to the third tier and had stayed there ever since, finally winning promotion in the 1962/63 season. They stayed in the second tier for two seasons before dropping back down into the familiar territory of the third. It was back in this league that the club enjoyed their finest ever moment just a few seasons later.

Swindon kicked off their campaign in the first round at home to Torquay United on 13 August 1968 and with it a 2-1 victory. Two second-half goals from Peter Noble and Roger Smart inflicted the damage for Danny Williams's side.

It took a replay for Swindon to progress in the second round, forcing a second match on home turf after a 1-1 draw at Bradford City, but the fans who attended the return were served up seven goals with Swindon taking it 4-3 as John Smith, a Rogers penalty and two further goals from Smart and Noble were on the score sheet.

Swindon ensured a place in the fourth round with a 1-0 home victory against Blackburn Rovers, Rogers scoring the only goal of the game. They were then back on their travels with an away trip to Coventry City. This also went to a replay with both teams sharing four goals, although the Robins were kicking themselves as they should have held on to a two-goal lead secured by Rogers and Smart as the match entered the final four minutes. Goals from John Tudor on 86 and Tony Hateley just two minutes later ensured a replay at the County Ground. Town had not previously been beyond the fourth round, but they were able to lay the hoodoo to rest with a comprehensive 3-0 win. The match was effectively over in the first half an hour as Swindon raced into a three-goal lead via Rogers, Smart and Willie Penman. There would be no further Coventry comeback this time. Arsenal continued their quest to reach another final and make amends for the previous season with a 2-1 home victory versus Liverpool.

The Gunners eased past Blackpool with an emphatic 5-1 at Highbury in the quarter-finals and they were joined in the semi-finals by local rivals Tottenham Hotspur, who beat Southampton 1-0, and also Burnley who progressed with a 2-0 home victory against Crystal Palace. Swindon went through once more using the replay method. A goalless draw at Derby County was followed up with a 1-0 victory at the County Ground, Rogers providing the fireworks on Bonfire Night.

Like two years earlier, a team from the Third Division reached the semi-finals. Could Swindon emulate

Queens Park Rangers and go on to lift the trophy? It was an all-north London derby in the semi-final with Arsenal taking on Spurs in the first leg at home. The other semi saw Burnley meet Swindon. Arsenal and Swindon took their first legs, but the winning margin was only one goal which meant that it was all to play for in the return matches, Arsenal beating Spurs 1-0 and Swindon overcoming Burnley 2-1. Stan Harland and Peter Noble were on goalscoring duties this time.

Wiltshire's biggest town was on the verge of playing its greatest ever match and the excitement was at fever pitch as Swindon took to the field at home against Burnley on 4 December 1968. However, it was the team from the north-west who exacted revenge, themselves winning 2-1 to make the aggregate score 3-3 – the champagne being put firmly on hold for the Robins, who had John Smith on target.

Tottenham and Arsenal drew 1-1 on the same night, but this match was concluded, and Wembley knew the first team that would play in the League Cup Final of 1969 – Arsenal winning 2-1 on aggregate. Burnley and Swindon had to wait until 18 December to find out which one of them joined Arsenal, but this time Robins fans were able to crack open their cold bottles of champagne as they defeated the Clarets 3-2 in a thrilling match. It was played at The Hawthorns and Smith was once more on the goal trail, putting Swindon in front after just nine minutes. This lead was held until the closing stages before Dave Thomas equalised to take the game into extra time. It was Burnley who then took the lead in the first minute of the additional period before Swindon came back with an own goal scored by the unfortunate Arthur Bellamy. The winning goal that took Swindon to the final was scored by Peter Noble, who had scored the first on the road to Wembley and now he had got the last.

For the second time in two years a Third Division club had made the final against First Division opposition. The bookies had made Arsenal firm favourites, but then they had done this when West Bromwich Albion had fallen foul of Queens Park Rangers.

Could the baton be handed over to Swindon? Well not on a perfect pitch that any cup final should be worthy of.

The early months of 1969 had seen some of the heaviest downfalls and it was pretty much nonstop. The Horse of the Year Show had been at Wembley just a few days before the final and had turned the pitch into a real quagmire. This suited the Third Division team and the omens for a cup upset increased when the Arsenal camp complained of a flu bug doing its nasty rounds on players and staff alike.

Arsenal took the game to Swindon in the early stages; however, it was the underdogs who took the lead in the 35th minute after a mix-up in the Gunners' defence allowed Roger Smart to put the ball into the net. The pattern of the second half pretty much mirrored the first, with Swindon's Peter Downsborough producing crucial saves. There were just four minutes left on the clock when Arsenal finally breached Swindon's defence as Bobby Gould headed in the equaliser to take the match into extra time. The heavy pitch was now taking its toll on the First Division favourites as Swindon started to dominate. Enter Don Rogers, who scored two goals to put himself into football folklore. His first came after a corner which wasn't cleared properly by Arsenal allowing Rogers to retain a cool head before smashing the ball home from close range. Then with just one minute left and Arsenal pushing to get back in the game, Rogers scored his second when he ran unmarked before rounding Bob Wilson to put the ball into the net with legendary status assured.

Rogers recalls the mood in the Swindon camp at the start of the 1968/69 season, 'We had a very good pre-season, and the feeling within the team was that we would have a good campaign in the league. We had been improving over the past few years and we had bonded well with the newer players that had come in. Our aim was promotion to the Second Division and, in fairness, we never really gave the cups any real thought other than to go as far as we could and get some money into the club.

'I scored my first goal in the second-round replay back at the County Ground against Bradford City. It was a penalty and we played well that night, as did Bradford. It could have gone either way and I remember that they had gone two up as well. My goal was the equaliser. I scored the only goal in the next round against Blackburn Rovers, so I was pretty happy with my contributions so far. We played Coventry away in the next round and my wife, Jane, came along. Not with the players, though, as we were on the coach. Jane had left with 15 minutes to go with us being two up and wanted to avoid the traffic outside the ground. They ended up having a drink in Coventry and a bite to eat, satisfied that we were through as we were two up and I had scored the first. It was only when the Coventry fans came into the pub with smiles on their faces that she knew we hadn't won but drew. We won the replay with relative ease, and I remember that our league crowds were getting bigger. We had a very confident team but still we never believed that we would go all the way.

'It was in the next round where I really started to think of Wembley. We played Derby County away, and we got absolutely battered but came away 0-0. In the replay it was pretty much nip and tuck. I had a shot in the 27th minute which wasn't one of my best efforts, but the ball bounced off Dave Mackay and into the net. It was at that moment that I started to think about the Twin Towers, and it could be our year. We had a marathon semi-final with Burnley. We beat them 2-1 in the first leg away and I remember that we played a chunk of that match without many of our supporters in the away end as the train had broken down. They beat us by the same score at the County Ground, so it was a replay at The Hawthorns. We won that match in extra time. The coach journey back was fantastic as was the weeks leading up to the final and everyone wanted to talk about us. We had to keep our minds on the league, though, as we were going well in it, just as we aimed to.

'It was only the week before the final that we were able to concentrate on the final, and we actually went up to Wembley to have a look around at the start of the week. It was just wonderful, and we could not wait to get there for the final which was played on the Saturday. Before the match, [Swindon manager] Danny Williams gave his team talk but we never really needed it as we were so pumped up. I know that we were playing Arsenal, but we had self-belief. When Roger Smart opened the scoring we all looked at each other thinking that we were going to win the cup. Even when they equalised with just minutes to go with the match going into extra time, we kept our shape – and our heads. We had played so much football in extra time in the competition before the final.

'I got my first goal because of a corner we were awarded, which bobbled about before I was able to slot the ball home by trapping the ball with one foot and scoring with the other. My second goal was the one everyone still talks about today, when I picked up the ball just inside our half before running down the right side and taking the ball round Bob Wilson. I knew that I was going to take it round him when I received the ball in the first instance. It was a great feeling because then we knew we had won it.

'Going up the steps to collect the cup and our medals and celebrating in front of our fans is a memory that I will never forget. We celebrated deep into the night. The one thing that I regret is not going back with the players on the coach the following morning, as I had to stay for interviews with the media and have pictures taken. It was just a brilliant time in that season as the stars aligned, and the whole town was with us with Swindon being firmly put on the map.'

Trevor Byron Jones was in the crowd that day at Wembley as a very excited 12-year-old Swindon fanatic, 'My dad wouldn't let me go to night games, so I never saw the semi-finals, but once we won and were on the way to Wembley my dad organised a coach that went from our village of Drayton near Abingdon in Oxfordshire, with all his mates and their partners. There are only a few memories; one being my Aunty Hilda was the only lady of our group that went to the game itself, the others possibly went shopping! I remember having to stand on the seat to see the game, and after the game we all went to see a Brian Rix stage play. I guess my dad assumed we would not win so needed something to do in the evening. Looking back, we all sat in a quiet theatre somewhere in London while Swindon fans celebrated out on the streets of London.

'Later that same year, Don Rogers presented awards to the winners of the darts league at Marcham social club near Abingdon. My dad, I guess, arranged to take me and have my photo taken with the man who is still my only football hero. Don has his '69 cup final tie on in the photo. In 2010 after Paolo Di Canio left Swindon I went to Don's sports shop in Swindon and asked him to sign over Di Canio's name I had printed on my shirt. At first, he refused, saying he would ruin the shirt; once I explained what HE meant to me he duly signed my shirt.'

The underdogs had done it again – the second time in just two years. A European berth had not been afforded to Queens Park Rangers as qualification for the Inter-Cities Fairs Cup had not been introduced until 1968. In any case the Football League would not have offered it to Third Division teams, as Swindon were. However, it gave rise to the short-lived Anglo-Italian Cup, organised as a way of compensating the Robins.

Swindon's exploits had made the rest of the country sit up and take note. The following season was the first in ten attempts when all 92 clubs competed in the League Cup for the first time, although it was not mandatory. Swindon and QPR had blazed a trail for the so-called 'minnows' and won a prestigious competition that all Football League clubs could enter, and for the Goliaths it meant serious European adventures.

Season 1969/70

The Final
7 March 1970
Manchester City 2 (Doyle, Pardoe) West Bromwich Albion 1 (Astle)
Wembley Stadium, London
Attendance: 97,963
Referee: V. James

All 92 clubs competed for the trophy, the competition kicking off on 12 August 1969 with the first round consisting of teams in the lower divisions. The most goals scored in the first round came at Burnden Park as Bolton Wanderers trailed 3-1 to Rochdale at half-time but came back to score five in the second half and win 6-3.

John Byron took the ball home as he scored a hat-trick. The biggest winning margin was a 5-1 home victory for Southport against Oldham Athletic. As defending champions, Swindon did not have to participate until the second round.

The Robins got off to a great start in the defence of the cup with a 3-1 victory at Swansea City on 2 September 1969, Peter Noble scoring all three. There was a local derby at Villa Park with West Bromwich Albion beating Aston Villa 2-1, the home side once again going out in the second round. Manchester City were also winners on their travels, 3-0 at Southport. The biggest winning margin of the second round occurred at Portman Road with Ipswich Town's comfortable 4-0 success against Colchester United. There were also victories for Leeds, Manchester United and Liverpool, while Arsenal were hoping to go one better as they had been runners-up in the last two finals. Their campaign started with a 1-1 draw at Southampton before a 2-0 home win just two days later, on 4 September. Previous winners Queens Park Rangers also had to play two games to qualify for the third round, sharing four goals away at Mansfield Town. There were four goals in the replay, but this time they were not to be shared with Rangers scoring them all.

Arsenal had to go through a replay in the third round as well, after a goalless game at home to Everton. Any chance of the Gunners making it third time lucky went out of the window in the replay with Everton winning 1-0. There was no second match for QPR who had once again set their sights on more cup glory, turning over Tranmere Rovers 6-0 at home on 24 September. Manchester City saw off Liverpool in a thrilling game at Maine Road, winning 3-2 on the same evening. Mike Doyle opened the scoring after 12 minutes before Liverpool's Alun Evans equalised in the 21st minute. Second-half goals from Neil Young and Ian Bowyer gave the impetus to the home team although Liverpool did pull one back moments after the third through Bobby Graham. The night after saw West Bromwich Albion having to settle for a replay after a 1-1 draw at Ipswich before finishing the job 2-0 at The Hawthorns. The flame of romance that had been Swindon Town in the past 12 months finally flickered and was put out in the third round, 1-0 at Oxford United.

Oxford progressed by the same score in the fourth round at Nottingham Forest. There was no replay for West Brom as they were comfortable 4-0 winners at home to Bradford City. QPR were back in the groove with a 3-1 home victory against Wolverhampton Wanderers, while Manchester City defeated Everton at Maine Road. Manchester United and Derby County were also winners, but both had to go to replays before going through.

The only team to reach the semi-finals at the first attempt were Manchester City who beat QPR 3-0 at home, and thus ending Rangers' hopes of a second win in the competition. Amazingly all the other games finished 0-0 with Derby at home to Manchester United, Leicester City at home to West Brom and Oxford at home to Carlisle. All three teams that had played away went through in the replays, Manchester United and Carlisle both 1-0 and West Brom 2-1.

The semi-final saw Carlisle at home to West Brom and the first ever Manchester derby in the competition with City having home first-leg advantage, both home teams taking a slender lead into the second legs – Carlisle 1-0 and City 2-1.

Albion showed their pedigree by thrashing Carlisle 4-1 on 3 December, then the very last League Cup game of the 1960s took place at Old Trafford on 17 December 1969. Ian Bowyer had given City the lead in the 17th minute to stretch the advantage before Paul Edwards equalised just six minutes later. Denis Law had restored parity on the hour before Mike Summerbee levelled the tie in the 66th minute. No more goals were scored which meant that City had made the final with a 4-3 aggregate win. Albion had done it 4-2.

The final was played on 7 March 1970. City had also reached the final of that season's European Cup Winners' Cup, although their league form had dipped as the campaign played out, most probably because of their cup exploits.

It was a very cold day in London and snow could be seen on Wembley's perimeters. It did not take long until the first goal was scored when Jeff Astle was on target for Albion after five minutes, becoming the first player to score in the final of both the League Cup and FA Cup at Wembley. This had warmed the thousands of Albion fans packed into the stadium as dreams were now held on another cup final victory, and it was looking very likely until City equalised through Mike Doyle to send the game into extra time, and they eventually won 2-1, with Glyn Pardoe netting the winner. Albion fans' hearts had been broken for the second time in three seasons. For Manchester City and Joe Mercer, though, it meant more glory and they could now display the League Cup in the cabinet. This was soon followed by the European Cup Winners' Cup as they beat Polish team Górnik Zabrze 2-1 on 29 April 1970 at the Praterstadion in Vienna, Austria.

2

The 1970s

Season 1970/71

The Final

27 February 1971

Tottenham Hotspur 2 (Chivers 2) Aston Villa 0

Wembley Stadium, London

Attendance: 100,000

Referee: J. Finney

The 1960/61 season had been kind to Aston Villa and Tottenham Hotspur. Both were members of the top tier. Villa had won the inaugural League Cup and Spurs had won the FA Cup and claimed the First Division championship to win the double. They followed this up with further trophies in the FA Cup and the European Cup Winners' Cup as the 1960s progressed. For Villa, it turned out to be the opposite. The League Cup victory was as good as it got for the club and as 1967/68 had commenced, they were competing in the Second Division following relegation the season before.

Many had predicted that Villa would bounce back into the First Division very quickly, but this did not happen. In fact, it got even worse for the fallen giants as

63

they were relegated to the third tier for the first time in their history at the end of the 1969/70 season.

York City and Northampton Town played out the marathon match in the second round. A goalless game at Boothferry Park meant a replay at Northampton, which ended up 1-1, and a second replay took place on 28 September 1970 at Villa Park. It was the Cobblers from Northampton who went through 2-1 to set up a tie against Aston Villa at home in the third round. Once again, Northampton were involved in further replays after a 1-1 draw on 6 October. Seven days later, Villa beat them 3-0 to reach the fourth round. Tottenham Hotspur overcame a determined Sheffield United 2-1 at White Hart Lane. There were 1-0 away victories for Arsenal and West Bromwich Albion, the Gunners at Luton Town and the Throstles at Preston North End. Manchester United also went through by the same scoreline but this was at Old Trafford when they beat Portsmouth. Queens Park Rangers fell 2-0 to London rivals Fulham at Craven Cottage. The winners of the 1969 competition, Swindon Town, were back in the mood as they beat Liverpool 2-0 at home in the third round, Don Rogers scoring both.

Aston Villa progressed into the quarter-finals with a slender 1-0 victory against Carlisle United at Villa Park with a Brian Tiler scoring the only goal. Bristol Rovers beat Birmingham City 3-0, Fulham breaking Swindon's hearts with a 1-0 home victory and Coventry City beating Derby County by the same score. On the same night that Villa were beating Carlisle, Manchester United were doing the same at Old Trafford, seeing off Chelsea 2-1.

The biggest win of the night and indeed the round came at White Hart Lane where Spurs entertained West Brom. At the ground on that evening were Cliff Crancher and his father. Cliff was an Albion supporter, and his dad was staunch Arsenal, so both wanted to see a Baggies win. Cliff takes up the story, 'I was born in Basildon, Essex. I had absolutely no Albion connection. My dad was a staunch Gooner, but for some reason didn't push me to support them. When I was six, I said on the morning of the FA Cup Final between Albion and Everton that I would support the winners. I knew nothing about the Albion who won 1-0 and I knew they were not one of the big clubs. My dad did inform me that the Albion were a good cup team and I liked the sound of it. So, I became a Baggie in Basildon! My first game watching them live was in 1970 against Dad's beloved Arsenal. He was the happiest coming out of Highbury as they beat us 6-2. My next match was the League Cup fourth-round match where the Baggies took on Spurs at the Lane. As we were a cup team, I was so sure we would win.'

It wasn't to be for Master Crancher with the final score of Tottenham Hotspur 5 West Bromwich Albion 0.

It was a similar sinking feeling for Colin's father in the fourth round as well, although not as bad as losing 5-0. A goalless draw at Selhurst Park meant a replay at Highbury on 9 November; however, it was the Eagles who soared to a 2-0 victory.

The other replay came at Ashton Gate where Bristol City beat Leicester City 2-1 after a 2-2 draw at Filbert Street.

The quarter-finals paired Bristol Rovers at home to Aston Villa and Bristol City were at Fulham. Both these games ended up going to replays, with Rovers and Villa playing out a 1-1 draw and Fulham and Bristol City ending goalless. There were no second attempts for Manchester United and Spurs, United reaching the semi-finals with a 4-2 victory over Crystal Palace and the Londoners beating Coventry City 4-1, both at home. The replays ended with victories to the home teams as well and by the same 1-0 scoreline, Villa and Bristol City joining the two First Division giants in the semi-finals.

The semi-final first legs were both played on the same night, 16 December 1970. Manchester United and Villa drew 1-1 at Old Trafford and Bristol City did the same with Spurs at Ashton Gate.

It was all to play for as the return legs commenced on 23 December 1970. Spurs put paid to Bristol City's hopes with a 2-0 victory at White Hart Lane and Aston Villa ensured it was a very merry Christmas as they beat United 2-1 in front of a packed and delirious Villa Park faithful. Here is how the *Birmingham Evening Mail* recalled the match, 'United arrived with an attacking quartet of George Best, Denis Law, Bobby Charlton and Brian Kidd. They were full of star quality and understandably confident of bagging their £1,000-per-man win bonus. When Kidd fired them into a 12th-minute lead, Villa's hopes of a memorable upset stalled. But not for long. A memorable upset followed. And, strangely, the catalyst for it was an injury. Just before the half-hour mark United's Paddy Crerand needed treatment and, during the hiatus,

Villa's supporters got involved. Chants of "Villa, Villa" filled the stadium. Eight minutes later, right in front of the Holte End, Lochhead equalised with a header from Brian Godfrey's cross. Another Godfrey centre, 18 minutes from time, led to Paddy McMahon firing home the winner and, amid a claret and blue cacophony, Villa closed out victory.'

Aston Villa were in their third final. What fate was in store for the Third Division side against the might of Tottenham Hotspur from the first?

It was a day for the top-tier giants as Tottenham won 2-0 late on, but it never really told the story of the match as Aston Villa gave a great account of themselves and could have so easily taken the lead just in the 78th minute when striker Andy Lochhead had a shot which was cleared off the line by Steve Perryman. Moments later, Martin Chivers gave Spurs the lead against the run of play. A second was added by the same player three minutes later and that is how it stayed. After years of decline, Aston Villa could be proud of themselves once more.

Season 1971/72

The Final
4 March 1972
Stoke City 2 (Conroy, Eastham) Chelsea 1 (Osgood)
Wembley Stadium, London
Attendance: 100,000
Referee: N.C.H. Burtenshaw

Tottenham once again knocked out West Bromwich Albion as they had done in the previous season, but this time it was a 1-0 away win in the second round. The defending champions were off the mark. Runners-up Aston Villa recorded a 3-2 victory at Chesterfield. Stoke City were also victorious on their travels, winning 2-1 at Southport with Jimmy Greenhoff and Denis Smith on target. At Stamford Bridge, Chelsea avoided a banana skin with a 2-0 win against Plymouth Argyle. The tie of the round took place at Maine Road as Manchester City beat Wolverhampton Wanderers in a seven-goal thriller, 4-3, on 8 September 1971. The previous night had paired two former winners of the cup together, Queens Park Rangers beating Birmingham City 2-0. Carlisle United recorded the biggest win of the round with a 5-0 home victory over Sheffield Wednesday.

Arsenal and Blackpool both recorded 4-0 victories at home in the third round, against Newcastle United and Colchester United respectively. Aston Villa progressed to the fourth round as well, but their path was a little harder, drawing 2-2 at Crystal Palace before a 2-0 home victory was secured on 13 October. Spurs were back on the goals trail as they romped to a 4-1 victory at Torquay United. Stoke drew 1-1 away at Oxford but went through to the fourth round 2-0 in the home replay. Manchester United continued their quest with a 1-0 victory at Burnley after a replay that had seen a 1-1 draw at Old Trafford. Chelsea followed a similar path with a 1-1 draw at Nottingham Forest before a 2-1 home victory in the replay followed.

Aston Villa were not happy to be beside the seaside as they went down 4-1 at Blackpool in the fourth round to end any dreams of another Wembley final. The only other game that did not require a replay was at West Ham United where they defeated Liverpool 2-1. Arsenal and Sheffield United played out a goalless draw and all the others finished 1-1, including Chelsea at home to Bolton Wanderers, Manchester United versus Stoke and Tottenham at home to Preston North End. Chelsea made amends with a comprehensive 6-0 win at Bolton in the replay and Spurs won 2-1 at Deepdale. Bristol Rovers, Norwich City and Sheffield United also progressed. It wasn't clear-cut in the final replay as Stoke hosted Manchester United. The teams could not be separated in a 0-0 draw. The second replay took place on 15 November, and this time Stoke secured a 2-1 victory to progress. Two second-half goals from Peter Dobing and John Ritchie sent the home fans wild after George Best had given United a first-half lead.

Tottenham's chances of winning the cup for a second successive season increased with a 2-0 home victory over Blackpool, and the biggest win saw West Ham thrash Sheffield United 5-0. A hat-trick from Bryan 'Pop' Robson and a brace from Clyde Best made the difference. Chelsea and Stoke also went through to the semi-finals without replays but did so on their travels, the Potters beating Bristol Rovers 4-2 and Chelsea winning 1-0 at Norwich.

Stoke played West Ham at home in the first leg of their semi-final and Chelsea entertained Tottenham in an all-London affair in the other. West Ham secured a 2-1 victory, putting them in the driving position for the second leg, as were Chelsea who beat Spurs 3-2.

Stoke had not read the script as they overturned the lead that West Ham had given themselves in the first game, winning 1-0. This made the aggregate score 2-2 and away goals didn't count as they had done in Europe. Therefore, a replay was required, and this took place on 5 January 1972. The game finished goalless, meaning a second replay was necessary. Also playing on the same night was the other semi-final which saw a 2-2 draw at White Hart Lane, meaning that Chelsea went through 5-4 on aggregate and made sure Tottenham were not the first team to successfully defend the cup. Chelsea had to wait until 26 January to find out who they would be playing. It was not an all-London final, with Stoke winning the second replay in a thrilling 3-2 encounter at Old Trafford. Mike Bernard gave Stoke the lead on 33 minutes. Two goals for the Hammers either side of half-time, by Billy Bonds and Trevor Brooking, put the Londoners into the driving seat. However, two goals in five minutes shortly afterwards sent Stoke into the final, to be played on 4 March 1972, Dobing and Terry Conroy sending them to Wembley.

Stoke took the game to Chelsea and after only five minutes, a long throw-in from Dobing was headed on by Denis Smith. Chelsea's rearguard were slow to react and Terry Conroy was quickest to pounce to put his team into the lead. This woke Chelsea up and they started to regain the impetus. However, it was Stoke who should have stretched their advantage with both Dobing and Jimmy Greenhoff being denied by Peter Bonetti, who was nicknamed 'the Cat' and had a great game. Stoke rued their chances and cursed the former England keeper as Chelsea equalised just before half-time. A mistake from Alan Bloor in his own penalty area allowed Peter Osgood a chance to score and he duly made it one apiece as the half-time whistle blew.

The second half was a somewhat scrappy affair, until George Eastham restored Stoke's lead in the 73rd minute, pouncing after Bonetti could only block a goalbound attempt from Greenhoff. Chelsea peppered Stoke's defence, but they held firm as Gordon Banks produced some fine saves. Stoke had won their first ever major trophy and yet another name would appear on the trophy.

Stoke had also reached the semi-final of the FA Cup before once again going out to Arsenal as they had done the previous season.

Tony Waddington's first real success with Stoke had started some ten years earlier when he had wisely brought back a 46-year-old Stanley Matthews. He had not needed to do the same in 1972 as the great man was going in the direction of his 60th birthday. The likes of Gordon Banks and George Eastham had set the standard after England's 1966 World Cup triumph and the younger generation had watched and decided that they were heroes themselves in 1972.

Alan Hudson had broken into the Chelsea first team in the late 1960s and the young playmaker had started to make an impact and make people sit up and take notice, including Stoke manager Waddington. Hudson explains exclusively for this book, 'I hadn't taken much notice of our route to Wembley except for the latter stages when we played Spurs in the semi-final. I was originally from south London but at that time I was living in north London. I often would go past the national stadium, and it dawned on me that I could actually play there soon. I had missed the 1970 FA Cup Final [which saw Chelsea beat Leeds after a replay]. I scored the final goal at White Hart Lane in the second leg to get us through to Wembley. I was so relieved as I had given away the penalty a few minutes before.

'The next day, I was having a bite to eat with Terry Venables, and he told me that that was the best Chelsea performance he had ever seen. I was made up. We lost the match and George Eastham scored the winning goal. Looking back, I was close to him, and I rue that I never tried to block him. It wasn't my best performance but strangely enough I must have done something good as I signed for Stoke City 18 months later, and funnily enough I replaced Eastham.

'I had a great time in the Midlands playing for them and under Tony Waddington who came up trumps for City in that final on the day. Perhaps it was divine intervention as Tony had met the Pope when Stoke were in Rome when they played Roma in the Anglo-Italian Cup some months before!'

Liam O'Gorman was involved in two games of football on cup final day. Firstly, he represented his school in the morning, before making a painful trip to Wembley to follow his beloved Chelsea. He recalls, 'During the match I played in, I went over after being tackled and tore all the ligaments in my ankle. I practically hobbled to Wembley in agony which was made worse by the scoreline. After the match, I fainted on the Tube back home three times because of the pain. I got home and my ankle was the size of a football.'

Season 1972/73

The Final

3 March 1973
Tottenham Hotspur 1 (Coates) Norwich City 0
Wembley Stadium, London
Attendance: 100,000
Referee: D.W. Smith

History was once more made in the 1972/73 season. Up until this point, no team had won the Football League Cup more than once. Previously, there had been 12 finals and 12 different winners.

Both finalists in 1973 had won it before so a record was going to be broken either way.

Defending champions Stoke City eased through with a 3-0 home win against Sunderland in the second round. Runners-up Chelsea also qualified for the third round with a 1-0 victory on the east coast at Southend United. Norwich City defeated Leicester City 2-1 at Carrow Road to get off to a winning start and Tottenham Hotspur also won 2-1 at home against a spirited Huddersfield Town. There were 4-0 wins at home for Bristol Rovers, Leeds United and Manchester City – on the receiving end were Brighton & Hove Albion, Burnley and Rochdale respectively. Charlton

Athletic and Mansfield Town played out a classic with the Addicks edging it 4-3.

Arsenal cruised to a 5-0 victory at home against Rotherham United, but the biggest shocks of the round came at Gigg Lane as Bury beat the might of Manchester City 2-0 (George Hamstead and John Murray scoring) and St James' Park where Blackpool came away with a 3-0 win against a shell-shocked Newcastle United. Leeds United, Manchester United, Chelsea and Liverpool were all involved in replays. Leeds saw off Aston Villa 2-0 at Elland Road after a 1-1 draw at Villa Park, Chelsea beat Derby 3-2 at the Bridge after a goalless draw at the Baseball Ground, Liverpool beat West Bromwich Albion 2-1 at Anfield after a 1-1 draw at The Hawthorns and Manchester United came away from Bristol Rovers with a 1-1 draw and were expected to finish the job back at Old Trafford. However, this was not to be the case with Rovers winning 2-1. John Rudge and Bruce Bannister both scored and sent shockwaves through Old Trafford.

Another team involved in replays were Tottenham Hotspur and they finally went through in the second one. They had drawn their tie 1-1 at the Ayresome Park home of Middlesbrough, and like Manchester United they were expected to go through at home in the first replay. However, neither side could find the net and so it went to a second replay at White Hart Lane on 30 October where Spurs won 2-1. Norwich went through at the first time of asking by winning 2-1 at Hull City.

The tie of the fourth round took place at Anfield when Liverpool were paired with Leeds. This was the only match that needed a replay with the final score being 2-2. It was Liverpool who went through with a 1-0 victory at Elland Road, with Kevin Keegan scoring in the last minute. Stoke were beaten 3-1 at Notts County and there were also victories for Blackpool, Chelsea, Arsenal and Tottenham. The other teams that went through did it in style with significant victories. Norwich came away with a 5-1 away win at Stockport County, and Bristol Rovers' reward for knocking out Manchester United in the previous round was a 4-0 thrashing dished out by Wolverhampton Wanderers at Molineux.

Ron Saunders's Norwich were back on the goalscoring trail in the quarter-finals when they beat Arsenal 3-0 at Highbury. Graham Paddon took home the match ball after scoring all three. Tottenham beating Liverpool 3-1 after a replay.

The semi-final draw paired Chelsea at home to Norwich in the first leg and Wolves at home against Spurs. Both fixtures ended up with away victories, with Norwich winning 2-0 and Spurs 2-1. The return leg at White Hart Lane was on the penultimate day of 1972 and finished 2-2, meaning Spurs went into the final for the second time in two seasons. Norwich finished off the challenge put forward by Chelsea just three days into 1973 with a 1-0 victory. The Canaries went through to Wembley with a 3-0 aggregate victory and Spurs won their semi 4-3.

The final was not one for the purists and was a mostly disappointing affair. It was settled in the 73rd minute via a term that was used a lot in the 1970s, by a 'super-sub', and in this case his name was Ralph Coates. A long throw from Martin Chivers was helped on by Martin Peters but cleared to the edge of the penalty area, where Coates, a first-half replacement for the injured John Pratt, thumped home a low shot.

For Norwich defender Dave Stringer, this was the first of two League Cup Final defeats, and his recollection of the day will always be synonymous with a certain song performed by Cliff Richard as reported years later by the *Eastern Daily Press*. 'It was not a classic as is very often the case,' he said. 'We lost 1-0 but we would have wanted the game to be a little more spectacular.

'We played very well to get there; we came through the semi-final against Chelsea after the fog came down at Carrow Road and we had to replay the second leg, but against Spurs, a bit like our second final against Villa in 1975, we didn't get going.

'Nobody wants to know the losers … I remember at the end that the band played Cliff Richard's song "Congratulations". Every time I hear it, it reminds me and I think, "Oh, switch that off!"'

There were some notable quotes from other people on that day as well. Spurs midfielder Doug Livermore: 'I remember that before the game our manager stood up and told us to enjoy the day because it was a fantastic occasion for our lads to get there.'

Norwich striker David Cross: 'I think we left it all on the training ground … it was a slog, a big, big slog. I thought we did well to only lose 1-0. We never threatened Tottenham.'

Norwich manager Ron Saunders: 'We can be proud of every one of our team in this final. It was a physical game but never dirty. The goal came against the run of play when we were getting on top.'

Norwich goalkeeper Kevin Keelan: 'Spurs were almost playing at home, having played there so many times, and it was up to them to come out and play. They didn't. The only goal was scrappy.'

Spurs forward Martin Chivers: 'Late in the game I took a long throw. The ball was partially cleared to the edge of the area and Ralph belted it into the net. His hair went mad as he went on his famous run.'

Spurs midfielder Martin Peters: 'Being captain of the side and going up to receive the trophy at Wembley is very special. It was a great day for Tottenham, and it took us into Europe again.'

Tottenham Hotspur had become the first team to win the trophy twice – their second in three seasons.

Season 1973/74

The Final
2 March 1974
Manchester City 1 (Bell) Wolverhampton Wanderers 2
(Hibbitt, Richards)
Wembley Stadium, London
Attendance: 100,000
Referee: E.D. Wallace

Sport had been in turmoil somewhat in the early part of the 1970s. In 1972 at the Munich Olympics, 11

Israeli athletes had been taken hostage and killed by an organisation known as 'Black September'. The following year the planet saw the first oil crisis where an embargo was put on many parts of the world. The proclamation was made by members of the Organization of Arab Petroleum Exporting Countries, led by Saudi Arabia. The embargo was targeted at nations that had supported Israel during the Yom Kippur War, a conflict carried out in Syria and Egypt. The initial nations targeted were Canada, Japan and certain parts of Europe, including the United Kingdom. It also affected the United States of America, and other countries were later added to the list, including Portugal, Rhodesia and South Africa.

The embargo was to have an effect that went way beyond its original action. It caused a world recession and prices shot up as a result of having to procure alternative oil that fed cars and lighthouses. Many parts of Europe banned driving, flying and boating on Sundays to lighten the burden. In the Netherlands, people were even going to prison for using too much electricity, although the country experienced a total embargo, while the UK and France were treated much better than most. That was their reward for refusing to allow the US to use their airfields and stopping arms and supplies to both the Arabs and the Israelis. The other six EEC (now EU) nations faced partial cutbacks, but the UK had other problems that it faced when it came to its own energy crisis, due to a series of strikes in the coal and rail industries. It eventually brought down the Labour government.

Football had to play its part during these troubled times and the original idea that Alan Hardaker had for the League Cup, in terms of making ties midweek matches under the floodlights, had to be temporarily reversed. Matches were still played in midweek in the evenings but also took place during the day and weekends and were also used to fulfil fixtures.

The first-round ties of the 1973/74 season commenced just a few weeks before the oil crisis began, but they still caused a fixture backlog as 12 of the 28 went to replays. Fortunately, there were no second replays to endure. The biggest win of the first round came at Walsall who thrashed Shrewsbury Town 6-1 in front of a crowd of 4,772. By far the biggest crowd and one of the 12 games that went to a replay was at Burnden Park where 17,101 fans witnessed a 1-1 draw between Bolton Wanderers and Preston North End. There were even more fans on the terraces in the replay as Bolton made amends with a 2-0 win in front of 18,571, sending the vast majority at home unhappy.

The second-round matches took place between 2 and 10 October 1973, just as the oil crisis was taking shape. Ron Saunders's Norwich City made amends for their goal-shy exploits in the previous season's final by securing a 6-2 home victory against Wrexham. Tottenham Hotspur's defence of the cup was a weak one as they were beaten 1-0 at Queens Park Rangers. Wolverhampton Wanderers got off to a winning start with a comprehensive 3-0 victory at Halifax Town, while the biggest crowd of the second round came at Derby

County with 29,172 in attendance to see a thrilling game finish 2-2 against Sunderland, the north-east side eventually going through after a second replay.

The game of the third round was at Loftus Road where QPR hosted Sheffield Wednesday on 6 November. The fans were treated to ten goals, but unfortunately it was a long journey back to Sheffield for the fans and players as Rangers scored eight of them. A Danny Cannon own goal in the second minute and a goal from Gerry Francis, braces from Mick Leach and Don Givens, a goal from Stan Bowles and another own goal – this time by Jimmy Mullen – completed the rout. Manchester City avoided any replays as they beat Carlisle United 1-0 on the same evening and Norwich were also 1-0 winners at Everton. Wolves came away with a 1-1 result at Tranmere Rovers before winning 2-1 at home in the replay.

Norwich continued another quest to reach Wembley in the fourth round after disposing of Southampton 2-0 at The Dell, but they did it without Ron Saunders. He had resigned just four days earlier after a 3-1 home defeat to Everton in the league which had put them in a precarious position. It was a boardroom row that prompted Saunders to resign. Manchester City drew 0-0 at York City on the same evening that Norwich had progressed. The following day, Saunders was installed as Manchester City's new manager, their fourth of 1973, with Malcolm Allison, Johnny Hart and Tony Book having been the previous incumbents. On 5 December, Saunders took charge of the League Cup replay at Maine Road and got off to a great start with a 4-1 home victory.

Saunders's new charges endured another replay in the quarter-finals after a 2-2 draw at Coventry City with goals from Tommy Booth and Dennis Leman. They went through 4-2 in the replay, but Coventry put them to the test. Mike Summerbee's 65th-minute goal had cancelled out a lead that Coventry held at half-time. However, a second Coventry goal for Brian Alderson (he had bagged a brace in the first match) just three minutes later restored the lead for the Sky Blues. Francis Lee equalised in the 78th minute before getting his second and Manchester City's third just two minutes later. Denis Law settled matters three minutes from time. Could Saunders take a team to Wembley for the second successive season? His old club Norwich were also trying to make amends. A 1-1 draw at Millwall saw them involved in a replay, which they duly won 2-1. The other teams going through and not requiring a replay were Wolves, who beat Liverpool 1-0 at home courtesy of a goal just after half-time scored by their hotshot John Richards, and Plymouth, who made the last four with a 2-1 victory at Birmingham City.

The semi-final draw saw Saunders's team avoid a clash with Norwich. Instead, Plymouth faced Manchester City in the first leg and Norwich took on Wolves in theirs. Both games were played on 23 January 1974, and both games ended 1-1. Steve Davey gave Plymouth a half-time lead before Tommy Booth restored parity in the second half. John Richards continued his fine scoring run with an equaliser at Carrow Road after Ian Mellor had put the Canaries a goal up.

Manchester City's game had kicked off at 2pm on the Wednesday at Plymouth and Wolves did the same on Saturday, 26 January for the return leg, with Richards scoring the only goal to put his team into the final 2-1 on aggregate in front of a crowd that tallied 32,605.

City then took care of Plymouth on Wednesday, 30 January with a 2-0 home victory in their second leg, going through to the final 3-1 on aggregate, with Francis Lee and Colin Bell ensuring victory.

In the final, Wolves had taken the lead on the stroke of half-time through Kenny Hibbitt, before Colin Bell sent the City fans packed into Wembley into a frenzy when he equalised. The game was living up to expectations and was set for a thrilling finale. The popular West Midlands paper, the *Express and Star*, continued with its report as the minutes ticked down with the match evenly poised, 'But with the scores level and no more than ten minutes remaining came the one moment of drama from the touchline and the element of luck that can be so vital when a cup final is at stake. Substitute Barry Powell has begun warming up and it was [Bill] McGarry's intention to bring off Richards, whose stomach injury was causing so much discomfort. But the Wolves boss knew winger Dave Wagstaffe was in some trouble with a thigh strain and for a couple of minutes longer, he pondered over the situation. It was just long enough for Wagstaffe to solve McGarry's predicament for a right-wing run had him pulling up sharply and limping out of the game. On went Powell and within three minutes Richards fired Wolves ahead to kill the hopes of Manchester City and land the biggest prize which Wolves has so valiantly fought for.'

Wolverhampton Wanderers had become the 13th team to win the trophy and, at the final whistle, their fans found themselves in dreamland. It certainly wasn't unlucky for them.

Season 1974/75

The Final
1 March 1975
Aston Villa 1 (Graydon) Norwich City 0
Wembley Stadium, London
Attendance: 100,000
Referee: G.W. Hill

Aston Villa and Norwich City had been the first two winners of the League Cup. Villa had done so as members of the First Division and Norwich from the second tier. Now they had the chance to claim their second titles and emulate Spurs. However, they were both participating as Second Division clubs, and it still remains the only time that the final was contested by teams not in the top flight. It also proved to be third time lucky for Ron Saunders, who had been on the losing side in the previous two finals, with Norwich and Manchester City respectively.

Two divisions below both clubs were Chester City. As the season started, Chester had not experienced promotion since joining the Football League in the 1931/32 season where they were members of the Third Division (North) until the 1957/58 campaign when they had been relegated to the fourth tier where they had stayed ever since. Ron Saunders had been a prolific scorer in his career as a player. The Birkenhead-born striker had played for Everton, Tonbridge Angels, Gillingham and Watford before finishing his playing career at Charlton Athletic in 1967. However, it was at Portsmouth a few seasons earlier where he was more fondly remembered, scoring just shy of 150 goals for them. The fitness fanatic began his management career with Yeovil Town and Oxford United, before making his mark with Norwich from 1969 to 1973, taking them to the League Cup Final in his last year at Carrow Road. He guided them to the Second Division championship in 1972 thus ensuring top-flight football for the Canaries for the first time in their history. Saunders resigned after a boardroom battle in November 1973 and duly took the reins of Manchester City shortly afterwards, once more guiding his new club to the League Cup Final, of 1974, where he experienced further Wembley heartache as City ended up on the losing side. Saunders did not last at Maine Road as he took up the helm at Aston Villa in the summer of the same year.

Manchester United had been crowned champions of Europe in 1968, but years of decline followed after Sir Matt Busby had retired (although he did a second stint as interim manager after the sacking of Wilf McGuinness) before Frank O'Farrell took over. This culminated in relegation from the First Division in the 1973/74 campaign. The club were playing in the League Cup for the first time as a Second Division outfit, but it never showed as they beat Charlton Athletic 5-1 in front of the Old Trafford faithful in the second round. United's local rivals were also in the mood as they thrashed Scunthorpe United at Maine Road 6-0, the evening before the Red Devils' big win. Aston Villa drew 1-1 at home to Everton but upset the First Division giants in the replay, winning 3-0 at Goodison Park. Norwich also required a replay after a goalless game at Bolton Wanderers, the Canaries winning the second match 3-1. There was a big win for Derby County as they went to Portsmouth and came away from the south coast with a 5-1 victory. West Ham enjoyed a 6-0 win as Manchester City had done, but the difference was that it was not at the first time of asking after a 0-0 draw at Tranmere Rovers.

Villa and Norwich would also be involved in replays in the third round. Villa went through after a 2-2 draw at Gresty Road against a valiant Crewe Alexandra team, before winning the replay back at Villa Park 1-0, and Norwich played against Second Division rivals West Bromwich Albion. After a 1-1 draw at The Hawthorns, the Canaries took care of business 2-0. The draw of the round was at Old Trafford where Second Division United played First Division rivals City, with a Gerry Daly penalty deciding the tie as the hosts won 1-0.

Fourth Division Chester had knocked out Walsall and Blackpool at home in the first two rounds and the home advantage and winning run continued in the third round as they beat Preston North End 1-0. Derby's reward for a 5-1 victory on the south coast in the previous round was another trip there, but they were on the receiving end of a 5-0 thrashing at the hands of Southampton, and thus became the biggest shock of the round. There was a repeat of the 1971/72 final when Chelsea played host to Stoke City. This was settled on the third attempt and again Stoke came out on top. A 2-2 draw at the Bridge was followed by a 1-1 draw at Stoke, but they made no mistake in the replay as the side from the Potteries thrashed Chelsea 6-2. Chelsea fans must have become sick of the sight of Stoke in the early parts of the 1970s in the League Cup.

Norwich and Villa continued to make their paths to the final as difficult as possible as both teams yet again required replays. Villa were held at Hartlepool 1-1 before a 6-1 win in front of home fans at Villa Park, and Norwich drew 2-2 at Sheffield United but claimed a 2-1 home victory in their replay. Manchester United continued to beat First Division opposition with a 3-2 home victory against Burnley. Middlesbrough pulled off a shock with a 1-0 win at Liverpool. However, by far and away the biggest upset came at Chester. They had played at home in all the previous rounds and won against opposition in or around them, and they had done this largely unnoticed. It all changed when the mighty Leeds came to town on 13 November, as 19,000 fans packed into Sealand Road to witness a game between a team in the Fourth Division and the champions of England. There could only be one winner, but Chester had not read the script, winning 3-0 against a side that had such household names as Billy Bremner, Johnny Giles and Peter Lorimer. Trevor Staunton and a John James double did the damage to ensure that their names would for ever be etched into Chester (and indeed football) folklore history. The headlines on the back pages the day after were full of the match. The *Daily Mirror's* read 'SHOCKER! LEEDS OUT – CHESTER CRUSH THE CHAMPS' while the *Daily Mail* devoted front-page coverage along with the news of early morning hunts to find the body of Lord Lucan, the aristocrat who had gone missing in London, exclaiming 'CHESTER HEROES KO THE LEAGUE CHAMPIONS'.

Chester had crept through previous rounds without any fanfare. Now this was about to change as the draw was made for the quarter-finals. This time, they had to travel and once more it was First Division opposition in Newcastle United, as they forced a replay at home after a 0-0 draw at St James' Park. This was the same score at Ayresome Park where Middlesbrough entertained Manchester United. It was also a stalemate in the third game played on the evening of 4 December when Norwich drew 1-1 at home to local rivals Ipswich Town. Aston Villa were the only team through at the first time of asking as they beat Colchester United 2-1 away. Ron Saunders had reached the semi-finals for the third season on the trot, and they were soon joined by his old club, Norwich, who also made it three semis on the spin as they won 2-1 at Portman Road. Manchester United eased by Middlesbrough 3-0 at Old Trafford and the giant-killers of 1974 in the League Cup continued as Chester won their replay 1-0.

These results ensured that no team from the top flight contested the semi-finals. There were three from the Second Division, with Chester representing the Fourth Division.

Chester were paired at home to Aston Villa in the first leg and Manchester United entertained Norwich in theirs. Both matches were played on 15 January 1975, and both ended up 2-2 in two very entertaining games. Bobby McDonald had given Villa the lead on 15 minutes before Tommy Owen restored parity on the stroke of half-time. Incidentally, Tommy and his wife in later years had a son called Michael who went on to have a fantastic career with England, Liverpool, Real Madrid, Newcastle United and Manchester United. Ray Graydon restored Villa's advantage in the 50th minute before Gary Moore made it 2-2.

In the other match at Old Trafford, Tony Powell gave Norwich the lead on the stroke of half-time before a brace from Lou Macari in the 51st and 71st minute turned things around. This lasted until two minutes from time when Ted MacDougall equalised.

Two weeks later, Villa and Chester served up another feast of goals with Villa taking the match 3-2, and 5-4 on aggregate. The players of Chester and the Sealand Road faithful could hold their heads up high after a fantastic campaign which was made even better with promotion as well. Villa had raced into a 2-0 lead before the half-hour mark thanks to a brace from their young hotshot striker, Keith Leonard. Stuart Mason pulled a goal back on 33 minutes and then John James scored just after the hour and the game, and the tie, was once again all square. Villa settled it in the 80th minute when Keith Leonard turned provider for Brian Little to make it 3-2 on a pulsating night at Villa Park.

There was less drama at Carrow Road, but that didn't bother the home fans as they beat Manchester United 1-0 to return to Wembley 2-1 on aggregate, with Colin Suggett scoring the only goal, on 54 minutes.

Ron Saunders was in his third final on the trot managing his third team, Aston Villa, against the club he did it with first with, Norwich City, in an all-Second Division affair. It also guaranteed that one of them would match Tottenham Hotspur by winning the competition for the second time. Both had also lost to Spurs in their previous appearances in the final. There was a lot at stake, as both were going for promotion as well.

It was a dour final played on the first day of March. The game was settled with just nine minutes remaining when Villa were awarded a penalty. Ray Graydon took it and scored after a rebound when his original kick had been pushed on to the post by Kevin Keelan. The final ended 1-0 to Villa and they joined Spurs at the top of the League Cup leaderboard. For Norwich, it was their second 1-0 defeat in two seasons in the final and they had simply not turned up in either of them; not that Villa had been much better, but it was their captain Ian Ross who collected the trophy as well as leading the customary lap of honour. However, there was one player who missed it, and that just happened to be the goalscoring hero. Ray Graydon recalls the moment, 'One of my dreams was to be in the victory lap of honour round the stadium, but somebody pulled me through the fence that was around the ground in those days and by the time I got going again, the rest of the players had left me behind. I couldn't catch up. I was last back in the dressing room but that gave me another memory that will never fade. It was a big communal bath, big enough to swim in, and all the other players had gone so I was on my own. There were cardboard cups of champagne still around, and I just swam around with one, just taking the day in.'

It had been third time lucky for Ron Saunders as he could now finally call himself a Wembley winner.

It had been a wonderful campaign for Chester City in the League Cup, their run ending at the semi-final stage. However, the season finished with them finally getting their first ever promotion in the Football League, making it a wonderful season for manager Ken Roberts and his team.

Season 1975/76

The Final
28 February 1976
Manchester City 2 (Barnes, Tueart) Newcastle
United 1 (Gowling)
Wembley Stadium, London
Attendance: 100,000
Referee: J.K. Taylor

It was time for another change at the start of the 1975/76 season for the League Cup and it centred around the first round with games now being played on a home and away basis as had been commonplace at the semi-final stage. Away goals did not count double, so if the match was still tied after the two legs, then replays were required.

The late 1960s and the early part of the 1970s had afforded good fortune to both Manchester City and Newcastle United, but in particular for the team from the north-west of the country. A clean sweep of the three domestic trophies had been completed from 1968 to 1970 with the club winning each competition once in that time. It had got much better for them in 1970 when they also claimed the European Cup Winners' Cup, ensuring a golden time for Joe Mercer who had been manager since 1965. Newcastle were also victorious in the Inter-Cities Fairs Cup in 1969 and had been runners-up to a rampant Liverpool team in the FA Cup Final of 1974, all under the stewardship of Joe Harvey who had also served them well as a player. By the time of the final in 1976 both clubs were under new management, though. Like Harvey, Tony Book had served City well as a player and was now in charge of the team and Gordon Lee was in the hot seat at Newcastle.

Aston Villa and Manchester United had been promoted at the end of the previous season and they met in the third round of the League Cup, with United winning 2-1 at Villa Park and knocking the defending champions out. Manchester City saw off the challenge posed by Nottingham Forest at Maine Road, winning 2-1. Newcastle needed a replay at St James' Park after a 1-1 draw at Bristol Rovers, with the second meeting ending up 2-0 to the hosts. The goals came from Irving Nattrass and a penalty converted by Tommy Craig.

The fourth round threw up a Manchester derby with the reds of United travelling to the blue half of the city on 12 November, Dennis Tueart scoring a brace and Asa Hartford and Joe Royle netting one apiece as Book's side claimed the derby bragging rights by winning 4-0 in front of 50,000 fans at a jubilant Maine Road. Newcastle also went through into the quarter-finals at the first time of asking with a 3-1 win at Queens Park Rangers, who were flying in the First Division. Mansfield Town and Notts County pulled off the shock results of the round. Mansfield beat the 1974 winners Wolverhampton Wanderers 1-0 at home, while Notts County got past Everton at Meadow Lane, although it took a replay after drawing 2-2 at Goodison – the oldest league club winning 2-0 second time around.

All four quarter-finals were decided without the need for replays with Newcastle United Notts County 1-0 at home, Manchester City seeing off the challenge of Mansfield 4-2, Middlesbrough winning 2-0 at Burnley, and the most goals coming at White Hart Lane where Tottenham thrashed Doncaster Rovers 7-2.

The semi-final first legs were played on 13 and 14 January 1976. First up were Middlesbrough at home to Manchester City with Tottenham taking on Newcastle the day after – both finished 1-0 to the home teams. However, the second legs saw both results overturned, with City beating Middlesbrough 4-0 to go through 4-1 on aggregate and Newcastle joining them in the final after a 3-1 home win over Spurs, going through 3-2 on aggregate.

It didn't take long for the first goal to be scored in the final. Glenn Keeley fouled City's Joe Royle in the middle of the Newcastle half. The resulting free kick was hoisted into the penalty area by Asa Hartford, and Mike Doyle was there to head the ball across the goal. It fell to the feet of the youngster, Peter Barnes, who turned away to celebrate as he put it into the net and gave City the lead. Newcastle fans were in rapture themselves after 33 minutes as Alan Gowling finished from a Malcolm Macdonald cross. The teams went in all square at the break but this was all to change just after the start of the second half. A ball by Willie Donachie to the far post was headed across by Tommy Booth. While this was happening, City's Dennis Tueart had his back to goal, but this did not deter the boyhood Newcastle fan producing an overhead kick that bounced beyond Mike Mahoney into the bottom-left corner of the net. Royle had a goal disallowed and there was no more scoring as City joined Aston Villa and Tottenham Hotspur as winners of the competition for a second time. There was also another record of note. City captain Mike Doyle lifted the trophy, and Tony Book became the first man to win the competition as both a player and a manager, having played in the 1970 League Cup Final when City had beaten West Bromwich Albion. Book's caretaker roles in the previous seasons had bode well for him and Manchester City in 1976.

Karen Kennedy was a very excited young Geordie who was Newcastle-mad in 1976. She had been looking forward to travelling down to Wembley for weeks, and takes up the story here: 'I was 11 years of age and went down with my father. I had to collect the tokens from the programmes of all the home games. When I had collected enough, I had to post them to St James' Park and hope for the best. I was so happy when I got the letter to say I had a ticket. So off we went for the weekend, and we stayed in a B&B in Fulham. One of our elderly neighbours had knitted me a black and white jumper with League Cup patterned all over the front. But the overall memory for me was the travel down to Wembley. The motorway was full of cars with Newcastle scarves hanging out of them. I started to count them but there were so many I soon lost count. My father passed away in 2021 and up until that time we would often reminisce about those wonderful times.'

The 1976 League Cup Final had been fiercely contested by both clubs and it took a wonder goal worthy of any final to win it. To this day, Dennis Tueart calls his winner the best goal that he ever scored – it was probably one of the best ones ever seen at Wembley, if not just about anywhere in the world.

Two very proud teams who had won many major honours in the past had contested the final, but it would take several decades for one of them to get their hands on another trophy of real significance as both clubs found themselves in football's wilderness for long periods of time that seemed unthinkable back in 1976.

Season 1976/77

The Final
12 March 1977
Aston Villa 0 Everton 0
Wembley Stadium, London
Attendance: 100,000
Referee: G.C. Kew

Replay
16 March 1977
Aston Villa 1 (Kenyon own goal) Everton 1 (Latchford)
(after extra time)
Hillsborough Stadium, Sheffield
Attendance: 55,000
Referee: G.C. Kew

Second Replay
13 April 1977
Aston Villa 3 (Nicholl, Little 2) Everton 2 (Latchford,
Lyons) (after extra time)
Old Trafford, Manchester
Attendance: 54,749
Referee: G.C. Kew

The long, hot summer of 1976 broke several records at the time, and the Football League Cup was no different as it was the first final that went to not only one replay but two as Aston Villa became the first team to win the competition three times.

The first round's first legs took place on 14 to 16 August in sweltering conditions with the second legs taking place just a few days later. The biggest aggregate win was for Blackburn Rovers who defeated Rochdale 5-1 and the most goals saw a 6-5 victory for Cardiff City at the expense of Bristol Rovers across both legs.

The second-round draw saw the 1975 winners play the 1976 winners at Villa Park as the home team entertained Manchester City. Villa ran out 3-0 victors with Brian Little scoring a brace and Ray Graydon the other. The first goal scored by Little was an absolute beauty as he emulated Dennis Tueart with a spectacular overhead kick that gave Joe Corrigan no chance. Everton's campaign saw them also win at home by the same margin as Villa, beating Cambridge United.

Ron Saunders faced an old team once more in the third round with a 2-1 victory over Norwich City. Everton avoided a potential banana skin with a 1-0 win at Fourth Division Stockport County. The biggest upset came at White Hart Lane as First Division Tottenham Hotspur lost 3-2 against Third Division Wrexham on 26 September 1976. Wrexham were 3-0 up by the 50-minute mark with Mickey Thomas scoring two and Billy Ashcroft the other. Spurs managed to pull two back through Glenn Hoddle and Ian Moores soon afterwards but could not get that all-important equaliser. Newcastle, the previous season's runners-up, beat Stoke City 3-0 at home.

Wrexham's reward for their cup upset saw them travel to another First Division outfit. This time there was no slip-hup for the top flight as Aston Villa won 5-1. Newcastle's hopes of reaching the final again were completely derailed at Old Trafford with Manchester

United winning 7-2. Everton continued their quest to reach their first final with another sound 3-0 home win, this time against Coventry City.

Six teams from the top flight and two from the second tier made it through to the quarter-finals. Villa beat Millwall 2-0 at Villa Park and the shock of the round came at the Baseball Ground where Bolton Wanderers beat Derby County 2-1, ensuring at least one representative from the second tier went through. The other two all-First Division clashes saw Everton win 3-0 once more, this time at Old Trafford, and Queens Park Rangers saw off the challenge of local rivals Arsenal with a 2-1 success.

The semi-finals paired Everton at home to Bolton in the first leg. Queens Park Rangers hosted Aston Villa in their first leg, and both ended in draws, 1-1 at Goodison and 0-0 at Loftus Road. Everton took the second leg at Burnden Park with a 1-0 victory courtesy of a goal from Bob Latchford after 24 minutes, although they should have scored again in the 65th minute when they were awarded a penalty which was put wide by Duncan McKenzie.

Villa and QPR served up a great second leg which ended 2-2 and meant a replay at Highbury on 22 February. Villa ruled the game and ran out 3-0 winners with Brian Little bagging a hat-trick, and they were back at Wembley for their third League Cup Final of the 1970s.

The final, played on 12 March 1977, was a complete anticlimax and was one of the worst finals in living memory, with the 'highlight' being that the game was held up for several minutes as one of the horses had lost its spur on the turf. No goals were scored – but the horse was OK. The League Cup had its first final go to a replay, at Hillsborough, the home of Sheffield Wednesday, on 16 March, where 55,000 Villa and Everton fans witnessed a game that was only slightly better than at Wembley. A Roger Kenyon own goal on 79 minutes looked to have given Villa the cup, but Bob Latchford was there to put the ball into the net two minutes from time to take the game into extra time. No more goals were scored and so a first replay became a second one which was played at Old Trafford on 13 April with a crowd just shy of 55,000.

This time they were served with a game that would live long in the memory. Everton took the lead in the 38th minute through Latchford, who had rescued the Toffees in the dying minutes of the first replay. This advantage lasted until the 80th minute when Villa equalised with a wonder goal from all of 40 yards as centre-back Chris Nicholl hit a rocket that flew past David Lawson. A minute later, Villa went in front through Brian Little who put the ball into the net from a tight angle with a shot that was all about precision. The final had sensationally sprung into life – at last – but it didn't stop there as Mick Lyons forced the ball over the line just one minute later, and Everton fans breathed a huge sigh of relief. Just three minutes earlier they had looked like they were going to lose it, but now they had levelled. Gordon Kew had been the man in black for this marathon final (and the replays) from the start. Now he brought the 90 minutes to a close and extra time beckoned. Both teams gave no quarter, and Villa lost their influential right-back John Gidman on 103 minutes, due to a groin strain he had picked up.

It looked very much like it would be deadlock once more, but at least the teams had played their part this time around. Then, in the 118th minute, Villa took the lead and won the match to break the hearts of the blue side of Merseyside. Gordon Smith, who had replaced Gidman, sent a cross into the Everton box, but the ball took a deflection that seemed to slow it down. Perhaps this had confused left-back Terry Darracott who just let the ball roll past him and in stepped Little to tap home at the far post and past Lawson. After 330 minutes, the game was finally settled, and Aston Villa had become the first team to win the trophy three times – but they did it at the third attempt.

Chris Nicholl's screamer had got Villa back into the game, but he very nearly couldn't see much for the rest of the match, 'After I scored to make it 1-1 in the final, I was on the halfway line, and I remember some of the lads jumping on me. Leighton Phillips jumped on me and put his right foot into my eye and my contact lens fell out. When everyone went to kick off again, I spent the next minute and a half scouring Old Trafford for my contact lens, but it didn't affect my timing as my timing was rubbish anyway. After the final whistle and we had won the cup, I remember coming back out on to the muddy pitch to look for it again. In those days, contact lenses were quite valuable and pricey so it was a big deal to lose one. I still couldn't find it!'

Michael Pye also went to the three finals as a young Everton fan, as he had done for most of the previous rounds. He takes up the story, 'I think we had vouchers for the Wembley final and I bunked off school and queued from 8.30 in the morning to 3pm in the afternoon at Goodison along with fellow classmates from Formby High School for a ticket. It was my first time at Wembley and the coach was booked from Crosby.

'To be honest it was a bit of an anticlimax. We had the east side players' entrance which was packed and a good atmosphere but nothing of any note on the pitch and the game fizzled out into a 0-0 draw. The replay was on a Wednesday night so again we bunked off school and went to Hillsborough on the same coach. Liverpool were playing the same night at home to Saint-Étienne in a European Cup semi-final. We had picked up points all over the city. I remember giving the Victory sign (in reverse) to the Liverpudlians. We were late getting to Sheffield due to congestion at Snake Pass and missed, along with hundreds of others, the first 25 minutes. Everton had the Leppings Lane end. It was rammed. The game was end-to-end but nothing in the final third. Then I remember Villa putting a cross in from the left. It was never cleared, and it seemed to bobble in off Roger Kenyon. We were gutted, but we never stopped singing the whole match and in injury time the ball was whipped in and Bob Latchford rammed it home. I was swept about 15 yards from where I was standing but the noise and relief was immense, and I did not care. It went to extra time but nothing of note came of it so it was now going to a second replay at old Trafford.

'My late dad and I managed to get tickets for the replay at Old Trafford, so Dad drove there. He had been to the 1968 cup final, and I was worried he might be a jinx. We got to the ground early. We had been given the Stretford End and had most of both side stands. We seemed to outnumber the Villa fans again. The atmosphere and build-up was immense with thousands of blue and white scarves and flags being waved. We were singing' "Tell me mama I don't want no tea no tea we're going to Wembley tell me ma."

'In the first half we played really well and Bob Latchford put us 1-0 up. I think we sat back in the second half too much. Chris Nicholl equalised with a screamer for them. Then they went 2-1 up and I believe that our keeper, David Lawson, was at fault for both goals. Our captain, Mick Lyons, equalised with a header for us; 2-2 and the scarves were twirling again. If memory serves me right, it was extra time, then in the final two minutes the ball came in from the left and our left-back Terry Darracott let it roll past him and Brian Little put it past Dave Lawson right in front of me and Dad. We had lost it and Dad just looked at me shaking his head. I felt physically sick, with tears in my eyes. All them finals, all them League Cup rounds and we had lost it like that! I lived and breathed Everton at 16 years of age and had never seen them win anything. I now had to go to school and get the piss taken out of me by my Liverpudlian mates!

'We left Old Trafford and could hear the Villa fans celebrating. It was a long drive home and to make matters worse we had to pick up Mum from my nan's house, and my grandad was there in his final weeks dying of lung cancer. He took one look at me and said, "Never mind, son." God love him. I felt ill for a week with football-induced depression.'

Season 1977/78

The Final
18 March 1978
Nottingham Forest 0 Liverpool 0 (after extra time)
Wembley Stadium, London
Attendance: 100,000
Referee: P. Partridge

Replay
22 March 1978
Nottingham Forest 1 (Robertson) Liverpool 0
Old Trafford, Manchester
Attendance: 54,375
Referee: P. Partridge

A popular consensus doing the rounds on the terraces and in the studios in the mid-1970s centred around whether Brian Clough's days as a great manager were over and he had become a spent force. With Peter Taylor at his side, Clough had overseen the rise of Derby County in the latter part of the 1960s and early 1970s, taking them from the Second Division to the First. This resulted in the provincial club becoming champions of England in 1972. Boardroom battles and his outspoken views eventually took their toll, resulting in his resignation, with Taylor still by his side. A spell at Brighton & Hove Albion and his infamous 44 days in charge at Leeds United in 1974 (without Taylor at Elland Road) further dented Clough's reputation. On 6 January 1975, Clough, once more reunited with Taylor, took the manager's role at Nottingham Forest. This move echoed what he had done with Derby, taking a provincial club who seemingly were going nowhere in the Second Division and gaining promotion to the top tier soon afterwards. The promotion came in the 1976/77 season. Up to this point, Clough's relationship with the League Cup had been a finite one.

It had rained goals in the first round of the 1977/78 League Cup campaign over the two legs, where scores like 4-4, 5-3, 6-3, 4-5 were not uncommon. The biggest aggregate win saw Sheffield Wednesday go through 8-2 against Doncaster Rovers.

Aston Villa's defence of the cup saw them travel to Exeter City and come back with a 3-1 victory. Nottingham Forest had taken to the First Division like a duck to water, and they made a splash in the second round with a comprehensive 5-0 victory at home against West Ham United. Liverpool beat Chelsea 2-0 at Anfield. Everton had recorded three 3-0 wins as they progressed to the previous season's final, and they were at it again, seeing off Sheffield United at Bramall Lane.

Villa had beaten Queens Park Rangers at the semi-final stage the previous season, and they were doing the same again, but this time winning 1-0 in the third round. Forest were scoring goals for fun once again in the third round with a 4-0 thumping of city rivals Notts County. Liverpool once more recorded a 2-0 home victory, this time against Derby, and Everton went through after a replay, drawing 2-2 at home against Middlesbrough before putting the Teesside club to the sword with a 2-1 win. It took Manchester City two replays to go through but go through they did with a 3-2 success after extra time against a valiant Luton Town.

Forest continued to bang in the goals in the fourth round with a 4-2 home victory over the holders, Aston Villa, effectively ending the game with three goals in the first 30 minutes with Larry Lloyd, Viv Anderson and Peter Withe putting them in total control. Tony Woodcock scored the fourth before damage limitation was undertaken with two late Villa goals via Brian Little and Frank Carrodus. It took Liverpool two attempts to go through after a 2-2 at home to Coventry City, but the Reds made amends with a 2-0 victory at Highfield Road. Jimmy Case and Kenny Dalglish were on the mark.

Leeds stopped Everton reaching a second successive semi-final by thumping them 4-1 in the quarter-finals. Forest continued their excellent form in both the league and cup with a 3-0 away win at Bury. Liverpool were also successful on their travels with a 3-1 win at Wrexham. Manchester City and Arsenal found the target elusive as they drew 0-0 at City's ground, but it was the north London club who marched on with a 1-0 win at Highbury.

Don Revie had left Leeds some years before his old team had been drawn at home in the semi-final first leg to Nottingham Forest on 8 February 1978; however, his issues with Brian Clough had been well documented when Clough had those 44 days in charge at Elland Road. There was still bad blood between Leeds and the Forest manager, but it was Clough who came out on top with a 3-1 away victory and then followed it up with a 4-2 home win in the second leg on 22 February for a thumping 7-3 aggregate win. Liverpool beat Arsenal 2-1 on aggregate in the other semi-final after a goalless draw at Highbury in the second leg.

The League Cup had another new name on the winners' board as well as for the runners-up. Neither Forest nor Liverpool had been in any of the previous finals.

The final at Wembley was another damp squib. David Lacey was covering it for *The Guardian*, and he was quick to note another showpiece ending 0-0. The headline was 'RECITING THE NIL TIMES TABLE'.

The replay was four days later at Old Trafford and wasn't exactly a great game itself either, but at least it produced a goal and a talking point, John Robertson scoring from the penalty spot in the 53rd minute after a professional foul by Phil Thompson on John O'Hare. However, controversy followed as TV replays confirmed the foul was just outside the penalty area.

The only other real moment of note happened to Ian Callaghan when the stalwart received a yellow card, the first and only time he had received a booking in a long and illustrious career with Liverpool.

Nottingham Forest had been tipped to go down at the start of the season. A few weeks after this success, they followed it up by winning the First Division championship. One cannot say for sure, but it's doubtful that the bookies were paying out to any punter on this prediction at the start of the 1977/78 season

Season 1978/79

The Final
17 March 1979
Nottingham Forest 3 (Birtles 2, Woodcock)
Southampton 2 (Peach, Holmes)
Wembley Stadium, London
Attendance: 100,000
Referee: P.G. Reeves

Nottingham Forest marched on into the second round with a 4-2 home win against Oldham Athletic after a replay. Everton were in the goals with an 8-0 home win against Wimbledon in the second round – Bob Latchford netting five of them, and Martin Dobson was unlucky not to take the ball home after his three. Southampton, under the guidance of Lawrie McMenemy, had won the FA Cup just two years previously and were now in the mood to get to Wembley again. This was vindicated with a 5-2 away victory at Birmingham City. The biggest shock of the round came at Millmoor when Third Division Rotherham United knocked out the mighty Arsenal 3-1, with goals from John Green, Dave Gwyther and Richard Finney sending the majority of the 10,481 in the stadium into heaven. Frank Stapleton at least spared the blushes somewhat for the Gunners. Liverpool also joined Arsenal through the exit door with a 1-0 loss at Sheffield United.

Forest followed up with another large victory, 5-0 at Oxford United in the third round. Southampton beat Derby County 1-0 at The Dell and Charlton left Chesterfield with a 5-4 victory. Meanwhile, Aston Villa went through but only after two replays when they defeated Crystal Palace 3-0.

However, there was a shock waiting for Villa in the fourth round when they were soundly beaten 2-0 by Luton Town at Villa Park. Nottingham Forest beat Everton 3-2 in an entertaining game at Goodison. It took Southampton two attempts to see off the challenge of Reading after a goalless game at Elm Park, the Saints winning the replay 2-0.

Leeds United, Nottingham Forest and Southampton all took advantage of home ties in the quarter-finals with wins over Luton, Brighton & Hove Albion and Manchester City respectively. The other game in the round went to a replay, Watford going through to the semi-finals for the very first time by beating Stoke City 3-1 at home after a goalless draw in the Potteries.

The Hornets' reward was a trip to the City Ground in the first leg of the semi-final on 17 January 1979, Forest winning 3-1.

The second semi-final a week later saw Leeds and Southampton share four goals in an entertaining first leg at Elland Road.

Forest saw the job off in the return leg at Vicarage Road by effectively shutting up shop and no further goals saw them through to their second successive final, 3-1 on aggregate. On the same night at The Dell, Southampton beat Leeds by a slender 1-0 scoreline. Terry Curran had scored the goal and now he had got Southampton in the final against one of his previous clubs.

It was Southampton who drew first blood in the final, in the 17th minute, when David Peach scored after some great interlinking play between himself and Alan Ball. Forest were back in the game in the 51st minute when Garry Birtles equalised before putting his team into the lead with just 12 minutes remaining. Tony Woodcock was on the mark just four minutes later before Nick Holmes reduced the Forest lead to just one in the 88th minute to set up an exciting last few minutes, with Forest holding on to become the first team to successfully defend the competition.

After a few years of dour finals played at Wembley and a few replays, it was refreshing to see a great game of football being played. Saints' fans may have left Wembley feeling disappointed but they had most certainly played their part.

As did actors Ian McShane, Paul Nicholas and Adam Faith in a film later released that year called *Yesterday's Heroes*, also starring Suzanne Somers and written by Jackie Collins. The film was about a has-been, alcoholic former football star determined to make a comeback. He gets help from his former girlfriend, now a rock star, and her partner. Real-life footage of the 1979 League

Cup Final was used to complement the scenes filmed, although there were errors. To correspond with the footage used, the Saints actors wore replica Southampton kits, featuring yellow shirts and blue shirts. However, not all the players featured in the fictional Saints side had the same strip. While some had the correct kit, featuring a blue band running down the sleeves with yellow Admiral logos, other players wore a shirt that had plain sleeves. Furthermore, a couple of players, including Ian McShane's character, had the wrong typeface for their numbers on the back of the shirts. Admiral had a distinctive font at the time, but some players had plain numbers more familiar with Umbro shirts of the period.

Season 1979/80

The Final
15 March 1980
Nottingham Forest 0 Wolverhampton Wanderers 1 (Gray)
Wembley Stadium, London
Attendance: 100,000
Referee: D. Richardson

There were more changes made to the format with the second round now being played on a home and away basis. There were some significant aggregate wins for Arsenal, Crystal Palace, Southampton and, not surprisingly, Nottingham Forest at that stage. Arsenal may have lost the 1968 final to Leeds United but won 8-1 over the two legs against them in 1979. Crystal Palace won by the same margin as their north London counterparts at the expense of Stockport County. The biggest winning margin in the second round went to the previous season's runners-up, Southampton, 8-0 against Wrexham, and Nottingham Forest went through 7-2 against Blackburn Rovers. The most goals over the two legs were 13 with Mansfield Town scoring seven of them to Reading's six.

Everton took revenge on Aston Villa in the third round, winning 4-1 at home in a replay after a goalless draw at Villa Park. Manchester United were beaten by the same scoreline at Norwich City, although no replay was required. Wolverhampton Wanderers came away from Selhurst Park with a 2-1 victory over Crystal Palace. Nottingham Forest were also victorious on their travels with a 3-1 win over Middlesbrough.

The two finalists in the 1980 showdown both needed fourth-round replays, both drawing 1-1 on their travels with Forest then beating Bristol City 3-0 and Wolves going through 1-0 against Crystal Palace thanks to Willie Carr's goal after just eight minutes. Norwich and Arsenal also went through after replays, and both were comprehensive wins, Arsenal putting paid to Brighton 4-0 and Norwich beating West Bromwich Albion 3-0.

Arsenal had reached two finals in the 1960s and lost them both but had taken revenge against Leeds in the second round and were presented with the opportunity to do the same against Swindon Town when they met in the quarter-finals on 4 December 1979 in front of a crowd of 38,024, but it was not to be as the game finished 1-1. A penalty converted by Alan Sunderland in the eighth minute was cancelled out by Billy Tucker's equaliser with just seven minutes remaining. A replay was held at the County Ground a week later, and history repeated itself with Swindon winning 4-3 after extra time in front of 21,795. Arsenal did not help themselves as they conceded two own goals via the unfortunate John Hollins and Steve Walford. The only team through to the semi-finals at the first attempt were Liverpool who won 3-1 at Norwich, while Forest won 3-0 in a replay after extra time against West Ham United. It took Wolves three attempts to get through to the semi-finals after a resolute couple of matches against Grimsby Town. A goalless game at Blundell Park meant a replay at Molineux on 11 December, but it ended 1-1 after extra time which meant a second replay took place exactly a week before Christmas. This time there was no upset as Wolves ran out winners 2-0 at the Baseball Ground.

The first legs of the semi-finals took place on 22 January 1980 with Forest at home to Liverpool and Swindon hosting Wolves. Forest took a slender 1-0 lead to Anfield through a John Robertson penalty with a minute to go. Swindon beat Wolves 2-1 and the Robins were dreaming of yet more glory in the League Cup. Andy Rowland put them 1-0 up in the 13th minute before Peter Daniel levelled the game on 26 minutes. There were no further goals until the 86th minute when Alan Mayes sent the home crowd into rapture. It looked good for Swindon when they appeared to draw first blood in the second leg but Billy Tucker's effort was disallowed. This prompted Wolves to get out of first gear and they scored two goals in six minutes, through John Richards on 53 and then Mel Eves on 59. Swindon were awarded a penalty just three minutes later, which was duly converted by Ray McHale. It was game on, but the tie was decided in the 73rd minute when Richards got his second of the evening. Wolves were going back to Wembley as they had done in 1974, winning 4-3 on aggregate. It had been another valiant effort from Swindon, but the class of 1980 were not going to emulate the class of 1969.

John Robertson had scored Forest's winning goal in the 1978 League Cup Final replay, and the first leg of this season's semi-final first leg – both penalties and both ending 1-0. It looked like it was to be a third such outcome when he converted his spot kick at Anfield, but David Fairclough had levelled things on 89 minutes to give the Anfield faithful some hope. It was not to be, however, as Forest went through 2-1.

And so, East Midlands met West Midlands at Wembley on 15 March 1980. Andy Gray had played in the first game of the mammoth final of 1977 at Wembley for Aston Villa but was injured for the two replays, and this time he got his chance to play once more as he led the Wolves front line on that day alongside John Richards.

Living up to their tag of favourites and hoping to make it three wins on the spin, Nottingham Forest took the game to Wolves from the kick-off as they created several opportunities. However, Wolves keeper Paul Bradshaw was in inspired form with Trevor Francis and Garry Birtles being denied. The first half belonged to Forest but Wolves had hung in there without seriously threatening Peter Shilton's goal. The second half was a more even contest, but the match was decided in the 67th minute. A long ball upfield by Peter Daniel created confusion in the Forest defence. As a result, David Needham and Peter Shilton collided with one another, leaving Andy Gray completely unmarked, with the goal beckoning. It was the simplest of chances as the Scotsman prodded the ball into the empty net. Wolves had taken the lead and capitalised on a dreadful mix-up. There was now a sea of red unrelenting in its aim to get back into the game, but the Wolves defence answered any questions that the Forest players raised, and could have made it 2-0 with George Berry hitting the woodwork. There were to be no further goals and Wolves had denied Forest a third straight win and in turn made it two League Cup trophies for themselves in six years. The smile on the face of their captain, Emlyn Hughes, was palpable to say the least, and the former Liverpool legend had now won every domestic trophy.

Kenny Hibbitt had been a member of the team that had won the cup in 1974 and recalls the moment that Wolves had beaten the European champions, 'It was great beating Forest at a time when they were at their very best with Clough at the helm, but really my memories of 1974 will always stay with me the longest. In 1974, the organisation from the club seemed to be better. We were allowed to celebrate properly. In 1980, we just got back on the bus and headed back to Wolverhampton. Scoring at Wembley in 1974 was a dream come true. Me and my brother Terry watched all the cup finals growing up and it was something we both dreamed about. And we did it in the same year. I was in the League Cup Final and Terry was playing in the FA Cup Final for Newcastle v Liverpool in the same year. Unfortunately, Terry's team got beat but our dreams had become a reality.'

The run-up to the final was not a great time for Hibbitt, though as he once more takes up the story: 'The build-up of the '74 cup final was quite worrying as I had an injury and missed a couple of games, so I wasn't sure the manager was going to pick me. I didn't find out I was in the team until I walked into the dressing room and saw my boots under the seven shirt. We had been away for a few days before the game in Worthing, which was great, we got some good team spirit build up. It felt amazing to walk on to the Wembley pitch for the first time knowing that England had won the World Cup there only eight years earlier. It felt amazing.

'My lasting memory was of my mum sitting in the stand. My dad had died and would have been so proud to see his two sons walking out in cup finals at Wembley in the same year and she said to see my name up in lights made her cry the whole of the second half. My wife, Jane, was in the stands and as we walked out on to the pitch I couldn't see her but still gave her a wave, I knew the area our wives were sitting in. We celebrated at the Hilton Hotel, London. Me and Jane went to our room and felt hungry, so I ordered a chicken sandwich each but when it came the price was extortionate, well it was for a Yorkshireman, but we had a fabulous night celebrating afterwards. The next morning, we arrived in Wolverhampton and the streets were packed with fans waving the gold and black flags. It was too much for Dave Wagstaffe and he went and sat at the back of our coach. In the town of Wolverhampton, it was packed. I'd not experienced anything like it. It was an unbelievable feeling, just amazing.'

Darren Wootton was a very excited 14-year-old Wolves fan in 1980. He recounts his story here, 'My recollections of the day were all positive as a 14-year-old Wolves fan beating Forest who had a monopoly of league and European Cup wins at the time. I went to the game with my dad and just remember a sea of gold and black colour behind the goal. Andy Gray's winning goal was due to a mistake between David Needham and Peter Shilton, leaving him with a simple tap-in into an empty net. Wolves were under the cosh for most of the game but a great defensive display between Emlyn Hughes and George Berry along with keeper Paul Bradshaw kept them at bay. Despite winning almost every trophy possible previously with Liverpool, this was the first time Emlyn Hughes had won the League Cup. Sadly, it remains Wolves' last major trophy since that happy day. That summer my school held a fete, and the trophy was on display. Amazingly, as my dad was on the PTA we were able to keep the cup overnight at my house. So, I went to sleep with the actual trophy on my bedside table – this just wouldn't be allowed now! Jack Taylor [the World Cup referee], who was Wolves' commercial director at the time, happily handed the trophy to us to bring home.'

3

The 1980s

Season 1980/81

The Final

14 March 1981

Liverpool 1 (Kennedy) West Ham United 1 (Stewart)

(after extra time)

Wembley Stadium, London

Attendance: 100,000

Referee: C. Thomas

Replay

1 April 1981

Liverpool 2 (Dalglish, Hansen) West Ham

United 1 (Goddard)

Villa Park, Birmingham

Attendance: 36,693

Referee: C. Thomas

The 1970s had been a very busy time for the trophy engravers assigned to Liverpool. The team were crowned champions of England five times, European Cup winners on two separate occasions, and winners of the FA Cup and UEFA Cup to boot as well. The foundation for their success had been built by Bill Shankly, who joined the club as manager in 1959. Shankly stepped down in 1974 and many predicted that the golden era was coming to an end. Just how wrong this prediction was, and it bore fruit when Bob Paisley was promoted from within as part of the famous 'Boot Room', which allowed coaches and assistants to progress to full management. One could even argue that Paisley took the baton from Shankly and ran faster with it. However, the one trophy that had eluded both managers had been the League Cup. Liverpool's only appearance in the final had been in 1978 when they lost to Nottingham Forest, who were arguably the Merseyside club's main rivals both home and abroad in the latter part of the decade.

In the early part of the new decade, all this was about to change as the Reds set about dominating the competition in a way that no one could have predicted.

Wolverhampton Wanderers' defence of the cup was over before it started as Cambridge United beat them twice over their two legs in the second round, 4-1 on aggregate. Liverpool saw off the challenge of Bradford City by the same aggregate scoreline. West Ham United enjoyed the biggest win when they beat Burnley 6-0 over two legs, but by far and away the biggest comeback was from Watford. Under the guidance of Graham Taylor, they had shot up the divisions and were looking good for a place in the top flight, which they eventually got in the 1981/82 season. However, they came unstuck against First Division Southampton in the first leg at The Dell, losing 4-0. After the match, Taylor had stated that his team were 'lucky to get nil!' If Watford were lucky to have got nil in the first leg, then they were positively unlucky not to get into double figures in the return match. Only 15,992 fans turned up, with many believing it was all over. How wrong they were.

Malcolm Poskett and Ray Train netted in the first half for the Hornets to stun the visitors and halve the deficit by the break. Southampton, while being cautious, still had cause for optimism. Watford still needed three more goals and if the Saints could score at least one, then it made the task a lot harder for the home team. Martin Patching scored to bring it to 3-0 on the night and 4-3 in the tie, before Steve Sims's agonising own goal appeared to put the visitors out of reach to make it 5-3 on aggregate with just 17 minutes remaining. Southampton just needed to see the game out, but Watford had other ideas and on 74 minutes it was 4-1 on the night with Ian Bolton converting from the spot. It was game on, and in extra time Ross Jenkins, who had been fouled for the penalty, scored to make it 5-1 on the night and 5-5 on aggregate. Watford could smell blood and had Southampton on the ropes and one of the greatest comebacks was completed with two goals in extra time from Nigel Callaghan and another from Poskett. Watford had snatched victory from the jaws of defeat on an extraordinary night in September and went through 7-5 on aggregate after wrapping up an incredible 7-1 victory in front of their own fans.

There was a less conspicuous victory for the Hornets in the third round, though they knocked out Sheffield Wednesday 2-1 at Hillsborough. There was a big win for Nottingham Forest, who were vying to get to their fourth final on the trot, as they thrashed Bury on their home turf 7-0. Liverpool were also on the goals trail with a 5-0 home victory against Swindon Town. Cambridge continued their giant-killing with a 2-1 home win against Aston Villa. West Ham beat London neighbours Charlton Athletic 2-1 away.

Watford took another significant scalp as they ensured that Brian Clough's Forest did not get to that elusive fourth consecutive final as they won 4-1 at Vicarage Road in the fourth round, with Ross Jenkins bagging a hat-trick and Luther Blissett scoring as well. West Ham and Liverpool continued their roads to Wembley with fourth-round home wins, the Hammers beating Barnsley 2-1 and Liverpool going through with a 4-1 victory against Portsmouth. Cambridge's attempt to knock out yet another First Division team came to an end, losing 1-0 to Coventry City at home in a replay after holding them 1-1 at Highfield Road.

Coventry also put paid to Watford's attempt in the quarter-finals after a 2-2 draw at Vicarage Road, the Sky Blues winning 5-0 in front of their home fans in the replay, and Liverpool beat Birmingham City 3-1 at home. There was also home advantage for Manchester City and West Ham United as they both went through, with City beating West Bromwich Albion and the Hammers' Wembley dream continuing with a 1-0 win against Spurs.

Coventry were at home in the first leg of the semi-final against West Ham and the other semi-final saw Manchester City entertain Liverpool. It was a game of two halves at Highfield Road with gaffes and own goals galore. West Ham took a 2-0 lead into the break before Coventry came back to win 3-2 with Garry Thompson getting the winner. It was also advantage Liverpool as they left Maine Road with a 1-0 victory. The Reds then made it to their second final with a 1-1 draw at Anfield and West Ham overturned their deficit to go through 4-3 on aggregate after a 2-0 home win.

There was a new name on the trophy as both had been previous losing finalists. The final saw no goals scored in the 90 minutes and went to extra time. The game was still goalless as it headed into the last few minutes with a replay looming. Liverpool thought they had won it when they scored in the 118th minute in very controversial circumstances as Alan Kennedy put the ball into the net; however, it had passed over team-mate Sammy Lee who was standing in front of Phil Parkinson, the West Ham goalkeeper. Clive Thomas was the referee, and he allowed the goal to stand. West Ham's manager, John Lyall, was furious at the time, and Thomas had given the goal as he believed that Lee was not interfering with play. Justice was served moments later when the Hammers were awarded a penalty in the dying seconds which was converted by Ray Stewart. The final whistle went and the Second Division team had given the English champions a proper match.

This continued in the replay, which was held at Villa Park on 1 April 1981, with West Ham taking the lead on just five minutes in front of a crowd of 36,693 through Paul Goddard. Could they provide another cup upset after they had beaten Arsenal in the 1980 FA Cup Final? The answer was no, as their lead was short-lived and goals from Kenny Dalglish and Alan Hansen gave Liverpool the lead before the break. No further goals were scored in the second half and Liverpool won the final 2-1 to lift the trophy for the first time.

The Football League Cup was now in its 21st season and going from strength to strength. The world of big business had taken note and getting a brand associated to it was very much viewed as the next step up – especially now that Liverpool had won it.

It added some kudos to the competition, as well as a new name for the cup in the 1981/82 season.

Season 1981/82

The Final
13 March 1982
Liverpool 3 (Whelan 2, Rush) Tottenham Hotspur 1
(Archibald) (after extra time)
Wembley Stadium, London
Attendance: 100,000
Referee: P.N. Willis

The League Cup had not had sponsorship for its first 21 years, but this was about to change. The competition was now under a deal with the Milk Marketing Board and was now known as the Milk Cup.

There were goals galore in the second round as Liverpool broke the record for the biggest aggregate victory. The Reds won 5-0 at home against Exeter City in the first leg at Anfield. The return leg was played on 28 October and Liverpool bettered that score by winning 6-0, and 11-0 overall.

Liverpool and Spurs enjoyed home advantage that led to wins for both teams in the third round. Liverpool took on Middlesbrough and won 4-1 and Spurs qualified with a 2-0 victory against Wrexham.

There was a repeat of the 1966 final when West Ham played West Bromwich Albion at home, and it went to two replays to separate them both. They drew 2-2 at Upton Park before a 1-1 stalemate at The Hawthorns and then a trip back down to Upton Park where West Brom won 1-0 on 1 December 1981.

The last couple of seasons had been kind to Graham Taylor and his Watford team in the League Cup with the finest of comebacks and scoring seven goals, plus the humiliation of Nottingham Forest. This campaign saw them racking up the goals once more when they beat Queens Park Rangers 4-1 at Vicarage Road in the fourth round, but, in contrast, Liverpool's trip to Arsenal produced no goals. It was not the case in the replay as Liverpool won 3-0. Spurs didn't need a replay, but it was a close match with Fulham at White Hart Lane ending in a slender 1-0 victory. Barnsley produced a shock by beating Manchester City 1-0 at Oakwell.

There was a local derby in the quarter-finals when Aston Villa took on West Brom at Villa Park. The champions of England were knocked out 1-0, sending the away fans happy. As in the previous round, Tottenham ran out 1-0 winners in front of their own fans, this time against Nottingham Forest. Barnsley produced the upset in the previous round and almost did it again, coming away from Anfield with a 0-0 draw, but Liverpool made amends in the replay with a 3-1 victory. Watford's run came to an end with a 2-1 defeat at Ipswich Town.

The first semi-final took place on 2 February 1982 between two teams going for the league title, but it was Liverpool who came out on top with a 2-0 victory over Ipswich at Portman Road, Terry McDermott scoring the first on 47 minutes and then Ian Rush making it 2-0 just minutes later. The following evening saw a goalless game as West Brom hosted Spurs.

A goal apiece from Rush and Kenny Dalglish had put Liverpool in command in the second leg at Anfield, but two goals in three minutes saw a spirited comeback from the Tractor Boys, with Eric Gates scoring on 75 minutes and then Alan Brazil equalising on the night to make it 2-2, so Liverpool went through to their second consecutive final, 4-2 on aggregate. For the third round on the trot, Tottenham won 1-0 at home and that was the aggregate score at the expense of West Brom.

Watched by a crowd of 100,000 at Wembley, Tottenham opened the scoring in the 11th minute when striker Steve Archibald netted. It looked like he had lost the ball, but sheer persistence took him over as he slotted home. Tottenham held the lead until the 87th minute when midfielder Ronnie Whelan equalised. For the second season on the trot, the final went into extra time. Whelan scored again in the 111th minute to give

Liverpool the lead and then Rush's goal a minute from time ensured that Liverpool matched Nottingham Forest with two consecutive trophies. Liverpool won 3-1, but in truth Tottenham only had themselves to blame, firstly by not seeing the game out and then being punished with sloppy passing in extra time that led to the two goals being scored. At the final whistle, there were multiple unhappy faces in the Tottenham team and none more so than Ray Clemence who had won the cup with Liverpool the season previously, before becoming the number one in goal for Spurs.

Season 1982/83

The Final
26 March 1983
Liverpool 2 (Kennedy, Whelan) Manchester United 1
(Whiteside) (after extra time)
Wembley Stadium, London
Attendance: 100,000
Referee: G. Courtney

The first round saw some big scores when the competition kicked off on 30 August 1982, with sizeable aggregate wins for Newport County, Blackpool, Bolton and Burnley against Exeter City, Chester, Carlisle United and Bury respectively.

Watford had taken to life in the First Division for the first time in their history extremely well when the third-round draw saw them once again paired with Nottingham Forest, the teams having got past Bolton

Wanderers and West Bromwich Albion respectively in the second round. Forest were looking for revenge after a 4-1 mauling at Vicarage Road in the cup a few seasons back, and how they got it with a thumping 7-3 victory in Nottingham. Brian Clough had come out on top but he still found time to go into the Watford dressing room and heap praise on Graham Taylor's team. This delighted the young Hornets boss. 'He was very complimentary,' said Taylor, when asked what had happened by the media. 'He said he would love to manage the team.'

Liverpool and Manchester United were drawn against lower-division opposition and found the going tougher than they would have hoped for, with Liverpool beating Rotherham 1-0 and United going through but only after a replay against Bradford City.

The two biggest clubs in the north-west both won 2-0 in home matches in the fourth round, Liverpool against Norwich City and United versus Brentford. Only one tie went to a replay, after a thrilling game at Notts County as they entertained both West Ham United and those in the stadium with both teams sharing six goals, with the Hammers winning the replay 3-0.

There were to be no replays in the quarter-finals. Arsenal beat Sheffield Wednesday by a solitary goal and Liverpool went through courtesy of a 2-1 win against the team they had beaten in the 1981 final, West Ham. The other two matches were more convincing wins and both raised eyebrows. Manchester United tore Nottingham Forest apart at Old Trafford, winning 4-0, and Burnley beat Tottenham 4-1 away from home, in what was definitively the biggest shock of the competition to date.

Manchester United, in search of their first League Cup triumph, overcame Arsenal in the semi-final to reach Wembley for the first time in the competition. A 4-2 win at Highbury was followed by a 2-1 win at Old Trafford. Liverpool, winners of the previous two competitions, booked their place in the final for the third year running at the expense of Second Division strugglers Burnley, winning the first leg 3-0 at Anfield. Burnley's 1-0 victory at Turf Moor in the second leg wasn't enough to prevent Liverpool from getting through, but it had been a fine achievement for the team in claret and blue.

It was third time lucky for Liverpool as they beat United in a thrilling final with Norman Whiteside opening the scoring for the Red Devils, before Alan Kennedy equalised with 15 minutes to go. The winner was scored in the ninth minute of extra time by Ronnie Whelan to send the red half of Merseyside home the happiest.

Season 1983/84

The Final
25 March 1984
Liverpool 0 Everton 0 (after extra time)
Wembley Stadium, London
Attendance: 100,000
Referee: A.I. Robinson

Replay
28 March 1984
Liverpool 1 (Souness) Everton 0
Maine Road, Manchester
Attendance: 52,089
Referee: A.I. Robinson

For decades, Walsall had plied trade mostly in the Third Division of English football and had not achieved anything of note in the League Cup previously. However, under the guidance of player-manager Alan Buckley, they came very close to emulating the feats of Queens Park Rangers, Swindon Town and Aston Villa in representing the third tier in the competition's final.

The Saddlers' route to the semi-finals largely went under the radar until the fourth-round stage when they were paired with Arsenal. Before that, the Third Division club took care of matches against Blackpool in the first round (4-3 on aggregate) and Barnsley (3-0 over two legs) in the second round.

The third round saw Walsall hosting Shrewsbury Town at Fellows Park which resulted in a 2-1 victory for the home team. Outside of the region, no one gave them a chance to progress to the quarter-finals as they were drawn to play Arsenal at Highbury on 29 November 1983. It looked very ominous for the away team when Stewart Robson opened the scoring for the Gunners in the 31st minute. This was the only goal in the first half with the home team looking to add to their tally to make their passage safe to the quarter-finals. However, the game was level just after the hour when Mark Rees scored to send the away fans into rapture. They were in dreamland with just six minutes remaining when Ally Brown put Walsall into the lead and it lasted until the final whistle. History had repeated itself after Walsall's famous win against Arsenal in the FA Cup in 1933.

Walsall were once more drawn away in the quarter-finals, this time at Rotherham United. They had managed to avoid the big guns still left in the competition which included Liverpool, Aston Villa and Everton. Millmoor may not have been Highbury, but the 4-2 victory afforded to Walsall was equally as important, with Rees (two) and Brown once more on the score sheet. The other goal was scored by Richard O'Kelly. It was impossible to avoid top opposition in the semi-final draw as all three teams went through. Everton were drawn at home to Aston Villa and Liverpool had first-leg advantage against the minnows from the third tier. Once more, no one was giving Walsall a chance. The Reds were looking good for repeated success in the league and also in the European Cup at the time and the tie was seen as a mere formality for them as they chased the treble. Somehow, the memo was not sent to the Walsall players as they stepped on to the pitch at Anfield on 7 February 1984. Once more it was the big boys who took the game by the scruff of its neck when Ronnie Whelan opened the scoring on just 14 minutes. Walsall were back in the game just before half-time when Phil Neale put through his own net. Whelan was in fine scoring form and this continued in the 73rd minute, but amazingly Walsall were level a minute later when substitute Kevin Summerfield made the score 2-2.

It was all to play for as the teams met at a packed Fellows Park in the second leg on Valentine's Day a week later. However, there was no further romance for Walsall as goals from Ian Rush and Whelan settled the matter in favour of the Merseyside club.

It was a double Merseyside victory against West Midlands rivals as Everton beat Aston Villa 2-1 over the two legs in the other semi-final.

Liverpool and Everton went on to dominate English football in the coming seasons, but the Milk Cup Final of 1984 offered no real clues to this claim and the final at Wembley was a dour affair with no goals being scored. For Everton, it was their second cup final appearance in the competition where excitement had been at a premium, following 1977. A solitary first-half goal in the replay at Maine Road, scored by Graeme Souness, was enough to give bragging rights to the red half of Merseyside and was not much better as a spectacle, although it did provide Liverpool with their fourth consecutive trophy. That feat was matched in the 21st century by the team that hosted the replay in 1984, Manchester City.

Season 1984/85

The Final

24 March 1985
Norwich City 1 (Chisholm own goal) Sunderland 0
Wembley Stadium, London
Attendance: 100,000
Referee: N. Midgley

Liverpool got off to a winning start in the second round as they were going for their fifth final victory on the trot, and a 2-0 aggregate win over Stockport County was sufficient to keep the dream alive.

No fewer than 13 goals were scored between Norwich City and Preston with the Canaries winning 9-4. West Ham had recorded a massive win against Bury in the second round in the previous season and once again found themselves in the goals against Bristol City, winning 8-3 over the two legs, and Queens Park Rangers also went through with the same winning margin against York City. Manchester City and Manchester United scored seven goals, City beating Blackpool 7-3 and United winning 7-0 against Burnley. Sunderland went through 2-1 against Crystal Palace, and the previous season's darlings, Walsall, also went through 4-2 over Coventry City, taking yet another First Division scalp. Could lightning strike twice for the Saddlers? The answer was no, as they were beaten by Chelsea in the third round, but only after a replay, drawing 2-2 at Fellows Park before succumbing 3-0 at Stamford Bridge, but their escapades in the previous seasons would live on for ever for the Sadlers.

The last time that Liverpool had lost a tie in the competition had been in February 1980 against Nottingham Forest. On 31 October 1984 it happened again, this time at the hands of Tottenham Hotspur who won 1-0 at White Hart Lane when Clive Allen settled the game in the sixth minute. Norwich went through 4-0 away in a replay at Aldershot after drawing the original tie 0-0 at Carrow Road. Arsenal were once again beaten by lower-division opposition, although this was at Second Division Oxford who were flying at the time and racing to the promised land of the top flight, winning 3-2 in front of their home fans. Like Norwich, Sunderland needed a replay after drawing 1-1 at the City Ground. The Black Cats went through 1-0 in the replay at home against Nottingham Forest.

Sunderland required a replay in the fourth round once more, this time against Spurs. They drew 1-1 at Roker Park before travelling down to White Hart Lane. Tottenham were widely expected to win, especially after beating Liverpool in the previous round. However, it was Sunderland who continued their quest to reach the final, going through 2-1.

Norwich dispensed of Notts County 3-0 at the first time of asking on home soil. The biggest shock of the round came at Goodison Park as FA Cup holders and title challengers Everton lost at home to Grimsby Town. Paul Wilkinson's late header was enough to file this match under 'Giant-Killers'.

Only two games were conclusive in the quarter-finals, and they both concerned the finalists. Sunderland didn't need a replay to go through as they beat Watford 1-0 away, and Norwich won by the same margin away to Grimsby Town, who could not quite match the heroics of Walsall in the previous season and make the semi-finals. Ipswich Town beat Queens Park Rangers 2-1 at Loftus Road after a goalless draw at Portman Road and it took Chelsea three attempts to see off the challenge of Sheffield Wednesday. The first game had been played at Stamford Bridge and had finished 1-1 on 28 January 1985. The replay was played just two days later and was a classic affair which ended 4-4 after extra time, but Chelsea made no mistakes in the second replay, winning 2-1 a week later. Gary Shelton opened the scoring for Wednesday before David Speedie and a last-minute effort from Mickey Thomas settled matters.

The first semi-final was played on 13 February 1985 when Sunderland hosted Chelsea. A Colin West brace was enough to give the home team the advantage without any reply from the Londoners.

Ipswich took a 1-0 lead in their first leg against local rivals Norwich, Mich d'Avray making the difference. Once again, Norwich were the team with the bragging rights as they beat Ipswich 2-0 in yet another semi-final to go through 2-1 on aggregate. A goal each for John Deehan and Steve Bruce were enough to take them through to their fourth final in the competition.

A crowd of 44,000 fans packed into Stamford Bridge to see if Chelsea could overturn a two-goal deficit in their second leg. It was not to be but it was a great match that went from end-to-end, with Sunderland winning 3-2 on the night and 5-2 over the two matches. Colin West was back on the score sheet for the Black Cats along with two goals for Clive Walker, with David Speedie and Pat Nevin netting for Chelsea. However, the match was marred with a pitch invasion from the home supporters which turned very nasty and very quickly too.

Norwich had won only one of the three previous finals that they had contested and that had been back in 1962, while Sunderland were appearing in their very first final. It was the experienced team who won through courtesy of a Gordon Chisholm own goal a minute after the break, the defender deflecting Asa Hartford's shot past goalkeeper Chris Turner after tenacious work from John Deehan. This was Hartford's third appearance in the final after playing for West Bromwich Albion and Manchester City. Later in the second half, Clive Walker missed a penalty awarded for a handball by Norwich defender Dennis van Wijk. The Sunderland players had played their part and looked dejected, and it was left to captain Barry Venison to gather the players round after the match. What made this even more impressive was that Venison was only 20 and became the youngest ever captain to do so in the final of the competition.

John Holland and Keith Nevols were Norwich fans who attended the final. Both were extremely happy with the result, but only one could celebrate it at Wembley. John was the one who could live the moment, 'We had a couple of spare tickets for the final, and we decided to give them to my uncle and his friend. They both lived in a small village in Suffolk, and they had never been to Wembley before. I will never forget the looks on their faces as we approached the Twin Towers. It was just sheer amazement, and it was just wonderful. As was the fact that we won it. It was a perfect end to the day, although at first it was a sombre one for us as we travelled to London by train. The British Transport Police had got on board to inform us all that there had been a fatality on an earlier train.'

It was the first time that Keith had seen his beloved Canaries win at Wembley, but he just couldn't celebrate it, 'My mate got me a ticket, so I was delighted to go with him. That was until I found out he was a Sunderland fan, and I was going to be in their end! It was so hard trying to downplay any attacks we had, especially when we scored the goal. Or rather they did for us, but I managed to keep a dignified and joyful silence when Clive Walker missed his penalty. It was a sea of angry faces around me, and the fans were not slow in telling Walker just what they thought of his spot kick.'

Norman Haggerston was also in the Sunderland end, but he could vent his anger as he was an actual fan of the Black Cats, 'I was 11 years old, and the sight of the Twin Towers was just brilliant. A few days before I had been unwell, and then Dad came in with the actual ticket. It was perfect medication and I started to feel better straight away. The whole day was unforgettable, and the friendship between the fans had to be seen to be believed. The game itself was pretty dire, except for those few minutes between Norwich scoring and us missing the penalty.'

The Metropolitan Police and the football bodies in general had also noted the special relationship by the two sets of supporters, so much so that the Friendship Trophy is now contested when the two clubs meet, either in the league or cups. The first of these matches occurred during the following season with the two teams now in the Second Division after being relegated, with both sets of fans shining a light in a season that saw several incidents of crowd trouble both home and abroad in 1985.

Season 1985/86

The Final

20 April 1986

Oxford United 3 (Hebberd, Houghton, Charles) Queens Park Rangers 0

Wembley Stadium, London.

Attendance: 90,396

Referee: K.S. Hackett

By the mid-1980s, football had seen its fair share of enigmatic owners of clubs. Perhaps the biggest of these was Oxford United's chairman, Robert Maxwell. The Czech-born British media proprietor, member of parliament (and suspected Mossad spy) had saved the club from financial ruin but controversy was never far away, especially when he had tried to unsuccessfully merge Oxford and local rivals Reading into one club which was to be known as Thames Valley Royals. By the time the season had started, Oxford had been promoted to the First Division. No one could have predicted what happened next, though, especially as Oxford manager Jim Smith had resigned to take over at Queens Park Rangers after a pay dispute with Maxwell.

As usual, there were a plethora of balls hitting backs of nets in the early rounds. The biggest aggregate score in the first round occurred as Crewe Alexandra who beat Carlisle United 7-6. Only one team failed to score over the two legs, and that was Peterborough United who lost on aggregate 2-0 to Northampton Town.

The second round saw a lot more goals scored with the biggest winning margin being by ten. This took place when Aston Villa were paired with Exeter City. Villa had just signed striker Simon Stainrod from Sheffield Wednesday for £350,000. His first game for his new club was on 25 September 1985 and what a debut it was as Villa came away from Exeter with a 4-1 lead in the first leg, with Stainrod bagging all four. If poor Exeter had thought that the First Division giants would take their foot off the pedal in the return leg at Villa Park on 9 October, then they were sadly mistaken, Villa winning 8-1 and 12-2 on aggregate. The Midlanders were 6-0 up at half-time with braces from Andy Gray (making his return to Villa Park after a successful spell with Everton), Brendan Ormsby and Gary Williams doing the damage. Second-half goals from Paul Birch and Simon Stainrod (who else) saw Villa in cruise control before a late goal from Alan Crawford salvaged some pride for Exeter. Villa's West Midlands rivals Coventry City were also banging in the goals as they won 9-3 against Crewe.

Liverpool and Queens Park Rangers also experienced significant aggregate wins. Oxford went through 4-1 on aggregate against Northampton.

Liverpool were in the mood to seek out a fifth final win of the 1980s as they put four past Brighton & Hove Albion at Anfield with no reply in the third round. Villa came away with a 3-0 victory at Elland Road against Leeds United of the Second Division, while QPR also won on their travels, 1-0 at Watford. Oxford's winning ways in the competition continued with a 3-1 home victory against Newcastle United.

Half of the fourth-round matches went to a replay – Aston Villa against West Bromwich Albion, Southampton at Arsenal, Chelsea at home to Everton and Portsmouth at Spurs. Going through at the first time of asking were the two finalists for the season, Oxford once again winning at home and by the same scoreline as the previous round, beating Norwich 3-1, and Queens Park Rangers matching the home advantage and same scoreline against Nottingham Forest. The other teams through were Liverpool who put out Manchester United 2-1 at Anfield and Ipswich who tasted the biggest winning margin with a 6-1 home win against Swindon Town. Three of the four replays were settled without the need for a third match, and all were the away teams, these being Villa, Arsenal and Everton. It was stalemate at Fratton Park between Portsmouth and Spurs, with Pompey winning the second replay 1-0.

Two matches needed a replay in the quarter-finals, Arsenal holding Villa at Villa Park 1-1 and Chelsea earning the same result at QPR. Once again the away team came away with the spoils in the replays. Villa beat Arsenal 2-1 and QPR beat Chelsea 2-0 after extra time. Another home tie for Oxford brought yet another 3-1 victory, this time Portsmouth suffering the same fate as Newcastle and Norwich. The scorers were Gary Briggs, Les Phillips and Neil Slatter for the home team before Portsmouth got a late consolation through Gary Stanley. Liverpool were handsome winners once more as they beat Ipswich 3-0 at Anfield.

QPR were drawn at home to play Liverpool in the first semi-final, while Aston Villa entertained Oxford in theirs. The smart money was on a Liverpool-Villa final but neither made it through.

QPR picked up a 1-0 victory at Loftus Road courtesy of a goal scored by Terry Fenwick in front of a crowd of just over 15,000. There were only 23,000 at Villa Park as the teams shared four goals in a thrilling match, with Paul Birch and Simon Stainrod scoring for Villa and John Aldridge adding a brace for Oxford, with one from the penalty spot. In the return leg, Oxford again scored twice through Phillips and Jeremy Charles but Villa could not match them despite a late goal from Mark Walters as United went through 4-3 to the final and a rare day out at Wembley for their first final.

What a match it was that unfurled at Anfield in the second leg as Liverpool missed a penalty and had four different players on the score sheet. The problem was that two of them were own goals. Steve McMahon and Craig Johnston had both given Liverpool the lead but they allowed it to slip on both occasions with own goals scored by Ronnie Whelan and Gary Gillespie, which meant QPR were through to their first final since 1967, with an aggregate win 3-2.

Trevor Hebberd opened the Wembley scoring five minutes before the break and Ray Houghton added a second seven minutes after the restart. The game was wrapped up four minutes from time with Jeremy Charles getting his name on the score sheet when he put the ball into the net after John Aldridge had a shot saved by QPR goalkeeper Paul Barron. Oxford manager Maurice Evans was delighted but did not take his winners' medal. He had deemed that the 72-year-old long-serving physiotherapist Ken Fish was more worthy. A class gesture if ever there was one.

Andy McCormac had been an Oxford fan since the age of ten in 1973. He was 22 when Oxford were at Wembley on that historic day in 1986, 'I had been to pretty much every Oxford United match as we shot up from the Third to the First Division. Before then we had endured several unremarkable years. We were relegated from the Second Division in 1976 and had a number of torrid years in the third tier. Ian Greaves had steadied the ship and Jim Smith had made it go faster. Throughout all the dismal years, I would stand there on the terraces with my father and listen to his football wisdom. One thing he would always say was "they've got to survive ten minutes". This was quite often true. Whatever the score was at half-time, in the dark days, Oxford United teams always conceded in the first ten minutes after the break. And so, then at Wembley on 20 April 1986, he said his usual thing to me. Well guess what? We DID survive the ten minutes and in fact we scored again when Trevor Hebberd and Ray Houghton combined with breathtaking passing that left the blue and white-hoop-shirted players wondering what hit them before Houghton finished the move to put us 2-0 up and sent everyone into delirium. I turned round to Dad and almost cried when I reminded him of his legendary half-time talk to me. That's the way to do it, Dad!'

Keith Hackett was the referee at Wembley and was not required to give a player a red card. However, he felt the need to produce one on the morning of the final, 'I drove down to the hotel on the eve of the game and following dinner with my colleagues retired to my room early. I had watched the two semi-finals which I had recorded to avoid any surprises on the day by way of player misbehaviour or the impact of substitutes, etc. Following an enjoyable evening dinner, I was back in my room tidying up some of my outstanding business papers. We were amateurs in the professional game at that time, I received a match fee of £35 plus expenses for the game. Following breakfast on the day of the match, I was walking across the foyer and there sat in a corner was Sir Stanley Matthews.

'I approached him to introduce myself but just as I arrived, he was quick to his feet and said he knew who I was and had seen me officiate a few games. I was gobsmacked. I asked Sir Stanley for his autograph, and he agreed providing that I sign one of my red cards for him. I duly obliged of course. It was the only time that Sir Stanley ever got himself a red card, let alone a yellow one. And the only time that the yellow of Oxford United, to date, have laid claim to winning a major trophy.'

Season 1986/87

The Final
5 April 1987
Arsenal 2 (Nicholas 2) Liverpool 1 (Rush)
Wembley Stadium, London
Attendance: 96,000
Referee: L.C. Shapter

It was goodbye to the Milk Cup and hello to the Littlewoods Cup at the start of the 1986/87 season.

Aston Villa had beaten Exeter City 12-2 on aggregate in the second round during the previous campaign, but Liverpool went one better as they battered Fulham 13-2 over two legs. On 23 September, Fulham travelled up to Anfield knowing that it was going to be a very hard task waiting for them. What they didn't know was just how hard it was as they went back home with a 10-0 defeat. Liverpool had raced into a four-goal lead by the half-time break, with Ian Rush, John Wark, Ronnie Whelan and Steve McMahon all scoring. The tie was effectively over as a contest after just 45 minutes, and the second half saw the ball go past John Vaughan another six times with McMahon bagging two more to take the match ball home. He even had time to hit the post. Only 13,498 fans were in attendance to witness the mauling.

The second leg restored some pride in the Fulham camp as they lost by only one goal with the score being 3-2 to the Reds. The first-leg victory for Liverpool matched the record set by West Ham United for the largest winning margin in the competition. The Hammers had put ten past Bury in the second leg of their second-round tie in the 1983/84 season.

Everton, Liverpool and Tottenham continued to find the net in the third round with all three clubs being drawn at home, Everton putting four past Sheffield Wednesday without reply on 28 October. Spurs went one better than the Toffees the night after, again with no replay, against Birmingham City. On the same night Liverpool beat Leicester City 4-1 and Arsenal beat Manchester City 3-1.

Everton were again in the goals in the fourth round when they came away with a 4-1 victory at Norwich City. Oxford's defence of their cup came to an end when they were defeated 1-0 at West Ham, Tony Cottee separating the sides with an 81st-minute penalty. Liverpool required a replay after the initial game had ended without any goals being scored at Highfield Road, against Coventry City, the champions then winning 3-1 on home soil. Arsenal went through 2-0 at Highbury, this time taking care of Charlton Athletic. The biggest winners were Nottingham Forest who won 5-0 away at Bradford City.

Forest went out in the quarter-finals when they went to Arsenal and were beaten 2-0 – two first-half goals from Charlie Nicholas and Martin Hayes inflicting the damage. The mouthwatering tie of the round was on Merseyside when free-scoring Everton entertained Liverpool in a local derby clash. Only one goal was scored, though, and that went to the away team, courtesy of Ian Rush with just seven minutes remaining. The other teams going through to the semi-finals were Southampton and Tottenham.

There was another local derby in the semi-final with Arsenal taking on Tottenham, while Southampton had home advantage in the first leg at The Dell against Liverpool. There was only one goal scored in both first legs and that came at Highbury, for the away team, with Tottenham striker Clive Allen netting his 34th goal of a remarkable season.

The second leg at Anfield took place on 25 February 1987. Liverpool had lost at the semi-final stage the previous year, but this time they made no mistake by winning 3-0. It took up until the 67th minute for the deadlock to be broken via Ronnie Whelan after assistance from Gary Gillespie. Just eight minutes later, player-manager Kenny Dalglish doubled the lead before Jan Mølby ensured Liverpool's fifth final of the 1980s with just five minutes to go. Tottenham Hotspur and Arsenal locked horns in the second leg at White Hart Lane on 1 March 1987. A first-half goal from Clive Allen made the aggregate score 2-0. However, second-half goals from Viv Anderson and Niall Quinn took the game to a replay. Once more the match was to be played at White Hart Lane and there were no goals in the first half. The Spurs fans at half-time were optimistically cautious about their chances of getting through to the final to face Liverpool again and avenge the 3-1 loss in the 1982 showpiece. It appeared that the person who was doing the talking over the Tannoy was perhaps a little more confident as it was announced how the home fans could apply for cup final tickets.

That confidence was boosted in the 62nd minute when Allen once again scored to make it 1-0, which prompted the Spurs followers to remind the Arsenal supporters that the short journey to Wembley was beckoning for them. Then on 82 minutes, Arsenal levelled when Paul Davis fed the ball through to Ian Allinson who twisted and turned and fired a shot home that went past Ray Clemence. Arsenal were now back in the game and won it in the dying seconds of regulation time. A free kick taken by David O'Leary was partially cleared by the Tottenham rearguard. It fell to Allinson whose shot was blocked but it fell to David Rocastle who shot home to make the score 2-1 and take his team into the final. In just a few days, Arsenal had beaten their closest rivals 2-1 at White Hart Lane on two occasions. Within minutes of the game finishing, managers George Graham and David Pleat were sharing sandwiches and cups of tea before the Spurs boss gave his Arsenal counterpart a lift home. Pleat later recalled these moments as 'camaraderie' which was prevailing at that time.

Ian Allinson had more than played his part in the semi-finals, but he was not part of the Arsenal team that ran out at Wembley on 5 April 1987. His place was taken back by Charlie Nicholas who had been injured in the first leg of the semi-final. It was a decision that bore fruit for Graham as Arsenal won 2-1 at Wembley. Once again they had to come back from a goal behind after Ian Rush opened the scoring for Liverpool with a side-footed finish to the corner of the net. It looked like Liverpool were on course to claim their fifth trophy in seven seasons, before Nicholas equalised, turning in a cross from the right in the crowded penalty area. Then in the second half Nicholas put the Gunners in the lead with a fortuitous goal. Perry Groves had put a cross into the Liverpool box, and Nicholas was first to it but his shot was going wide until it deflected off Ronnie Whelan and was diverted past goalkeeper Bruce Grobbelaar's outstretched hand before landing in the left-hand corner of the net. Arsenal had won the cup for the very first time after defeats to Leeds and Swindon in previous finals. The win over Tottenham and the comeback against Liverpool in the final inspired a new Arsenal fanzine called *One-Nil Down, Two-One Up*. It was also the first time that Liverpool had lost a game after taking the lead with a goal scored by Ian Rush.

Season 1987/88

The Final
24 April 1988
Luton Town 3 (Stein 2, Wilson) Arsenal 2
(Hayes, Smith)
Wembley Stadium, London
Attendance: 95,732
Referee: J.B. Worrall

Up until this season, Luton Town's trophy cabinet had
consisted of championship top spots and runners-up
positions in the lower divisions. They had been members
of the First Division since 1982 and indeed enjoyed one
of the great escapes in May 1983 when a 1-0 victory
at Manchester City consigned the hosts to the Second
Division and gave the football world one of its great
sights as manager David Pleat danced on to the pitch to
celebrate with his players.

Their only other notable appearance had been in the
1959 FA Cup Final where they had lost to Nottingham
Forest. They had established themselves in the top flight
and were now managed by Ray Harford. Still, none of
this was enough for betting folk to part with their money
at the bookies to make Luton potential winners of the
League Cup when the tournament kicked off on 17
August 1987.

Manchester United and Crystal Palace had
comfortable 6-0 wins in the second round, with Hull
City and Newport County on the respective ends.
However, these results were not even close to the biggest
winning margin, which went to Watford. The Hornets

had beaten Darlington 3-0 away on 22 September 1987. The second leg was played on 6 October with Watford running amok, winning 8-0 on the night and 11-0 on aggregate. Steve Terry scored the last of his 20 goals for the club, Peter Hetherston scored two and then the rest were spread around with Iwan Roberts, Glyn Hodges, Tony Agana, Nigel Gibbs and Luther Blissett completing the rout. Luton's first foray after the previous season's ban saw them win both games against Wigan Athletic – 1-0 away and a 4-2 home victory completed the formality.

Luton's previous absence had occurred as a result of the club banning Cardiff City fans from attending a match at Kenilworth Road after the teams had been drawn together. Luton had taken the decision to ban away supporters from all clubs after an infamous match with Millwall at home in 1985. The Football League had requested that Luton relax the rule for the League Cup, but this was not adhered to.

Perhaps the biggest shock of the third round came at Villa Park when Aston Villa defeated Tottenham Hotspur 2-1. Villa, under the tenure of Graham Taylor, were now a Second Division outfit after the previous season's relegation. Luton had been drawn at home to Coventry City and the game was played at a neutral stadium, at Leicester City's Filbert Street. Luton were still insisting on not accommodating away fans but had been let back into the competition by the Football League, and they won 3-1. On the same night, Arsenal were hosting Bournemouth, and it was a comfortable 3-0 win to send them through to the fourth round. There was a Merseyside derby when Liverpool entertained Everton and it was the blue half of the city that was celebrating this time, with Gary Stevens scoring the only goal in the 83rd minute.

Aston Villa's reward for beating Spurs was another member of the top flight, although there was no further shock as Sheffield Wednesday came away with a 2-1 victory. Luton were also victorious on their travels as they beat Ipswich Town at Portman Road 1-0 on 17 November. Arsenal once again were at home and managed a 3-0 win against Second Division opposition – this time it was Stoke City.

The quarter-finals commenced in January 1988 with Luton dispatching Bradford City 2-0. The following night saw similar wins for Everton against Manchester City and Oxford United against the red half of Manchester. Arsenal beat Sheffield Wednesday 1-0 away.

The first semi-final saw Arsenal go to Everton and come away with a 1-0 advantage. Arsenal had not conceded a goal in this season's competition but did so in the return leg, just the one, and they scored three themselves to go to a second successive final after winning 4-1 over the two legs. Adrian Heath was the only player to put the ball into the Gunners' goal.

Luton went through 3-1 on aggregate against Oxford. The first leg had finished all square at 1-1 before Luton won 2-0 in the return.

The final was played on 24 April 1988 at a very sunny Wembley. Arsenal were red-hot favourites and firmly expected to be only the third team to successfully defend the cup after Nottingham Forest and Liverpool. What followed was certainly not in the script and is widely recognised as THE greatest League Cup Final of the 1980s.

Luton opened the scoring after 13 minutes, Brian Stein getting away after Steve Foster's flick and driving his shot past John Lukic. The Hatters were comfortable in the first half and nearly doubled their lead early in the second period but Lukic saved spectacularly from Stein's header.

But the final turned around in Arsenal's favour as the half progressed, substitute Martin Hayes equalising in the 71st minute and sparking resurgence from the Gunners that saw them in front three minutes later through Alan Smith.

It could – and perhaps should – have been all over soon afterwards but Smith and Hayes both hit the woodwork, while Andy Dibble made a string of outstanding saves, notably from Nigel Winterburn's penalty with nine minutes to play.

That was the spark for Luton to take advantage and they were back on terms a minute later, Danny Wilson heading home from a cross, and then just as it looked like extra time was on the cards Stein got on the end of a free kick to win it for the club from Bedfordshire.

Welsh goalkeeper Dibble was in no doubt about the importance of his penalty stop. 'I knew I had to save that penalty or things would be over for us,' he told *The Guardian* after the match.

For Luton fan Craig Baxter, it was a day he wouldn't forget for reasons on and off the pitch. He takes up the story, 'I was 21 and went with my dad and a mate. My mate knew a few dodgy sorts, and he bumped into them in the stadium. The three blokes had told us that they had stolen a car from Luton to get them to the match. We had the upper terrace level with the Arsenal fans directly beneath us. When they went 2-1 up, these guys went mad and jumped down into the Arsenal section "to have words". We thought that would be the last we would see of them on the day. However, my dad was driving us home up the M1 and just before we got to junction two, we saw the same three blokes walking up the hard shoulder. Dad pulled over and picked them up. They were really miffed as the car that they had stolen to get to the game actually broke down on the North Circular Road. I will never forget this day!'

Season 1988/89
The Final
9 April 1989
Nottingham Forest 3 (Clough 2, Webb) Luton
Town 1 (Harford)
Wembley Stadium, London
Attendance: 76,130
Referee: R.G. Milford

Birmingham City had beaten Aston Villa 3-1 on aggregate to claim the 1963 League Cup, and they were paired together in the second round in this season's competition. This time there was a totally different outcome as the Villa ran out 7-0 winners. A 2-0 victory had been secured at St Andrew's before they put five past a hapless Blues' defence in the return leg at Villa Park.

This was not to be the biggest aggregate winning margin, though, as Nottingham Forest ran Chester City ragged home and away to claim a 10-0 victory. Walsall had come close to knocking out Liverpool in the 1984 semi-final and had the chance to make amends when both teams met again, coming out on top 4-1 over the two games, and defending champions Luton went through 2-1 against Burnley.

Leeds United fell victim to the Luton Wembley-bound train in the third round – the Hatters winning 2-0. Liverpool and Arsenal had met three times after two draws. The Gunners did not make it three appearances on the trot in the final as Liverpool won 2-1. Arsenal gained serious revenge, though, on the very last game of the season when they pipped Liverpool to win the First Division crown with a 2-0 victory at Anfield. Nottingham Forest progressed with a 3-2 home win over Coventry City, and West Ham United had the biggest win of the round when they thrashed Derby County 5-0 at home.

Aston Villa were once more on the goal trail in the fourth round after thrashing Ipswich Town 6-2 at Villa Park on 30 November 1988. There were shocks for both Merseyside teams as West Ham won 4-1 at home against Liverpool, and perhaps more surprising was that Bradford City put three past Everton at Valley Parade to win 3-1. Luton took care of Manchester City 3-1 on home turf, and it took Nottingham Forest a replay to also go through after a goalless draw against Leicester City at Filbert Street – the Reds eventually winning 2-1.

All the quarter-finals were played on 18 January 1989. Three were decided at the first time of asking with Bristol City winning 1-0 at Bradford, West Ham beating Aston Villa 2-1 and Nottingham Forest winning 5-2 against Queens Park Rangers at the City Ground. Luton also went through to the semi-finals, but it took a replay as they had drawn 1-1 at home against Southampton but then they beat them 2-1 after extra time at The Dell.

Luton made easy work getting through to a second successive final against a shell-shocked West Ham team, the Hatters winning the first leg 3-0 away and then following it up with a 2-0 home victory to go through 5-0 overall. Goals from Mick Harford, Roy Wegerle and a Danny Wilson penalty were enough to damage the Hammers in the first game and practically enabled Luton supporters to book their hotels for the final. By contrast, Nottingham Forest had to do it the hard way against Bristol City as the Robins came away from the City Ground with a hard-earned 1-1 draw. Forest had won ten out of their previous 11 matches and even the one they didn't win was a draw. The visitors were 9/1 to win the match but they came close to doing it when Paul Mardon scored his one and only goal for Bristol City, and it looked like that was a very good bet until John Pender scored an own goal to equalise. Still, it was all to play for in the second leg on 26 February 1989. The game went into extra time as there were no goals scored in the regulation 90 minutes, and it was seemingly heading to a replay at Villa Park, but Garry Parker had other ideas six minutes from the end when he scored to break Bristol hearts and put Forest through 2-1 on aggregate.

It was to be a repeat of the 1959 FA Cup Final which Forest had won 2-1, and the same club won again but this time with a 3-1 margin.

As in the previous final, Luton took a one-goal lead into the half-time break. Mick Harford had made the breakthrough in the 35th minute with his head. Forest equalised in the 54th minute when Nigel Clough calmly converted a penalty to get Forest back in the game. This especially pleased his father, Brian, in the dugout. Soon afterwards, Tommy Gaynor provided a cross for Neil Webb to control and slot into the Luton net. Arsenal had pulled a goal back and then went into a 2-1 second-half lead in the previous final, only for Luton to come back and win it 3-2. Was the same thing about to happen again for Ray Harford's men? Alas, it was not the case for the Hatters as Nigel Clough claimed his second of the match with a low shot drilled into the back of the net from just outside the penalty area and Forest were 3-1 up. There were no more goals scored in the final 14 minutes, and Forest joined Villa as three-time champions.

Season 1989/90

The Final

29 April 1990
Nottingham Forest 1 (Jemson) Oldham Athletic 0
Wembley Stadium, London
Attendance: 74,343
Referee: J.E. Martin

Luton Town had not been able to defend the cup in the previous season, but the second round in 1989 saw them most definitely in the mood to get to the final again and break records at the same time. The Hatters were paired with Mansfield Town with the first leg away on 19 September. The 5,361 crowd, much higher than Mansfield's average, were treated to a great spectacle which ended 4-3 to Luton, with two goals each for Lars Elstrup and Roy Wegerle, while Trevor Christie also bagged a brace for Mansfield, whose other goal was scored by Ian Stringfellow. The return leg saw even more action with Luton winning 7-2 at Kenilworth Road on 3 October. The 16 goals scored over the two matches was a record. Liverpool, Arsenal and Sheffield Wednesday also scored eight goals over the two matches, Liverpool beating Wigan 8-2, with the Gunners overcoming Plymouth 8-1 and Wednesday bagging eight with no reply against Aldershot. Nottingham Forest made hard work of their defence by drawing 4-4 with Huddersfield on aggregate and going through on away goals after a 1-1 draw in the first leg at the City Ground. The other second leg went to extra time, as Oldham went through 4-2 on aggregate having won both matches 2-1.

There was another record broken in the third round as Frankie Bunn almost single-handedly thrashed Scarborough against Oldham. The Latics won 7-0 with Bunn netting six of them to become the first player to score a double hat-trick in one game in the competition, netting five of them in the first half alone. By the end of the season, Oldham would break another record with Andy Ritchie's 12 goals being the most scored in a League Cup campaign. Forest once again made it hard work as they came away from Crystal Palace with no goals scored. They made amends on home soil with a resounding 5-0 victory. The marathon tie of the round saw Swindon Town and Bolton Wanderers lock horns over FOUR matches, with Swindon eventually winning 2-1 in the third replay, and even that went to extra time.

The shock of the fourth round was when Oldham entertained the 1987 winners, Arsenal. Andy Ritchie scored two and Nick Henry added the third to put the Second Division team in total control, but Niall Quinn pulled one back for the north London giants in the 90th minute to make the 3-1 score a little more respectable. Lee Chapman was on the mark in the 83rd minute to ensure Forest continued on the road to Wembley by beating Everton 1-0 on 22 November 1989. Swindon's love affair with the draw continued as they drew with First Division Southampton at home with no goals scored. The replay took place on 16 January 1990 with Southampton winning 4-2 after extra time. This was the first game of the 1990s for the competition as it reached its fourth decade.

The following evening saw three of the four quarter-finals being played and they all finished needing a replay, with Forest drawing 2-2 at home against Tottenham, Sunderland and Coventry playing out a game that finished goalless, and West Ham and Derby drawing 1-1. The Southampton v Oldham tie was played a week later on 24 January, and this was not settled as it finished 2-2 – Matt Le Tissier with two for the home team and Ritchie once again on target twice in a game. The replays also took place on the same evening as Forest edged out Tottenham in a five-goal thriller at White Hart Lane, and Coventry demolished Sunderland 5-0 at Highfield Road, with Steve Livingstone getting four of them. Derby and West Ham required a second replay after a 0-0 draw at the Baseball Ground, the Londoners winning the match 2-1 to reach their second consecutive semi-final. Oldham beat Southampton 2-0 at Boundary Park to make up the quartet vying for a place in the final.

West Ham had been thrashed in the previous season's semi-final, 5-0 by Luton, so they were determined to make amends this time around as they were paired with Oldham at Boundary Park in the first leg on Valentine's Day. It turned out to be a massacre for the Hammers as they went down 6-0 to an Oldham team that were simply on fire. This really was a team effort for Joe Royle's side as goals from Neil Adams, Earl Barrett, Rick Holden, Roger Palmer and the obligatory two for Ritchie condemned the Hammers. West Ham won the second leg 3-0, but it hardly mattered as the damage had already been done. Nottingham Forest beat Coventry 2-1 on aggregate, with all three goals being scored in the first leg at the City Ground.

And so, Oldham met Forest in the final on 29 April 1990. Earlier in the month the Latics had faced heartbreak in the FA Cup semi-final when they lost to Manchester United after a replay, so they were determined to make amends in the final. Both teams went into the match with a loss of form, and it was the Second Division side who looked like putting that right with a cross-come-shot from Neil Adams in the first minute. The rest of the first half fluctuated between tedium and few chances created. However, the second half was a much better affair and came to life straight from kick-off. Frankie Bunn had a chance to put Oldham ahead when a looping ball was crossed in, but his shot went well over. Bunn rued the miss straight away, as the resulting goal kick downfield caught Oldham napping, with a flick-on header falling to Nigel Clough. Clough was able to play the ball into the path of Nigel Jemson, whose momentum carried him into the box and fired left of Latics keeper Andy Rhodes. The man in green dived the wrong way to his right, but his feet were able to block the ball. However, to Rhodes's dismay, Jemson was in to put away his effort at the second time of asking and Nottingham Forest were 1-0 up with only two minutes of the second half played.

For the next 15 minutes, it was all Forest as they pressed forward to try and seek out a second goal. Then Oldham came back, and it seemed that the Forest strategy was then to protect the lead – and it worked out that way.

It seemed, though, that Forest had strangely settled for a 1-0 victory and allowed Oldham back in, Roger Palmer, Denis Irwin and Andy Ritchie all coming close but to avail. The final whistle went, and Forest had successfully managed to retain the cup, just as they had done in 1978 and 1979. The 1978 triumph had been Brian Clough's first major trophy as the boss of Nottingham Forest, but the one in 1990 was to be his last.

4

The 1990s

Season 1990/91

The Final
21 April 1991
Manchester United 0 Sheffield Wednesday 1 (Sheridan)
Wembley Stadium, London
Attendance: 80,000
Referee: R.S. Lewis

The competition had yet another new sponsor in Rumbelows, the electrical and electronics retailer.

There were significant aggregate wins for multiple teams in the second round as Everton beat Wrexham 11-0, and Crystal Palace also made double figures. On 25 September 1990 they hosted Southend United in the first leg, winning 8-0, a hat-trick from Mark Bright and Ian Wright with a goal apiece for Garry Thompson and Glyn Hodges doing the damage. They then won the second leg 2-1 to make it 10-1 on aggregate. Chelsea defeated Walsall 9-1 and Southampton beat Rochdale 8-0. Sheffield Wednesday beat Brentford 2-1 in both legs to go through 4-2 and Manchester United went one better with a 5-2 aggregate win over Halifax Town.

Derby County inflicted the highest score in the third round as they thrashed Sunderland 6-0, with Mick Harford scoring three, a brace from Ted McMinn and an own goal by Gary Bennett rounding off a miserable night for the Black Cats. The tie of the round to whet the appetite came at Old Trafford as Manchester United beat Liverpool 3-1. Steve Bruce and Mark Hughes had put the home side in the driving seat in the first half, before Lee Sharpe put the game beyond the four-time winners with a goal in the 81st minute. A consolation goal two minutes later was scored from Ray Houghton. Sheffield Wednesday went through 1-0 in a replay at Swindon Town after both teams had failed to find the net in the first game at Hillsborough.

There were two classic matches in the fourth round, which yielded 17 goals between them, and both took place on 28 November. Arsenal were paired at home with Manchester United, where Clayton Blackmore opened the scoring for United in only the second minute before Lee Sharpe and Mark Hughes tripled the lead just ahead of half-time. There were a further five goals in the second half with Sharpe netting two more and Danny Wallace also getting on the score sheet for the visitors, before Alan Smith scored a brace for Arsenal to limit the damage already done by United, who won 6-2. Coventry City hosted Nottingham Forest in the other high-scoring and entertaining match. The previous two seasons had seen Forest win the League Cup and on both occasions they had seen off the challenge of the Sky Blues, and now they had the chance to make it three on the trot. Coventry were under the management of Terry Butcher, and this was only his third game in charge. Unbelievably, Coventry raced into a 4-0 lead within the first 35 minutes, with Kevin Gallagher twice on target. Cyrille Regis and Steve Livingstone were the other scorers to shock Brian Clough and his Forest team. However, a crazy ten-minute period followed before the break when Nigel Clough scored three goals. As the second half started Forest were only one goal down, but that lasted for just a few minutes and amazingly Forest clawed their way level with a Garry Parker goal after he had turned David Speedie on the edge of the box. Coventry had shell-shocked the Trees and now the boot was firmly on the other foot.

The home team were awarded a corner on the half-hour, which was taken by Micky Gynn. The ball was partially cleared and Cyrille Regis volleyed it back in where it was met by the head of Livingstone, who bagged his second goal to put Coventry back in the lead. Amazingly there were no more goals, and Coventry won a memorable match 5-4. Sheffield Wednesday once again went through after a replay. They had hosted Derby and drew 1-1, before a 2-1 victory at the Baseball Ground.

Joining Manchester United, Sheffield Wednesday and Coventry City in the quarter-finals were Aston Villa, Chelsea, Leeds United, Tottenham Hotspur and Southampton.

Wednesday went through at the first time of asking this time with a 1-0 victory over Coventry at Highfield

Road. Leeds thrashed Aston Villa 4-1 while the other two matches needed a replay. Manchester United drew 1-1 at Southampton and Chelsea and Tottenham ended up goalless at the Bridge, United winning the replay 3-2 at Old Trafford and Chelsea coming away from White Hart Lane with a comprehensive 3-0 success.

Manchester United took on Leeds in the semi-finals, and were at home in the first leg. The first half was a goalless affair, and the game came to life in the 67th minute when Lee Sharpe put his team ahead, only for Chris Whyte to level three minutes later. The night swung back in United's favour in the 79th minute with Brian McClair bagging the winner to earn a slender 2-1 lead. Leeds could not break down their opponents' defence in the second leg and Sharpe scored a goal in the last minute to secure a 1-0 win at Elland Road, going through to the final 3-1 on aggregate.

The other semi-final saw Sheffield Wednesday take a 2-0 lead into their home second leg, with Peter Shirtliff and David Hirst scoring second-half goals. Wednesday took the second leg 3-1 and 5-1 on aggregate to get to their first final in the competition, with Nigel Pearson, Danny Wilson and Paul Williams sending the home team into raptures and planning a trip to Wembley. Chelsea pulled one goal back through Graham Stuart.

Second Division Sheffield Wednesday faced First Division Manchester United in the final, with Ron Atkinson now in charge of the Yorkshire club having previously managed Manchester United before Alex

Ferguson took over. Ferguson had experienced some torrid times at the Old Trafford helm; however, he had won the previous season's FA Cup and was going great guns in the European Cup Winners' Cup in the first season that English clubs had been allowed back into Europe after the Heysel Stadium tragedy in 1985.

Only one goal was scored in the final, but that doesn't tell the whole story. It was a great end to the showpiece with both teams going for it, but it was the steel of Sheffield that won the match when John Sheridan scored in the 38th minute. It was the first time that a team from the Second Division had won the competition since Aston Villa in 1975.

Gregg Reynolds was a fanatical ten-year-old Owls fan and was transfixed by what was going on at Wembley that day, 'I couldn't see anything but a sea of blue and white scarves, banners and tops. It was so exciting to be at Wembley. During the season and the cup run, it had been commonplace for fans to throw stuffed animals around in the stands.

'There seemed to be so much more at Wembley, and I remember it was like watching a tennis match as they were thrown from one side to the other. The game went so quickly for me but I soaked it all up. My abiding memory was Roland Nilsson marking Lee Sharpe out of the game. We all went mad at the final whistle knowing that we would be playing in Europe and the icing on the cake was getting promoted as well. They were just brilliant times to be an Owl.'

Season 1991/92

The Final
12 April 1992
Manchester United 1 (McClair) Nottingham Forest 0
Wembley Stadium, London
Attendance: 76,810
Referee: G. Courtney

This was the second and final season that the competition was known as the Rumbelows Cup. The most notable first round, first leg took place when Barnet, newly promoted to the Football League, took on Brentford. The game ended 5-5. Barnet were 5-3 up with ten minutes to go but two goals from Dean Holdsworth restored parity for the Bees. Barry Fry's newcomers were left to rue not holding on to the lead when they lost 3-1 in the second leg and went out 8-6 on aggregate. This was not to be the only tie that ended up with the same scoreline over the two matches. Tranmere Rovers had won 4-3 at Halifax Town in the first leg, then repeated the scoreline at home to progress, albeit only after extra time.

Grimsby Town provided the biggest shock of the second round as they went through against Aston Villa. It had been a goalless draw in the first leg and it was widely expected that Villa would finish the job at home, but it was Grimsby who went through on the away goals rule following a 1-1 draw after extra time. Oldham Athletic enjoyed the biggest aggregate win when they defeated Torquay United 9-1, closely followed by Nottingham Forest who beat Bolton Wanderers 9-2. Defending champions Sheffield Wednesday went through 4-1 against Leyton Orient, as did Manchester United against Cambridge United.

There were several 4-1 victories in the third round, with Everton beating Wolverhampton Wanderers at home, and Norwich City also did the same on home soil against Brentford. Swindon went against the grain by winning 4-1 on their travels against Huddersfield Town. Sheffield Wednesday's defence of the cup came to an end as Southampton beat them 1-0 in a replay at The Dell after no goals had been scored at Hillsborough. Crystal Palace claimed a spot in the fourth round after two replays against Birmingham City. Successive 1-1 draws meant that Palace won the toss and played at Selhurst Park, and the advantage counted as they finally put down the Blues with a 2-1 scoreline. Manchester United also went through in the third round with a 3-1 home victory against a plucky Portsmouth team.

Everton were on the wrong end of a 4-1 loss in the fourth round as Leeds United marched on at Goodison Park on 4 December 1991. On the same night, Manchester United continued their quest to reach another cup final with a 2-0 home win against Oldham Athletic. The biggest shock of the round came at Peterborough as they beat the mighty Liverpool 1-0 in front of 14,000 fans, with Garry Kimble for ever etching his name into Posh folklore by scoring the winning goal. Nottingham Forest went through with a 1-0 victory at Southampton in a replay after a goalless game at the City Ground.

The tie of the quarter-finals saw two teams vying for the First Division title when Manchester United were drawn at home against Leeds. It was played on 8 January 1992 along with the three other matches, which saw Peterborough entertain Middlesbrough, Tottenham meet Norwich in a repeat of the 1973 final, and Crystal Palace were up against Nottingham Forest, but perhaps the most interesting part of the draw was who made it.

By far and away the biggest football show on TV at the time was *Saint and Greavsie*, hosted by two legends of the game of the 1960s – Ian St John and Jimmy Greaves. The pair had travelled to Manhattan to do the draw at Trump Towers, with none other than the USA's most famous property tycoon, Donald Trump. This was how the *Daily Mail* recalled the bizarre events that day, which was overseen by the Football League secretary, David Dent.

'Greaves was drawing the home teams, Trump the away sides and St John stood beside them ready to interview the American billionaire afterwards. Before the draw started, St John turned to Greaves and said, "I don't know how you managed it," clearly surprised they had managed to secure such a high-profile booking for the draw. "This is some pad you've got here," Greaves said to Trump, claiming he hadn't "seen a boardroom like this since I was in Doug Ellis's at Aston Villa".

'Nothing of excitement came out of the first three ties to be drawn but then Trump saved the best for last when he pitted Manchester United against northern rivals Leeds in the standout fixture of the round. Trump admitted, "That's a game I want to go to," and said, "I think we're going to go over there [England] and watch a couple of those games."

'The three then engaged in chat about the development of "soccer", as Trump called it, in the United States and the country's upcoming World Cup [in 1994]. Asked if he had ever played football, Trump replied, "Well, I used to. Over here we call it soccer, but it's never worked out quite as well over here in the United States as it has elsewhere. But we're having the World Cup in the United States soon so that should be great. It's a great game. I love soccer. I actually used to play in high school. It'll be interesting to see how it catches on in the United States. When you look at England and other countries it's so big. It hasn't really caught on here yet but it's starting."'

Greaves then ended the draw ceremony by presenting Trump with an iconic *Saint and Greavsie* mug.

Manchester United got the better of Leeds with a 3-1 victory. Gary Speed put Leeds in front on 17 minutes, but three goals for United followed, with Clayton Blackmore, Andrei Kanchelskis and Ryan Giggs all scoring. Tottenham beat Norwich 2-1 and the other ties required replays. Peterborough and Middlesbrough drew 0-0 and Crystal Palace held Nottingham Forest 1-1. It was home wins in the replays with Forest triumphing 4-2 and Middlesbrough going through 1-0.

The semi-finals pitched Middlesbrough at home to Manchester United and Nottingham Forest against Tottenham. Both first legs ended in draws – there were no goals in Teesside, and it ended 1-1 in Nottingham.

United and Forest won their second legs 2-1, and both after extra time. United were looking for the first win in the final and Nottingham Forest were looking for their fifth and as a result became the competition's most successful club in it as they took to the field at Wembley on 12 April 1992. It was the red of Manchester who came out on top, with the only goal of the game coming in the 14th minute when centre-back Gary Pallister played the ball midway inside the Nottingham Forest half to Brian McClair, who laid it off to Ryan Giggs. As was becoming a common sight when Manchester United played, the Welsh wonder-kid Giggs then drove at the Forest defence, drawing players to him. This allowed the left-winger to play the ball to McClair who was able to dribble into the penalty area and shoot left-footed past Forest goalkeeper Andy Marriott into the bottom-right corner of the goal. This was the first time that 'Choccy' McClair had scored in a final for his club, although his scoring contributions in the FA Cup and European Cup Winners' Cup in previous seasons had been most significant. It was a moment that was deserved by the popular Scotsman.

Despite the optimism for a great final, it was a mostly disappointing match for the purists.

Manchester United went on to rule English football for the rest of the decade, winning trophy after trophy – although this was the last time that they won the League Cup until the 21st century. The zenith of United's dominance was cemented in the 1998/99 season when they won the Premier League, FA Cup and the Champions League and Alex Ferguson was soon knighted for his achievements.

Donald Trump would go on to move into reality TV with shows like the American version of *The Apprentice* in the early part of the 21st century. He would later become the president of the United States. It is not known if he did actually attend any of the League Cup quarter-finals that he had drawn out.

As the late and great Jimmy Greaves would often say to Ian St John, 'It's a funny old game, Saint!'

Season 1992/93

The Final

18 April 1993

Arsenal 2 (Merson, Morrow) Sheffield
Wednesday 1 (Harkes)

Wembley Stadium, London

Attendance: 74,007

Referee: A. Gunn

The League Cup was now sponsored by Coca-Cola – the first time that the competition had attracted a huge, worldwide brand.

Torquay United were on the receiving end of the highest aggregate win in the second round, losing 9-2 against Swindon Town, who won the first leg 6-0 away from home, so the match was pretty much over by the return leg which saw the Robins win 3-2. Holders Manchester United went through 2-1 on aggregate against a dogged Brighton & Hove Albion. Arsenal's pairing with Millwall resulted in both games finishing 1-1, with the Gunners going through 3-1 on penalties, shoot-outs now being used instead of replays to decide drawn ties in the early rounds. Sheffield Wednesday also reached the third round with a 5-2 aggregate win against Hartlepool United. The game that produced the most goals over the two matches was when Liverpool played Chesterfield. There were 13 recorded and it was the first leg which captured the imagination at Anfield on 22 September. After 48 minutes, the away team were 3-0 up and in total dreamland. Steve Norris had given Chesterfield the lead on just seven minutes before a brace from Dave Lancaster on the 30th minute and just after half-time put Chesterfield in total control, but Liverpool came roaring back and reduced the deficit to only one in a ten-minute spell that saw Ronny Rosenthal and Don Hutchison score. Amazingly, Norris picked up his second goal of the match on 69 minutes to rock the Anfield faithful once more. Just three minutes later, Mark Walters pulled a goal back before Mark Wright restored parity and saved the mighty Reds embarrassment with just five minutes to go of a pulsating match. Liverpool won the second leg 4-1 and went through 8-5 over the two games.

The most intriguing game in the third round saw Aston Villa entertain Manchester United at Villa Park on 28 October, and they won by a single goal courtesy of Dalian Atkinson. Sheffield Wednesday went through with the biggest score after a comfortable 7-1 victory at home to Leicester City. Arsenal went through after a 2-1 home replay win against Derby County, this after a 1-1 draw at the Baseball Ground.

Wednesday continued their fine goalscoring form in this season's competition with a resounding 4-0 home victory against Queens Park Rangers in the fourth round. Arsenal went through with a hard-fought 1-0 win at Scarborough, who had endured a great cup run of their own. Aston Villa, Everton and Liverpool were all knocked out at home, with Ipswich Town, Chelsea and Crystal Palace respectively inflicting the defeats.

The first two quarter-finals took place on 6 January 1993, with Blackburn Rovers overcoming Cambridge United 3-2 at Ewood Park and Crystal Palace taking care of fellow London club Chelsea 3-1 at Selhurst Park. Just six days later, Arsenal saw off the challenge of Nottingham Forest 2-0 at Highbury. Only one game was decided after a replay and that was when Ipswich Town drew 1-1 with Sheffield Wednesday on 19 January. The replay took place on 3 February with Wednesday winning 1-0.

The first of the semi-final first legs took place just four days after Wednesday had made the final four when Crystal Palace entertained Arsenal in an all-London contest. It was the away team who came away with a 3-1 victory after a penalty from Palace old boy Ian Wright on ten minutes and a couple from his strike partner Alan Smith proved enough to hand the advantage to the Gunners. Simon Osborn pulled one back to give Palace a glimmer of hope, but two first-half goals in the second leg at Highbury were enough for Arsenal to go through 5-1 on aggregate. Wright once more inflicted some damage before a goal from Andy Linighan on the stroke of half-time saw Arsenal through to their third final in six years.

Sheffield Wednesday reached their second final in three seasons with a 6-3 aggregate victory over Blackburn. The damage was done in the first leg at Ewood Park on 10 February when Roy Wegerle had given Rovers the lead on ten minutes before Wednesday came back, scoring four goals in just 16 minutes, with John Harkes equalising before John Sheridan gave them the lead, then a brace from Paul Warhurst on the 26th and 30th minutes put them in total control. Despite Carlton Palmer putting through his own goal just a few moments later, there were to be no further goals. Wednesday claimed a Wembley slot once more with a 2-1 home victory and 6-3 overall. Patrik Andersson gave Rovers a first-half lead but all hopes were dashed with two late Wednesday goals courtesy of David Hirst and Mark Bright.

The final took place on 18 April 1993 and was the first played in the Premier League era. It was also the first final that players wore their squad numbers as well as their names on their shirts. Harkes opened the scoring in only the eighth minute, becoming the first American to score in a major English final, before Paul Merson squared things in the 20th minute, and the teams went in all level at the break. The game was decided in the 68th minute when Steve Morrow scored to give Arsenal a 2-1 lead which they held on to. It was a bittersweet day for Morrow who not only scored the winning goal but was involved in a freak accident during the celebrations after the match. Tony Adams attempted to pick up Morrow and parade him on his shoulders, but the skipper slipped, and Morrow awkwardly hit the ground. He broke his arm and had to be rushed to hospital. The accident almost caused Morrow to sever his main artery, such was the damage caused. Fortunately, he made a full recovery and ensured a lifetime membership in the 'cult status' club. Morrow was unable to pick up his winners' medal due to the accident but he was able to collect it before the start of the FA Cup Final in May 1993. It was a moment of déjà vu as Arsenal and Sheffield Wednesday again met in that final, the Gunners breaking Wednesday's hearts once more and becoming double domestic cup winners. The FA Cup Final required a replay, which meant that the teams had met three times in just over a month at Wembley.

Season 1993/94

The Final
27 March 1994
Aston Villa 3 (Atkinson, Saunders 2) Manchester
United 1 (Hughes)
Wembley Stadium, London
Attendance: 77,231
Referee: K. Cooper

There were several clubs winning their second-round ties by racking up eight goals over their two matches. Middlesbrough, Liverpool, Leicester and Everton were the goal-hungry teams with Brighton, Fulham, Rochdale and Lincoln City all on the receiving ends. Newcastle United went three goals better with an 11-2 victory against Notts County.

Birmingham City were paired against Aston Villa in the second round. It was the first competitive game between the Second City rivals in five seasons and saw Villa winning 2-0 on aggregate. Alex Ferguson's Manchester United progressed 3-2 over the two legs against Stoke City. The team from the Potteries won the first leg 2-1 before succumbing to a 2-0 home victory for the Red Devils in the return at Old Trafford.

United's route into the fourth round was easier than what they had encountered in the previous round as they recorded a resounding 5-1 home victory against Leicester City. A Steve Bruce brace and a goal apiece for Brian McClair, Lee Sharpe and Mark Hughes were enough to see off the Foxes' challenge. Aston Villa were also in the mood to make it big with a 4-1 away win at Sunderland. It could have been so different if it wasn't for some fantastic saves by Villa keeper Mark Bosnich, who seemed to defy gravity and break the hearts of the Roker Park faithful. Two goals from Dalian Atkinson, the second taking a wicked deflection, and goals for Kevin Richardson and Ray Houghton were enough to put the claret and blue giants through, with Phil Gray scoring the solitary goal for the Black Cats. John King's Tranmere Rovers had seen off the challenge of the winners of the competition in 1986, Oxford United, 5-1 over two legs and they were very much in the mood to continue this, with a 4-1 home victory against Grimsby Town on 26 October 1993. The two finalists from the previous season, Arsenal and Sheffield Wednesday, once again progressed to the fourth round with victories over Norwich City and Middlesbrough respectively, both being replays and both on home soil, with Arsenal winning 3-0 and Wednesday 2-1.

Tranmere continued to win games by considerable margins as they beat Oldham Athletic 3-0 at Brunton Park on 30 November. Aston Villa ensured that Arsenal's defence of the cup came to an end with a 1-0 victory at Highbury. Manchester United also enjoyed a victory on their travels, 2-0 at Everton. Sheffield Wednesday joined Villa and United with a win on the road as they beat Queens Park Rangers 2-1 on 1 December.

Aston Villa's reward for beating Arsenal in north London was another trip to the vicinity in the quarter-finals, this time against Tottenham Hotspur. They were once again victorious, with a 2-1 win at White Hart Lane. Sheffield Wednesday came away from a tricky tie against Wimbledon, who had put out Liverpool in the previous round, by the same scoreline that Villa had enjoyed against Spurs. Manchester United and Tranmere also progressed through to the semi-finals but after a replay each. United had shared four goals with Portsmouth at Old Trafford on 12 January 1994, before winning by a solitary goal two weeks later at Fratton Park, Brian McClair netting on 27 minutes to break the hearts of the south coast club. Tranmere had been away to Nottingham Forest and gained a credible 1-1 draw, Rovers going through 2-0 in the replay.

The draw made for the semi-finals threw up two intriguing matches. The winners of the trophy in 1992 were drawn at home in the first leg against the winners in 1991 with Manchester United having the first-leg advantage in front of a crowd of 43,294 at Old Trafford on 13 February 1994, Ryan Giggs settling matters in the 20th minute to earn with a slender 1-0 victory. However, it was not to be a close affair in the second leg at Hillsborough on 2 March as United won 4-1 on the night and 5-1 on aggregate to take revenge for the 1991 loss to Wednesday in the final. The tie was effectively over just over ten minutes in as United raced into an early 2-0 lead on the night with goals from Brian McClair and Andrei Kanchelskis. David Hirst pulled a goal back on 34 minutes but just five minutes later, the Red Devils stretched the aggregate lead to 4-1 courtesy of Mark Hughes, and the Welsh striker added his second goal on 82 minutes. United were back at Wembley for the third time in five years in the competition and with a comprehensive 5-1 victory.

The other semi-final really had all the drama, and remains to date one of the greatest last-four ties ever in the competition. Tranmere were drawn at home to Aston Villa in the first leg which was played on 16 February at Prenton Park. It was a game that the vast majority of the 17,140 enjoyed as the second-tier club tore into the team that had finished runners-up in the Premier League the season before. Villa were shell-shocked and found themselves 2-0 down at half-time with Ian Nolan on five minutes and the aptly named Mark Hughes (no relation to the United forward) on the stroke of half-time putting the home team in wonderland and dreaming of that Wembley final. John Aldridge had received a winners' medal for Oxford United in 1986 and it looked very much like he'd get the chance once more when he extended Tranmere's lead on 78 minutes. Then, on the stroke of full time, Dalian Atkinson pulled a goal back to make the score 3-1. The Villa fans who poured out of the ground left feeling that this goal could turn the corner in their favour. This was not lost on the jubilant Tranmere supporters either, but for the moment celebrating was the order for the rest of the evening. The second leg took place on Sunday, 27 February 1994, and it was televised live on ITV. They had chosen wisely as it was a classic witnessed by the 40,593 in the ground and the millions watching on TV.

It was a game of cat and mouse for the first ten minutes or so with both teams sounding the other out. Villa had to go for it at some point and Tranmere needed to defend as if their lives depended on it. No quarter was shown or indeed given. Then in the 19th minute Dean Saunders arrived in the six-yard box to flick the ball past Eric Nixon at his near post after neat exchanges between Tony Daley and Andy Townsend to make it 1-0 to the home team and 3-2 to Tranmere overall. Four minutes later, Villa Park was once again lit up as central defender Shaun Teale scored with a diving header to level the tie. Now it was the turn of Rovers to feel shell-shocked.

The ascendancy was firmly with the home team and the Premier League giants. However, a third goal in ten minutes meant that Tranmere were back in the game and 4-3 ahead on aggregate. Villa were playing a high line and Rovers were able to play a long ball forward for John Aldridge to run on to and move into the Villa penalty area, where he was brought down by Mark Bosnich. Referee Alan Gunn pointed to the penalty spot without hesitation and Aldridge calmly slotted home. The Tranmere fans had booed the decision not to send Bosnich sent off. Amazingly there were no more goals until the 88th minute when Dalian Atkinson headed the ball home after a pinpoint cross from Daley. Atkinson's last-minute goal in the first leg had proved decisive. However, this was not to be the last moment of drama in regular time. Tranmere were awarded a free kick just outside the Villa penalty area. Liam O'Brien took it and his powerful drive hit the inside of the post, leaving Bosnich stranded, the Australian then watching the ball roll out on the other side. The game went into extra time with Villa having the most noticeable chances, Andy Townsend having a shot well saved and Earl Barrett hitting the post from it before Atkinson went close with a mazy run into the Tranmere penalty area. It went to penalties with Villa winning the shoot-out 5-4. It was one of those games where no team deserved to lose, and Tranmere players and fans could hold their heads high.

And so, the final of 1994 was to be played between Aston Villa and Manchester United. The only time that they had met in a final previously was the FA Cup Final of 1957 with Villa winning 2-1. Turf accountants up and down the land had made United firm favourites for the competition – and this was also the case for the media as well. This was to be the third time that Ron Atkinson led a team out for the final of the League Cup after previously guiding Manchester United and Sheffield Wednesday at Wembley.

Knowing that the domestic treble was well and truly on, Alex Ferguson decided to field a full-strength team, except for Peter Schmeichel who was suspended. Taking the great Dane's place was Les Sealey who had previously played for Villa. Ron Atkinson had decided to go more tactical as he went for a five-man midfield with Tony Daley and Dalian Atkinson on the wings. The surprise was that he included 19-year-old Graham Fenton behind Saunders, which allowed for Villa to play a faster counter-attacking formation. Possession was in favour of the English champions, but after 25 minutes it was the West Midlands team who drew first blood. Townsend played a ball into Saunders and the lone striker for the day was able to flick the ball over the top of United's defence and into the path of Dalian Atkinson, who put his side 1-0 up. It was rather apt that it was Atkinson who scored the opening goal as he had been the one to score the crucial away goal at Tranmere and then net again at Villa Park to take the semi-final into extra time.

The second half took the shape of the first with United having the possession once more and Villa looking dangerous on the break. On 70 minutes, it took a timely tackle from Villa's captain Kevin Richardson, stopped Lee Sharpe from getting United back on level terms. United were to rue this miss just five minutes later when Saunders stuck a foot out to divert a free kick taken by Richardson into the back of the net. Villa were two goals to the good and just 15 minutes away from cup glory.

United were back in the game in the 83rd minute when Mark Hughes pulled a goal back. Villa were rattled and Hughes nearly got his second just moments later but Bosnich was equal to his volley as he turned the ball past the post.

There was a fourth goal with just minutes to go, and it was Villa who scored it via a Saunders penalty. Daley had struck the post following a fantastic strike that came back off the United post. The ball fell into the path of Atkinson who hit it goalward only for the ball to strike Andrei Kanchelskis on the hand. The Ukrainian was immediately red-carded and could only watch as Saunders put the game well beyond United. While millions watched on TV, the final was significant on the radio as it was the last match covered on the original BBC Radio 5. The station closed down on the evening of 27 March and was replaced the very next morning by Radio 5 Live.

Season 1994/95

The Final

2 April 1995
Liverpool 2 (McManaman 2) Bolton
Wanderers 1 (Thompson)
Wembley Stadium, London
Attendance: 75,595
Referee: P. Don

Holders Aston Villa produced the biggest winning margin in the second round, with an 8-0 victory against Wigan Athletic. Arsenal dispatched Hartlepool United 7-0 and Middlesbrough took care of Scarborough with both legs finishing 4-1 to the Teessiders. The most goals scored over two legs occurred between Tottenham Hotspur and Watford. Both featured away wins, but it was Spurs who amassed the largest victory. The first leg was played at Vicarage Road where Watford took the lead in the first minute via Craig Ramage, but just a few minutes later Spurs were level courtesy of an equaliser by Darren Anderton. It then became the Jürgen Klinsmann show for the rest of the first half as the German bagged three goals. Tommy Mooney pulled a goal back for the Hornets in the second half, before Teddy Sheringham made it 5-2 and the game was put to bed by another goal for the north London club thanks to their Romanian international, Ilie Dumitrescu. Watford reduced the lead to three via a Gary Mabbutt own goal. The Hornets led three times in the second leg at White Hart Lane but were unable to stop Spurs equalising twice. Colin Foster and a brace from Lee Nogan scored the visitors' goals but Nick Barmby and another for Klinsmann meant that even though Watford had won 3-2, Spurs progressed 8-6 on aggregate. The biggest shock of the round was Premier League giants Leeds United losing 1-0 over the two legs against Third Division Mansfield Town. What made this even more remarkable was that Mansfield had won at Elland Road, Simon Ireland scoring the only goal. Another significant win was for First Division Bolton Wanderers under the guidance of Bruce Rioch, the Trotters comprehensively going through 4-0 against Ipswich Town over the two legs with a 3-0 win away to boot as well. Bolton's League Cup journey for the season was well under way.

Bolton's away adventures continued in the third round with a 2-1 victory at fellow First Division club Sheffield United. Liverpool also won by the same margin and on the same night as Bolton, the difference being that the Merseyside team were at home and the unlucky visitors were Stoke City. Mansfield's reward for beating Leeds in the previous round was a home tie against Millwall, with the Londoners winning 2-0. Taking Mansfield's place as this round's giant-killers were Notts County. The Football League's oldest club were to be relegated at the end of the season, finishing rock bottom of the First Division, and this made their 3-0 home victory against Tottenham Hotspur even more incredible. Meadow Lane was packed to the rafters as the home side tore into their Premier League opponents. Two goals from Gary McSwegan and one from Tony Agana were the difference. The Spurs manager, Ossie

Ardiles, was relieved of his managerial duties at White Hart Lane soon afterwards.

Crystal Palace made sure that Aston Villa were not able to defend their cup as the Midlands outfit were thrashed 4-1 at Selhurst Park in the fourth round. Dalian Atkinson had given Villa the lead on 33 minutes, but the second half saw Palace rampant and scoring four goals with two each by Gareth Southgate and Chris Armstrong. Liverpool and Bolton won 3-1 on their travels, with the Reds beating Blackburn Rovers, who went on to be crowned Premier League champions at the end of the season. West Ham United were Bolton's victims.

Palace were once more in the goals in the quarter-finals and this time it was Manchester City who fell on the Selhurst Park sword, losing 4-0. The other three ties ended up with home victories as well, with Bolton beating Norwich 1-0 and Liverpool winning by the same margin against Arsenal in a repeat of the 1987 final, and Swindon Town taking care of Millwall 3-1.

Bolton and Swindon were paired together in the semi-finals, meaning that at least one team from outside the top flight would be in the final. This was Bolton's first semi-final in the competition since 1977 and Swindon's first since 1980. The other semi paired two top-tier clubs together as Liverpool were drawn against Crystal Palace.

Just like in 1980, Swindon had home advantage in the first leg. They won 2-1 and then lost the second leg away 3-1 to go out 4-3 on aggregate. The difference in

1995 was that it was the Wanderers of Bolton as opposed to those of Wolverhampton who they contested the semi-final with. Alan Stubbs had given Bolton the lead on ten minutes at the County Ground, before Peter Thorne equalised in the first half and then put his team in front in the 78th minute. Jan Åge Fjørtoft stretched Swindon's lead in the second leg when he scored just before the hour. The Town faithful were once again dreaming of the triumphs of 1969, but Bolton had other ideas and booked a final berth for the first time with three goals in 24 minutes courtesy of Jason McAteer, Mixu Paatelainen and John McGinlay.

Liverpool went through to the final with two victories against Crystal Palace. The Reds won 1-0 at Anfield via a last-minute goal from local hero Robbie Fowler, who inflicted the damage at Selhurst Park by putting his team further ahead in the tie on 27 minutes and securing an overall 2-0 victory.

The final was played on 2 April 1995 at Wembley and produced three classic goals. If there was a gap in culture and status between the two clubs, then it didn't show in the early stages of the contest. Bolton winger David Lee was causing Liverpool mischief, and the first yellow card was awarded to the Reds' Phil Babb for a foul on him. Lee could easily have scored on the half-hour mark after a lofted pass from McAteer sent him clear of the Liverpool defence. The livewire was first to the ball instead of goalkeeper David James. Luckily for James and the Anfield faithful, the ball went just wide of the goal. Another player giving Liverpool a hard time was Alan Thompson in the Bolton midfield. Receiving a throw-in from Jimmy Phillips, the young Geordie unleashed a volley which took Liverpool's defence by surprise, except for James who was able to react and push the ball on to the crossbar. These chances for the underdogs seemed to give Liverpool a new lease of life, and just moments later they were in front with a great goal scored by Steve McManaman. Picking up a pass from John Barnes, the young midfielder ran past Stubbs and Scott Green with consummate ease before his shot went past goalkeeper Keith Branagan. The second half started as the first half had, with Bolton on the front foot as Paatelainen and Thompson went close. There was another sigh of relief for the Merseyside giants, before Stig Inge Bjørnebye hit the post, then McManaman went on a run which saw him once again ease past Green, McAteer and get in front of Mark Seagraves before putting the ball into the Bolton net. It looked like an uphill battle for Bolton, but they were back in the game almost straight away when Thompson scored a screamer. It was all to play for, but the class of Liverpool showed as they weathered the storm to win their fifth trophy in the competition.

Season 1995/96

The Final

24 March 1996
Aston Villa 3 (Milošević, Taylor, Yorke) Leeds United 0
Wembley Stadium, London
Attendance: 77,056
Referee: R.A. Hart

The game of the first round took place between Scunthorpe United and Rotherham United. The first leg was played at Glanford Park and it was the home team who prospered with a comfortable 4-1 victory as Scunthorpe put themselves in the driving seat for the second leg, but Shaun Goater pulled a goal back for Rotherham in the 14th minute and second-half goals from John McGlashan and Andy Hayward levelled the tie. There were no further goals scored until extra time when another from Goater put the Millers in front and Mike Jeffrey completed a fantastic comeback from the runners-up in 1962 to go through 6-4.

Rotherham's reward for their glorious comeback was against a Premier League team in the shape of Bryan Robson's Middlesbrough, but the Teesside club progressed 3-1 on aggregate after winning both legs. The four goals scored meant this proved to be one of the lowest-scoring games in the second round.

By far the tie with the biggest goal tally occurred between Wimbledon and Charlton Athletic. The first leg took place at Selhurst Park on 19 September 1995 with Charlton winning 5-4. A Lee Bowyer hat-trick and a goal apiece from Kim Grant and Peter Garland were enough for a remarkable away win. Wimbledon's scorers were Dean Holdsworth with a brace, and plus one each for Robbie Earle and Andy Clarke. Holdsworth scored a further two in the second leg alongside another from Earle. However, it was not enough for the Dons as Charlton also scored three themselves at The Valley courtesy of Carl Leaburn, Grant once more and John Robinson, the 3-3 seeing the Addicks through 8-7 on aggregate. Wimbledon's home leg was played at Crystal Palace because they were ground-sharing with Plough Lane being closed. Charlton had played home games at the same venue for several previous seasons due to The Valley closing for a few years.

But none of these matches mentioned above will stay in the memory of the fans as much as those of York City in the second round. City were paired with the mighty Manchester United, with the first leg being played at Old Trafford on 20 September. The bookies were offering odds of 20/1 for a York upset. It took the most foolhardy or optimistic fans to even think about taking this bet, especially as York were in the relegation zone in the Second Division while United were riding high at the top of the Premier League. Although Alex Ferguson included some of his less experienced, younger players, United still fielded a formidable side.

With Old Trafford full but at a reduced capacity due to ongoing stand reconstruction, City started brightly and quickly got into their stride and started to ruffle the Red Devils' feathers. Scott Jordan and Nigel Pepper both had decent shots on goal. Then on 24 minutes, the unbelievable happened when Paul Barnes took a shot from 25 yards that took a slight deflection which completely wrong-footed Kevin Pilkington in the United goal and the visitors were 1-0 up.

It was widely expected that United were going to get out of first gear with Brian McClair looking lively as ever, but to everyone's surprise it remained 1-0 to York at the break. The Old Trafford faithful were still not too concerned. Surely it was only a matter of time before United got back in the second half and would indeed go on and win at a canter. What absolutely no one could have predicted was for United to be three goals down on the hour, but this was precisely what happened and made sure that Barnes's name was for ever etched into legend status. On 51 minutes, Barnes raced into the United penalty area before being felled by Pat McGibbon, but he dusted himself down and scored from the spot kick. Now the United fans were deep in shock and the City faithful were deep into dreamland. The gap between the feelings of both sets of supporters widened just a couple of minutes later when Pepper swung in a pinpoint free kick right on to the head of Tony Barras and, with Pilkington in no man's land, the ball flew into the net for City's third. Barnes found the net once again, but he was judged offside, which on reflection was a harsh decision. He even had time to clear off his own line when it looked as if Steve Bruce had pulled a goal back for the home team.

The back pages of all the national papers were full of praise for City. *The Times* wrote, 'Mighty Manchester United were humiliated in front of their home crowd as lowly York City, from the bottom of the Endsleigh Insurance League Second Division, hammered three goals without reply in their Coca-Cola second round first leg tie.'

The headlines were simple and to the point as well, with one simply reading: 'YORKED'.

Smarting from the humiliation, Alex Ferguson was to bring back his big guns for the return leg. The class showed through as United won 3-1 at Boothferry Park but went out 4-3 on aggregate. It would not have been a surprise if the York manager had called his brother, who was also in football, to share his delight and be offered the sincerest of congratulations, blood being thicker than water for City's Alan Little and Aston Villa's Brian.

York were paired against another Premier League outfit in the third round, away to Queens Park Rangers. Perhaps beating one of the great teams in the country had taken it out of the Second Division club as they went down 3-1. But what a story they had created.

Brian still flew the flag for the Little family as his Aston Villa team beat Stockport County 2-0 at Villa Park. Liverpool were in the mood to retain the trophy with a comprehensive 4-0 victory at home against a lacklustre Manchester City team. Arsenal were still waiting to concede a goal in the competition as they won 3-0 at Barnsley, while Leeds United were also victorious away as they left Derby County with a 1-0 win.

Liverpool's hopes of a sixth trophy in the competition ended abruptly in the fourth round on 29 November

1995, losing to a solitary goal at home against Kevin Keegan's Newcastle United. Aston Villa continued their hunt to reach their second final in three years with a 1-0 victory over QPR. Arsenal and Leeds won their games 2-1, both at home, and the unlucky teams that fell foul were Sheffield Wednesday and Blackburn Rovers respectively. Another team going through and providing the biggest upset of the round were Reading as they beat Southampton at home, also 2-1.

All quarter-finals were played on 10 January 1996. Three of them were settled at the first time of asking, with Arsenal putting out Newcastle United 2-0 at Highbury, Villa beating local rivals Wolverhampton Wanderers 1-0 and Leeds ensuring that Reading's romance with the cup came to an end, winning 2-1 at Elland Road. The last quarter-final saw Norwich City entertain Birmingham City. The Blues' route thus far had been a trying one with them having to play two games to get through each time. The first two rounds had been two-legged affairs, firstly taking care of Plymouth Argyle 3-1 and then knocking out Grimsby 4-2 in the second round. Then it was all replays to get them to the quarter-finals. The third round saw them at home to Tranmere Rovers with a 1-1 draw before the Blues won 3-1 in the replay. The fourth round found them coming away from Middlesbrough after a goalless scoreline, before winning the replay 2-0. It stood to reason that they were going to progress to the semi-finals in a similar fashion. A 1-1 draw at Norwich meant a replay at St Andrew's on 20 January with the team from the West Midlands winning 2-1.

Villa were drawn with Arsenal, with the first leg at Highbury, and Birmingham met Leeds with the first leg at St Andrew's. It was not to be a Second City final again, though. Arsenal had found themselves two up before Villa came back to make it 2-2 with a Dennis Bergkamp brace being cancelled out by Dwight Yorke's two goals. The second leg at Villa Park was a cagey affair with chances at a premium. There were no goals added from the first leg in normal and extra time so away goals meant that it was Aston Villa going through to the final. In the first leg of the other semi-final, Kevin Francis had given Birmingham a 1-0 lead at half-time before Leeds came back with two second-half goals via Tony Yeboah and an unfortunate own goal from Chris Whyte. Whyte had played for Leeds previously and was a great servant to them as they won the last First Division title in 1991/92. The second leg was a formality for Leeds as they ran out 3-0 winners and 5-1 on aggregate. Phil Masinga, Tony Yeboah and Brian Deane were on target.

The final was played on Sunday, 24 March 1996, and was as one-sided as the 1986 final which saw Oxford United beat Queens Park Rangers 3-0. This time it was Leeds losing at the hands of a rampant Aston Villa.

Savo Milošević put Villa 1-0 up with a great shot from outside the penalty area. Leeds never recovered from this as Villa took advantage to eventually win 3-0, goals from Ian Taylor and Dwight Yorke completing the scoring. This was the beginning of the end for Leeds manager Howard Wilkinson, as he was heckled by the club's fans for his and the team's failure at Wembley.

Season 1996/97

The Final
6 April 1997
Leicester City 1 (Heskey) Middlesbrough 1 (Ravanelli)
(after extra time)
Wembley Stadium, London
Attendance: 76,757
Referee: M.J.D. Bodenham

Replay
16 April 1997
Leicester City 1 (Claridge) Middlesbrough 0
(after extra time)
Hillsborough, Sheffield
Attendance: 39,428
Referee: M.J.D. Bodenham

Leicester City's only major trophy had come in 1964 when they won the League Cup. Since then, the Foxes had spent time in the top flight interspersed with relegation to the second tier in the remaining part of the 1960s, 1970s and 1980s. Indeed, this continued with promotion to the Premier League in the 1993/94 season via the play-offs. There was an immediate return to the second tier the season afterwards before being promoted once more via the play-off final. At the helm was Martin O'Neill. The former Northern Ireland midfielder had played a major part in the rise of Nottingham Forest under Brian Clough in the 1970s when they won the First Division, League Cups and two European Cups. O'Neill's first foray into management was in the non-league arena with spells with Grantham Town and

Shepshed Charterhouse. However, it was at his third team that he really came to the fore when he took over at Wycombe Wanderers in 1990, overseeing promotion to the Football League in the 1992/93 season. A second successive promotion occurred in the following season before they narrowly missed out on another in 1994/95. One of the teams that Wycombe had played during the season was Stockport County.

The club from Greater Manchester had been crowned Third Division (North) champions twice in the 1920s and 1930s. They had been relegated in the first season that amalgamated the south and north divisions to become a nationalised Third Division in 1959. For the next three decades, County would ply the vast majority of trade in the fourth tier until they were promoted to the Third Division in the 1990/91 season. Two years later they were promoted to the second tier where they continued to play as they kicked off the League Cup campaign at home against Carlisle United at Edgeley Park. Goals from Gene Wilson and Tommy Anderson ensured a safe passage for Reg Flewin's team into the next round.

The team of the second round were Middlesbrough who took care of business quickly and succinctly with a 10-0 aggregate win over Hereford United. Bryan Robson had taken over as manager at the Teesside club and was able to spend big under the guidance of chairman Steve Gibson. Italian and Brazilian flair was the order of the day with Fabrizio Ravanelli, Emerson and Juninho joining the ranks, Ravanelli bagging four in the 7-0 home first-leg victory. There was a mighty scare for Chelsea, though. The Londoners were paired with Second Division Blackpool. The first leg was at Bloomfield Road, Chelsea coming away with a strong 4-1 victory. The second leg should have been a formality at Stamford Bridge, according to the bookies and punters. Blackpool didn't read the script, though, and while they went out 5-4 on aggregate, they upset Chelsea with a 3-1 victory with two goals by Tony Ellis, one by James Quinn.

The third round paired the finalists from the previous campaign when Leeds United were drawn at home to Aston Villa, nearly seven months on from the Wembley occasion. Again, it was Villa who won, but this time only 2-1, so not as comprehensive as the final. Lee Sharpe put the hosts 1-0 up on 69 minutes before Ian Taylor and Dwight Yorke scored. Leeds fans could be forgiven for being sick of the sight of both players, as they had scored in the 3-0 final victory as well. Leicester City went through with a 2-0 victory, also on their travels, against York City, so there was no further giant-killing as York had achieved against Manchester United in the previous season.

It was Manchester United who were knocked out in the fourth round by the Foxes. A 2-0 victory at Filbert Street was enough for progression with the goals scored by Steve Claridge and Emile Heskey. Aston Villa's hopes of a second successive final were quashed as they lost 1-0 away to Wimbledon. There was a repeat of the 1987 final and this time Liverpool came out on top with a 4-2 home victory against Arsenal. Middlesbrough were also victors on home turf, 3-1 over Newcastle United. The biggest win and shock came at Burnden Park when First Division Bolton Wanderers entertained Tottenham Hotspur of the Premier League. A John McGinlay hat-trick and further goals by Gerry Taggart, Nathan Blake and Scott Taylor stunned the north London club. Teddy Sheringham's goal just papered over the cracks as Wanderers won 6-1 to send shock waves through football.

It wasn't to be the only shock result of the round as Stockport claimed their second successive Premier League scalp. They had already beaten Blackburn Rovers 1-0 at Ewood Park with Tim Sherwood putting the ball into his own net, and West Ham were next to fall to the team from Edgeley Park. A 1-1 draw had taken place at West Ham before a 2-1 victory in the replay on 18 December 1996. Julian Dicks gave the Hammers the lead on 22 minutes but another unfortunate own goal just a minute later put Stockport back on level terms – Ian Dowie was the offender this time around. Brett Angell gave the home team the lead just five minutes later and no further goals meant that Stockport were through to the quarter-finals.

Stockport once again faced Premier League opposition, but this time the victims were Southampton who had put Oxford United out in the previous round after a replay, and this tie also went to a second match. The first game at Edgeley Park had finished 2-2 on 22 January 1997, Egil Østenstad putting the Saints one up after 16 minutes before two goals in a minute put Stockport in control just nine minutes later via Alun

Armstrong and Luís Cavaco. Østenstad grabbed his second and his team's equaliser with just five minutes to go. Again, the bookies and punters plumped for a Saints victory with the consensus being that Stockport could not put out three Premier League teams on the trot. How wrong could they be. The replay took place at The Dell on 29 January. Again, it was the Premier League team who took the lead, this time through Matt Le Tissier after just nine minutes. There were no more goals until the 63rd minute when Brett Angell levelled matters and 20 minutes later the fans and players were in raptures as Stockport took the lead through an Andy Mutch goal. Stockport had made it three wins in consecutive rounds against members of the elite division.

Wimbledon, Middlesbrough and Leicester also made up the semi-finals, with the Dons beating Bolton 2-0 away, Middlesbrough beating Liverpool 2-1 at home and Leicester winning 1-0 at Ipswich Town.

The semis paired Leicester at home to Wimbledon and Stockport at home to Middlesbrough in the first legs.

Aston Villa had reached the previous year's final via the away goals rule, and Leicester got to Wembley with the same route, drawing 0-0 at Filbert Street and 1-1 in London. It was Middlesbrough who joined them but it was not an easy ride against Dave Jones's brave Stockport team. The first leg at Edgeley Park saw Middlesbrough come away with a 2-0 victory, with the goals coming from their Danish striker Mikkel Beck and from Fabrizio Ravanelli. Stockport did not make it easy in the return leg at the Riverside, winning 1-0 with Sean Connelly putting County in the lead after just six minutes. Amazingly, despite best efforts there were no more goals. Stockport had represented the lower leagues with gusto, skill and determination and captured the hearts of the football nation. Middlesbrough went through to face Leicester in the final at Wembley on 6 April 1997. It had been 13 years since the final had not been decided at Wembley and a replay had been required.

The day ended in a 1-1 draw after extra time, and both goals came in that period, with Ravanelli opening the scoring in the 95th minute. It looked very much that Middlesbrough's name would be engraved on the trophy for the first time, until Emile Heskey equalised with just minutes to go. The Leicester striker was fortunate to still be on the field having committed a bookable foul on Middlesbrough captain Nigel Pearson. Heskey had already been booked and it was a second yellow. The replay took place at Hillsborough on 16 April. Again, there were no goals in regulation time, and this time there was only one goal scored in extra time, Leicester winning the replay, and their second League Cup, with Steve Claridge scoring the goal on 100 minutes. This was the last year that the final was decided by a replay.

There may have been semi-final heartache for Stockport County, but a wonderful season for them was capped off with a third promotion to the second tier at the end of the campaign, making the 1990s County's most successful period to date.

Season 1997/98

The Final
29 March 1998
Chelsea 2 (Sinclair, Di Matteo) Middlesbrough 0
(after extra time)
Wembley Stadium, London
Attendance: 77,698
Referee: P. Jones

The first-round draw included no fewer than six previous winners of the competition. Most noticeable were Nottingham Forest who had won it four times. The others were Manchester City, Birmingham City, Luton Town, Oxford United and West Bromwich Albion. Four of them progressed to the second round with Manchester City being the only team not to qualify. They were paired with Blackpool and both teams won their home legs 1-0, then the tie was eventually settled on penalties at Maine Road with the team in orange winning 4-2. Forest had the biggest aggregate win with a 10-1 victory over Doncaster Rovers.

There was a clash between two previous winners when Luton were drawn against West Brom in the second round, with the Baggies going through 5-3. The biggest win of the round fell to Wimbledon who thrashed Millwall 4-1 and 5-1 to go through 9-2. It was also job done for both Derby County and Everton who marched on with identical aggregate scores, both winning away games 1-0 against Southend United and Scunthorpe United respectively, with the home matches yielding 5-0 victories and 6-0 overall results. Leicester City's defence of the competition was a weak one as they crashed out of the third round 3-1 to Grimsby Town, who were plying their trade in the Second Division, with Kevin Jobling and a brace from Steve Livingstone enough to provide the shock of the round and Ian Marshall netting for the Foxes. On their way to the previous season's final, Middlesbrough had knocked out Newcastle United. This time it was the turn of Sunderland who fell foul of the Teesside club, losing 2-0, and Chelsea were held 1-1 at home by Blackburn Rovers. The previous season had seen the last of replays in any of the rounds leading up to and including the final, so ties would go straight to penalties if there was no winner in extra time. This was the case with Chelsea and they went through 4-1 after a shoot-out. The other team going through on penalties were Oxford when they played Tranmere at home; it finished 1-1 with Oxford winning the shoot-out 6-5.

There were four ties in the fourth round that finished all square after 90 minutes but were settled before the lottery of penalties, with Arsenal, Chelsea, Middlesbrough and Ipswich progressing at the expense of Coventry City, Southampton, Bolton and Oxford respectively. The biggest shock of the round came at Elland Road, where Reading came away with a 3-2 victory over 1996 runners-up Leeds United. It had been 1-1 at half-time with Carl Asaba giving Reading the lead on nine minutes and David Wetherall squaring matters just seven minutes later. Lee Bowyer had put Leeds in front on 54 minutes before Martin Williams levelled on 66. The game was settled in the 85th minute, Trevor

Morley putting the Royals into the quarter-finals with a 3-2 victory. West Ham United, Newcastle and Liverpool also made it through, with Liverpool's rising young star Michael Owen scoring three goals in a 3-0 victory over Grimsby Town.

Chelsea progressed to the semi-final with a 4-1 penalty shoot-out victory at Ipswich after a 2-2 draw. It was a clean sweep of away victories in the other games as well, with Arsenal beating West Ham 2-1, Middlesbrough winning 1-0 at Reading with a last-minute goal scored by Craig Hignett and Liverpool coming away from Newcastle's St James' Park with a 2-0 win.

The semi-finals saw some very interesting ties with Liverpool hosting Middlesbrough and Arsenal playing Chelsea. Both the home teams won with 2-1 victories. Paul Merson had given First Division Middlesbrough the lead at Anfield in the 29th minute with Jamie Redknapp restoring parity just two minutes later. The only other goal was scored by Robbie Fowler with just eight minutes remaining.

Arsenal raced into a two-goal lead against Chelsea courtesy of Marc Overmars and Stephen Hughes before a vital goal from Mark Hughes reduced the deficit to just one goal in the 68th minute. It may have been advantage the home teams in the first legs, but they were soon blown away in the return matches.

Incredibly, Middlesbrough found themselves 2-0 up and 3-2 on aggregate just four minutes into the match at the Riverside on 18 February. Merson continued his semi-final scoring feat when he converted from the spot after just two minutes, and then just moments later Marco Branca put his side into the lead overall. There were no further goals scored and Middlesbrough were back in the final for the second year running. They were soon joined by Chelsea to provide a repeat of the previous season's FA Cup Final. Chelsea found themselves 3-0 up after 53 pulsating minutes that had shocked an Arsenal team riding high in all domestic competitions, with the goals scored by Mark Hughes, Roberto Di Matteo and Dan Petrescu. Dennis Bergkamp pulled a goal back on 82 minutes from the penalty spot, but it was the Blues who held on and reached Wembley.

The final was played on 29 March 1998. A significant part of Chelsea's victories on the road to Wembley had been victories in extra time and penalties, and it was in extra time that they won again to claim their second League Cup and ensure a second successive victory over Middlesbrough at Wembley. Chelsea broke the resistance of Boro in the first few minutes of the additional period through Frank Sinclair, and Roberto Di Matteo extended their lead late on.

Season 1998/99
The Final
21 March 1999
Leicester City 0 Tottenham Hotspur 1 (Nielsen)
Wembley Stadium, London
Attendance: 77,892
Referee: T. Heilbron

The previous two seasons' finals had seen victories sealed in extra time; however, the final of 1999 did not go the same way, but it had been very, very close to making it three on the bounce. The competition was now sponsored by the brewery Worthington, following five seasons of sponsorship by Coca-Cola.

There have been a plethora of footballers who have crossed the north London divide and played for both Spurs and Arsenal, but some have caused more controversy than others. In terms of management, to date it has only happened twice. Terry Neill was the first in the 1970s when he went from Spurs to Arsenal. But none of these courted anything like the controversial decision for Spurs to appoint George Graham in 1998. The former Scottish midfielder had played for Arsenal from 1966 to 1972 and was a valuable member of the team that won the double of the First Division and FA Cup in 1971. Graham was back at Arsenal as their manager in May 1986 after a successful spell at the helm of Millwall, taking them from near the bottom of the Third Division before promotion to the Second Division in a short space of time. The homecoming proved to be a very successful one for the Gunners as they won two

First Division titles, two League Cups, the FA Cup and the European Cup Winners' Cup over the next eight seasons. All this was to end abruptly, though, in February 1995, when Graham was found guilty of accepting illegal payments from a Norwegian football agent called Rune Hauge over the transfers to Arsenal of two players. Graham was subsequently banned from football for a 12-month period. He was back in work as manager of Leeds United in 1996, before taking the red-hot hot seat at Tottenham Hotspur in 1998. The appointment was met with derision from both sets of supporters.

Leicester and Spurs picked up away wins in the third round, the Foxes beating Charlton Athletic 2-1 and Spurs going one better with a 3-1 victory at Northampton Town. Middlesbrough's hopes of reaching a third final on the trot and making amends for two defeats were dashed as they lost 3-2 at home to Everton, and Chelsea progressed with a comprehensive 4-1 victory at home against Aston Villa.

Tottenham were once again drawn away and enjoyed another 3-1 victory in the fourth round, this time against more stellar opposition with Liverpool making way for the north London club. Steffen Iversen, John Scales and Allan Nielsen put Spurs in total control until a late goal from Michael Owen reduced the deficit. Chelsea had knocked Arsenal out of the previous season's semi-final and once again ended up victorious at Highbury, recording a comprehensive 5-0 result. Frank Leboeuf started the rout with a penalty in the 34th minute before braces from Gianluca Vialli and Gus Poyet completed the scoreline. It was a case of the late, late show at Filbert Street as Leicester came from behind to beat Leeds 2-1. Leeds were ahead from the 17th minute when Harry Newell scored, but Muzzy Izzet's goal in the 88th minute and a last-minute penalty from Garry Parker kept the Foxes on course for their second final in three seasons.

A 3-1 scoreline was becoming a very common winning margin for Spurs as they saw off the challenge of Manchester United at White Hart Lane in the quarter-finals, with Chris Armstrong scoring twice before ex-Spurs player Teddy Sheringham pulled one back on 71 minutes. The game was put out of the grasp of Alex Ferguson's team when David Ginola put the result beyond doubt with just two minutes to play. Leicester's quest continued as they beat Blackburn Rovers 1-0 at Filbert Street. Chelsea's fine run came to an end with a 2-1 defeat away to Wimbledon and Sunderland saw off the challenge from Luton Town 3-0. These ties were played on the first two days of December 1998.

The semi-final first legs ended in narrow victories for Leicester and Tottenham.

Leicester drew first blood with Sunderland at the Stadium of Light with a 2-1 victory, Tony Cottee scoring both of their goals before Gavin McCann gave Sunderland some hope for the return leg. Niall Quinn enhanced that hope when he put Sunderland one up at Filbert Street in the 34th minute. However, a goal in the 54th minute from Cottee once more meant that it was Leicester who booked their passage to Wembley as his team secured a 3-2 victory. There wasn't a 3-1 victory for

Tottenham this time, against Wimbledon in the other semi-final. In fact, there was only one goal scored in the 180 minutes and that came in the second leg away via Steffen Iversen in the 39th minute at Selhurst Park. Leicester and Tottenham had both won the competition twice before, so something was to give as they took centre stage at Wembley on 21 March 1999. It was not the greatest of games for the purists to watch, but this did not bother Tottenham in the least as they won their first major trophy in eight years and were back playing in Europe. Tottenham earned the win after playing with just ten men for the last half an hour as Justin Edinburgh was sent off for violent conduct. The game was heading into yet another bout of extra time until Spurs won it in the dying seconds, Nielsen's goal giving Tottenham the Worthington Cup and George Graham a trophy in his first season as Spurs manager.

The Dane reacted sharply to poach a header and take the cup back to north London for the first time in six years, since Arsenal had last won it. Graham had overseen the Gunners then and now he had done it with their local rivals. Although in some quarters of the Spurs fanbase the victory was never fully acknowledged due to previous employment.

Season 1999/2000
The Final
27 February 2000
Leicester City 2 (Elliott 2) Tranmere Rovers 1 (Kelly)
Wembley Stadium, London
Attendance: 74,313
Referee: A.B. Wilkie

It was the strangest of seasons for the League Cup in 1999/2000, and it would also be the last final to be played at Wembley for several years as the famous old stadium was being demolished and rebuilt. There was a quarter-final that never was and for the first time in English football history, the entire draw for each round was made after the first round, meaning each team could plot their route to the final as well as predicting future opponents. It was basically tennis at Wimbledon without the seeding.

The competition began on 10 August 1999 and finished in a new century on 27 February 2000.

There were three clubs that won 6-0 on aggregate in the first round – Manchester City, Grimsby Town and Sheffield United providing the clinical finishes while not conceding.

The two future finalists also found themselves in goals galore territory, Leicester knocking out Crystal Palace 7-5 and Tranmere winning 6-4 over Coventry City from the Premier League in the second round. The 12 goals between Leicester and Palace were matched by Liverpool beating Hull City 9-3, the Reds taking the honours for most goals scored over the two legs that season.

Tottenham progressed in the third round with a very familiar score from the previous campaign. The latest team to be on the receiving end of a 3-1 loss was Crewe Alexandra. Spurs had also beaten Manchester United and Liverpool by the same score on their way to lifting the trophy, and both went out of the competition at this stage. Aston Villa beat United 3-0 at Villa Park and Southampton knocked out the Reds of Merseyside 2-1 at The Dell. Leicester and Tranmere both progressed with 2-0 home victories, the Foxes beating Grimsby Town and Tranmere seeing off the challenge of Oxford United.

Tottenham's defence of the trophy came to an end after a defeat at Craven Cottage at the hands of Fulham in the fourth round. Ironically, it was a 3-1 loss as well. Barry Hayles had given the hosts the lead on ten minutes, and it looked like the teams would go into the break all square when Steffen Iversen scored for Spurs, but just a minute later Fulham were back in the lead through Wayne Collins. Geoff Horsfield later made it safe for Fulham in the 77th minute. Tranmere and Aston Villa enjoyed 4-0 home victories, Rovers against Barnsley and Villa against Southampton. Leicester had met Leeds at home in the fourth round the previous season and history repeated itself once more. The game finished goalless after extra time with the Foxes coming out on top again, this time 4-2 on penalties. Middlesbrough also sailed through on penalties, beating Arsenal 3-1. The tie had finished 2-2 after extra time. West Ham beat Birmingham City 3-2 at St Andrew's and there were also wins for Bolton and Wimbledon.

Leicester and Fulham met at the quarter-final stage and both teams produced entertaining football as the match finished 3-3 after 120 minutes. Paul Peschisolido on 58 minutes and Geoff Horsfield after 75 minutes had seemingly put the Londoners in total control and heading for the semi-finals. However, Leicester had other ideas and drew level with two goals in the last five minutes by Ian Marshall and Steve Walsh to take the game into extra time. Chris Coleman restored Fulham's lead before Marshall added his second. There were no further goals so the game went to penalties, and once again it was the Foxes celebrating as they won 3-0 after scoring their first three while Fulham missed all of theirs. There was also a First Division double over the Premier League with Tranmere beating Middlesbrough and Bolton following suit against Wimbledon. Both matches ended 2-1 to the home teams.

The other quarter-final was an all-Premier League clash between West Ham and Aston Villa. It finished 2-2 after extra time and was decided by a penalty shoot-out, which was won by West Ham. However, this became the game that 'never was' and it had to be replayed. In the 113th minute in extra time, Paulo Wanchope was substituted, and in his place came a reserve-team player called Emmanuel Omoyinmi. Unbeknown to West Ham's manager, Harry Redknapp, Omoyinmi had played for Gillingham in the cup while on loan there, and thus was ineligible to play for the Hammers. Villa and the Football League were quickly made aware of this and, as a result, the game was to be replayed. This prompted the resignations of West Ham's club secretary, Graham Mackrell, and football secretary Alison O'Dowd.

Mackrell was in a philosophical mood when he stated, 'Whatever has happened, the buck stops with me.' The match was replayed on the 11 January 2000, Villa winning 3-1 after extra time and perhaps karma was very much in play. Frank Lampard had given the home team the lead just after half-time. Ian Taylor's goal with ten minutes to go ensured that the tie went into extra time once more, and this was where Villa ramped it up with two further goals from Julian Joachim and another from Taylor.

The semi-final draw meant that there was a guarantee of a Premier League versus First Division final. Bolton played Tranmere at home in their first leg and Villa were at home against Leicester in the other match. There was only one goal in these two games and that came at Burnden Park with Clint Hill giving Tranmere a valuable away lead. It was all to play for in the second legs. It was a cagey affair at Filbert Street with only one goal separating both teams, scored on the stroke of half-time via Leicester's Matt Elliott. The Foxes won 1-0 and booked yet another slot in the Wembley showcase. It was a much easier affair for Tranmere as they raced into a two-goal lead (and 3-0 on aggregate) after just 20 minutes. Nick Henry and Alan Mahon settled their nerves, and songs about Wembley were being sung in unison by the home fans. Rovers' veteran striker David Kelly added a third on the evening with just 20 minutes to go, securing a 4-0 aggregate win.

Wembley was split into two halves for its first final of a new decade and century. One was a sea of white for Rovers and the other the familiar blue of Leicester.

The League Cup Finals over recent seasons had been turgid affairs, but this was to be a better game for the purists to watch with Leicester asking most of the questions and Tranmere not giving up. The first goal came just before the half-hour mark. Scott Taylor's successful tackle on Robbie Savage forced the ball out for a corner which was taken by Steve Guppy and was met perfectly from the head of Matt Elliott. There were to be no more goals in a first half that was by and large dominated by the favourites, although Rovers were still in the game. That almost changed in the 60th minute when Muzzy Izzet found himself unmarked in the Rovers box, but hesitated and his shot flew wide. There was a bizarre incident just a couple of minutes later when referee Alan Wilkie was stretchered off with an injury to his right leg. Wilkie was replaced by the fourth official, Phil Richards. Richards was soon in the thick of it after he gave Clint Hill a second yellow card and, as a result, Tranmere were down to ten men. This spurred Rovers on, and their persistence paid off when they equalised in the 77th minute when the ball found its way to an unmarked David Kelly who was able to shoot low with Elliott poised to make the tackle. But just three minutes later, Leicester were back in front and it was almost a carbon copy of their first goal. A Guppy corner once more found the head of Elliott, who in turn found the net.

There were no further goals despite a valiant attempt from the First Division club and Leicester had won the League Cup for the third time, emulating the previous year's winners, Tottenham Hotspur. Martin O'Neill became the first manager to win the competition twice as a player and twice as a manager.

With Wembley being knocked down and rebuilt, the following season's final was to be played at the Millennium Stadium in Cardiff. This was also the case for the FA Cup Final as well, with the Welsh capital continuing to host the showpiece occasions until the 2007 FA Cup Final returned to London.

5

The 2000s

Season 2000/01
The Final
25 February 2001
Birmingham City 1 (Purse) Liverpool 1 (Fowler)
(after extra time)
Liverpool won 5-4 on penalties
Millennium Stadium, Cardiff
Attendance: 73,500
Referee: D. Elleray

Birmingham City's path into the second round was well and truly confirmed with a comprehensive 5-0 win away at Southend United in the first leg, goals from Nicky Eaden, Marcelo, Michael Johnson, Dele Adebola and Bryan Hughes making the return a formality for the Blues. It was damage limitation for Southend, though, and the second leg finished without any further goals being scored.

Birmingham's reward was a second-round tie with Wycombe Wanderers and the first leg in Buckinghamshire produced a classic. The away team took the match to their hosts almost from kick-off and by the 24th minute they had raced into a three-goal lead.

A Paul McCarthy own goal in only the third minute set the scene before the Blues threatened to take the game by the scruff of its neck with quick-fire goals in the 22nd and 24th minutes from Geoff Horsfield and Andy Johnson. A goal on the stroke of half-time converted by Andy Rammell reduced the deficit to only two, which was totally wiped out with goals from Andy Baird and Jamie Bates who equalised in the 86th minute. However, home hearts were broken when Johnson scored his second of the match just moments later to give Birmingham a 4-3 victory. The tie was sealed with a 1-0 home victory courtesy of Peter Ndlovu in the 66th minute of the match as the Blues went through 5-3 on aggregate.

There were two teams who progressed 8-2 on aggregate in the second round. These were Bradford City and Sheffield Wednesday who beat Darlington and Oldham Athletic respectively.

Liverpool's first game in the competition came in the third round when they were drawn at home against Chelsea in the biggest tie of that stage. It ended 1-1 after 90 minutes before Liverpool scored the winning goal in extra time. Danny Murphy had given the Reds the lead on 12 minutes before Gianfranco Zola restored parity for the Blues just before the half-hour mark. The winning goal came from local hero Robbie Fowler in the 104th minute.

The third round was the third stage on the trot in which Birmingham won away from home. This time they beat Premier League giants Tottenham Hotspur in the biggest upset in the round. Three first-half goals did the damage with a brace from Dele Adebola and one from Mark Burchill before a second-half penalty converted by Darren Anderton reduced the deficit.

Holders Leicester City also found themselves being beaten at home as they crashed to a 3-0 win to Crystal Palace. Clinton Morrison, Steve Thompson and Andrejs Rubins were enough for the Londoners.

The fourth-round matches were played on 28 and 29 November 2000 and they threw up some intriguing matches. It was Liverpool who made the biggest impact with an emphatic 8-0 victory at Stoke City. There were four goals in each half as Liverpool tore their hosts apart in front of a crowd of 27,109 with Christian Ziege, Vladimír Šmicer, Markus Babbel and one from Robbie Fowler had all but ended the match in a frantic first 45 minutes. Fowler was to add two more, with other goals from Sami Hyypiä and Danny Murphy completing the rout. It was a much tighter affair for Birmingham who progressed to the fifth round with a 2-1 victory over another Premier League outfit, Newcastle United. Kieron Dyer had given the favourites the lead on 14 minutes before Birmingham pegged them back through Dele Adebola just after the half-hour mark. There were no further goals until the last seconds of the match when Andy Johnson scored the winner for Birmingham and sent the vast majority of the 18,520 delirious.

Like Birmingham, Sunderland were also victorious in a home tie after coming from behind against much more favoured opposition in Manchester United. Dwight Yorke had given the Red Devils the lead on 31 minutes, and this lasted until just 15 minutes from time when Julio Arca equalised. The Black Cats were now in the ascendancy and took a deserved lead in the 101st minute of extra time when Kevin Phillips converted a penalty which they held on to for a famous victory in front of the biggest crowd in the fourth round, 47,543.

There were to be no goals in normal time as Liverpool took on Fulham in the quarter-finals. However, it still turned out to be a comprehensive win as the hosts scored three goals in extra time with Michael Owen, Vladimír Šmicer and Nick Barmby all netting to put the Reds in the semi-finals where they were joined by Birmingham after a 2-0 home win against Sheffield Wednesday. A Danny Sonner goal in the first half and one from Dele Adebola in the second half saw them through to the semi-finals for the first time since 1996. The other teams through were Crystal Palace and Ipswich Town, who won their matches 2-1 against Sunderland and Manchester City respectively.

Liverpool and Birmingham were drawn away in the first legs and both suffered defeats. Ipswich Town beat Birmingham 1-0 at Portman Road on 9 January 2001 with a Marcus Stewart penalty on the stroke of half-time, and Liverpool lost 2-1 to Crystal Palace the night after. Andrejs Rubins and Clinton Morrison both scored for the home team before Vladimír Šmicer reduced the deficit with his third goal of the campaign. If the first legs witnessed Liverpool and Birmingham lose by slender margins, then both saw off the opposition in emphatic style at home in the return legs.

Firstly, it was the turn of Liverpool as they entertained Palace on 24 January 2001. The Reds raced into a three-goal lead in the first 20 minutes through goals from Šmicer, Danny Murphy and Igor Bišćan. Two further second-half goals from Murphy and Robbie Fowler completed the rout with a 6-2 aggregate victory. Liverpool had now scored 17 goals in the last three rounds of the competition before the final. A crowd of 28,624 witnessed Birmingham overturning a one-goal deficit with a 4-1 home victory over Ipswich to win the tie 5-2 over the two legs and book their place in the final. Martin Grainger gave Birmingham the lead just before the break and a goal from Geoff Horsfield at the start of the second half seemingly put the home team in command before James Scowcroft made the score 2-2 on aggregate. The game went into extra time, and it was the home team who capitalised with two further goals to win 4-1 on the night and 4-2 overall, with a second from Horsfield and a final goal from Andy Johnson taking the Blues into their first final since 1963.

The 2001 showpiece was the first final not to have been played at Wembley Stadium since 1967, instead being played in Wales for the very first time at Cardiff's Millennium Stadium. This was the case for the next seven years as the latest development at Wembley took place.

It was a match that was supposed to be won at a canter by Liverpool, but Birmingham had other ideas.

It was all going to plan for Liverpool when Robbie Fowler hit a brilliant first-time shot from 25 yards just before the half-hour mark that sailed into the back of Ian Bennett's net. Instead of folding, this spurred Birmingham on, but it wasn't until the dying seconds of the match that they forced a well-deserved equaliser when captain Martin O'Connor was fouled in the box by Stéphane Henchoz and Darren Purse showed remarkable courage to score from the spot. There were no further goals in extra time before Liverpool emerged victorious 5-4 on penalties.

O'Connor recalls the day he led the Blues out for the final in Cardiff, 'Playing at Wembley was always a dream of mine growing up and I had not been to the stadium in Cardiff but as soon as I saw the Millennium Stadium, I knew it was the perfect place. It was big and majestic. We went a couple of days before to acclimatise when the roof was closed, and it was more than a suitable venue for a national final. It was breathtaking, and when they opened up the roof it was even more scary, but in a weird way even more inspiring to us. We believed in ourselves even though no one was giving us a chance. We soon changed people's minds, though, and even with minutes to go, we were in the game.'

On the penalty which gave the Blues their lifeline, O'Connor continues, 'It was just instinct to push forward and this was probably my only chance to play in a game like that at my stage of my career and I was going to enjoy it and leave nothing left at the whistle. It was luck more than judgement but I knew that if I had a shot it would have got blocked so decided to try and fake a shot and drive into the box, and yes I did make more of it than I should have but my knee got caught and went into spasm causing me to have extensive treatment off the pitch. In the meantime, I watched Darren Purse put the penalty away.

'Now I was running on pure adrenaline. Trevor Francis [Birmingham's manager] kept shouting to come off but there was no way that was going to happen. My knee was swollen and so painful, so running and mobility was limited. So, when we did get to penalties I would have been nowhere near fit enough to take one which again was a blow but then it was more about the team than personal glory.

'After the game was one of my worst experiences in football as it was deadly quiet in our dressing room but there was a party we could hear in Liverpool's. With the experience we had in staff regards their playing career, we were in good hands but whatever they said fell on deaf ears as everyone was spent and just void of energy, emotion and voice.

'To be fair to Liverpool they invited us into their dressing room and signed shirts for us but again it was something that couldn't and didn't fill that feeling that we all felt of losing the final. I look back with great pride, though.'

This was the first of three major cups won by Gérard Houllier's side that season as they also added the FA Cup and the UEFA Cup.

Season 2001/02

The Final

24 February 2002
Blackburn Rovers 2 (Jansen, Cole) Tottenham
Hotspur 1 (Ziege)
Millennium Stadium, Cardiff
Attendance: 72,500
Referee: G. Poll

There was a major change for the competition in the 2001/02 season, as the first and second rounds were no longer to be played on a two-legged basis. The first-round matches saw seeded teams being pitted against the non-seeded ones and this was dependent on league finishes in the previous campaign.

First Division Birmingham City considered themselves very unfortunate not to be the current holders and were in the mood to get to Cardiff once more with two comprehensive 3-0 victories against Southend United at home in the first round and then Bristol Rovers away in the second round. However, this was as good as it got for the Blues as they crashed out to First Division rivals Manchester City 6-0 at Maine Road in the third round, with Darren Huckerby netting four of them. Leeds United matched the same scoreline away at Leicester City who had only been winners of the competition two seasons previously, Robbie Keane taking away the match ball himself with three goals. The biggest shock of the round came at Anfield where Liverpool were beaten in extra time by Grimsby Town. The first 90 minutes had finished without a goal, and it looked all over for Town when Gary McAllister converted a penalty after 101 minutes but Grimsby hit back with just seven minutes remaining with Marlon Broomes equalising. The game looked to be heading into a penalty shoot-out before Phil Jevons put the visitors in front with just seconds to go.

Grimsby were then drawn away to another giant of the game in the fourth round, as they faced Arsenal on 27 November 2001. There was no repeat this time with the Gunners winning 2-0 with goals from Edu and Sylvain Wiltord. The biggest win of the round came at St James' Park as Newcastle United ran out comfortable winners over Ipswich Town with Lauren Robert, Shola Ameobi and a brace from Alan Shearer completing the rout in the first half. Darren Bent pulled a goal back for the visitors in the 77th minute, but the match ended 4-1 to the hosts.

All four quarter-finals produced home wins without any goals being conceded and some very comprehensive victories, the biggest coming at White Hart Lane with Spurs putting six past a hapless Bolton Wanderers. Les Ferdinand bagged a hat-trick in just nine first-half minutes. Blackburn Rovers beat Arsenal 4-0 with another quarter-final hat-trick courtesy of Matt Jansen. Sheffield Wednesday progressed by the same score but there was to be no three-goal hero in this match with four different scorers, with Gerald Sibdon, Matt Hamshaw, Phil O'Donnell and Trond Egil Soltvedt on the score sheet. Chelsea were the final team to qualify and it took a last-minute goal from Jimmy Floyd Hasselbaink to see off Newcastle.

The semi-final saw Sheffield Wednesday take on Blackburn and Chelsea face Spurs, which guaranteed a north v south final. Blackburn drew first blood with a 2-1 victory at Hillsborough on 8 January 2002 and the night after, Chelsea beat Spurs by the same margin at Stamford Bridge.

Blackburn and Spurs took to home advantage in the second legs to record comprehensive wins to take them through to Cardiff. Blackburn were 4-2 victors and sealed a 6-3 aggregate victory over Sheffield Wednesday with goals from Jansen, Damien Duff, Andy Cole and Craig Hignett, while Efan Ekoku and Soltvedt scored for Wednesday. Glenn Hoddle's Spurs made up for the first-leg defeat by putting five past Claudio Ranieri's Chelsea. Steffen Iversen opened the scoring as early as the second minute to level the tie before Tim Sherwood put the home team in front just after the half-hour mark. Further second-half goals from Teddy Sheringham, Simon Davies and Serhiy Rebrov completed the rout. Mikael Forssell pulled one back for the shell-shocked visitors but it was far too late, Spurs going through 6-3 on aggregate.

The final was played at the Millennium Stadium in Cardiff on Sunday, 24 February 2002. Perhaps the omens were not in favour of Spurs before the kick-off. The Football League had decided that both Tottenham's home and away shirts clashed with Blackburn's, who were deemed as the home team for the final. Therefore, a special one-off yellow kit was designed just for the occasion.

It wasn't all Blackburn's way for the final, though. Rovers were without Craig Short, Garry Flitcroft and Tugay Kerimoğlu due to suspension. Graeme Souness therefore decided that his veteran striker, Mark Hughes, would take one of the midfield places as a result.

Blackburn opened the scoring with a goal from Jansen in the 25th minute, but they were not able to hold the lead for too long as just eight minutes later, Christian Ziege equalised. Both teams went into the break in a propitious situation. It was the team from the north, though, who saw this through when in the 68th minute, Andy Cole scored the winner after mistakes in the Spurs defence. This was the signal for the team in yellow to play a higher line and press Blackburn with Les Ferdinand coming close while he was one-on-one with Brad Friedel in the Rovers goal. And in the final minute, Spurs had claims of a penalty turned down by Graham Poll.

Season 2002/03

The Final

2 March 2003
Manchester United 0 Liverpool 2 (Gerrard, Owen)
Millennium Stadium, Cardiff
Attendance: 74,500
Referee: P.A. Durkin

For the first time in the competition, there was a preliminary round played. This happened because Ipswich Town, newly relegated from the Premier

League, had taken a European place due to winning the UEFA Fair Play League and therefore it was necessary to reduce the number of teams in the League Cup by one. The match was played on 20 August 2002 when Bristol Rovers faced Boston United. Two second-half goals scored by Steve Burton and Simon Weatherstone ensured a safe passage through to the first round for the away side.

United's reward was a home tie against Cardiff City, and it was the Bluebirds singing all the way back home with a comfortable 5-1 away victory helped by Rob Earnshaw's first-half treble. Nottingham Forest were also winners by a four-goal margin as they thrashed Kidderminster Harriers 4-0 at the City Ground in front of a crowd of less than 5,000.

The second round was notable for some severe beatings dished out by Crystal Palace, Coventry City and Sunderland. The largest margin came at Highfield Road when Coventry entertained Rushden & Diamonds on 2 October 2002. The Sky Blues were a force of nature as they won 8-0 with a treble from Gary McSheffrey and braces from Lee Mills and Jay Bothroyd doing the damage alongside a solitary goal from Robert Betts. Palace and Sunderland ran out 7-0 winners in their matches.

Palace hosted Cheltenham Town and led 1-0 going into the half-time break after Dele Adebola's goal on 21 minutes. However, a six-goal blitz in the second period put paid to any hopes of a famous away win for Town. Adebola added his second with Dougie Freedman also bagging two himself. Hayden Mullins and Tony Popovic and an own goal scored by Richard Walker completed the rout.

Sunderland's win was more impressive as they were away at Cambridge United. Marcus Stewart and Tore André Flo shared four goals with the others scored by Claudio Reyna, Gavin McCann and Julio Arca.

There were third-round exits for both north London clubs – Arsenal losing 3-2 at home to free-scoring Sunderland and Spurs losing 2-1 at Burnley. Liverpool and Manchester United both got off to winning starts in home matches, with the Reds of Merseyside beating Southampton 3-1 with goals scored by Patrick Berger, El Hadji Diouf and Milan Baroš and the Red Devils of Manchester winning 2-0 with two late goals scored by David Beckham and Kieran Richardson.

United's 2-0 winning margin was also a feature of the fourth round as they defeated Burnley at Turf Moor, Diego Forlán and Ole Gunnar Solskjær making the difference. It was a harder route for Liverpool as they progressed on penalties against Ipswich Town at Anfield, winning the shoot-out 5-4. The match finished all square at 1-1. Tommy Miller had given the Tractor Boys the lead on 14 minutes before Diouf equalised from the penalty spot on 54 minutes.

The tie of the quarter-finals came at Villa Park on 18 December 2002 with the 38,530 in attendance treated to a classic as Aston Villa hosted Liverpool in a televised match. Villa started the brighter of the teams and took the lead on 23 minutes through striker Darius Vassell, but the advantage only lasted for four minutes as Danny

Murphy restored parity. There were no more goals in the first half, but it was the away team who came out the blocks looking stronger in the second period and found themselves 3-1 up with just 23 minutes remaining, Milan Baroš and Steven Gerrard scoring the goals. There was hope for Villa on 72 minutes when German playmaker Thomas Hitzlsperger scored, and the comeback was completed with just two minutes to go when an own goal by Stéphane Henchoz made it 3-3. The thrilling match looked like it was going to go into extra time until Murphy scored his second with just seconds to spare to break Villa hearts. Manchester United's passage into the last four was less dramatic but equally as important when a goal from Diego Forlán settled matters against Chelsea. Joining them in the semi-finals were Sheffield United, who dispatched Crystal Palace 3-1 at home, and Blackburn Rovers who beat Wigan Athletic 2-0 on their travels.

The giants of the English game were kept apart in the semi-final draw, making them clear favourites to progress to Cardiff. However, in typical football fashion, both teams struggled in their first legs.

Firstly, Liverpool lost 2-1 at Sheffield United in front of nearly 31,000 fans. The Reds took a one-goal lead into the break after Neil Mellor had opened the scoring with ten minutes left of the first half. However, it was the Blades who won thanks to a brace from Michael Tonge. The other semi-final saw Manchester United host Blackburn with the match finishing all square at 1-1. Paul Scholes gave the home team the lead on 58 minutes before Rovers equalised just three minutes later when David Thompson scored.

Parity was restored in the second legs much to the relief of the bookies when Liverpool won 2-0 at Anfield to go through 3-2 on aggregate – although the match went to extra time, with El Hadji Diouf scoring the only goal in regular play before Michael Owen bagged the decisive goal on 107 minutes. Meanwhile, a 3-1 victory at Blackburn was enough for the Red Devils to progress 4-2 over their two games. Andy Cole had given his former team-mates a scare when he put Rovers 1-0 up after 12 minutes, only to see Paul Scholes score a further two goals to add to his one in the first leg before half-time, and Ruud van Nistelrooy settled matters with just 13 minutes remaining, from the penalty spot.

The final was played on 2 March 2003, and the opening exchanges in the first 20 minutes were most sterile and turgid. It was United who nearly made the breakthrough on 21 minutes when Scholes found Ryan Giggs, and his cross to the far post was just missed by Van Nistelrooy.

Liverpool came out of their defensive shells as the half progressed and took the lead with just six minutes left when a shot from Steven Gerrard from 25 yards took a crucial deflection off David Beckham and looped over Fabien Barthez.

It should have been 1-1 on the stroke of half-time when a goalbound shot from Scholes was miraculously cleared off the line by Stéphane Henchoz from under the crossbar.

The hero of the second half was Liverpool's shot-stopper, Jerzy Dudek, who made some crucial saves to keep United at bay, and his reward was confirmed with just four minutes from time when the Reds broke to allow Michael Owen to score and put the game out of reach. There were no further goals as Liverpool won the competition for a record seventh time, and their second in three seasons.

Season 2003/04

The Final
29 February 2004
Bolton Wanderers 1 (Davies) Middlesbrough 2
(Job, Zenden)
Millennium Stadium, Cardiff
Attendance: 72,634
Referee: M.A. Riley

Another change of sponsorship saw the competition now known as the Carling Cup.

There is a saying in politics that informs us that a week is a long time in it. For Sheffield Wednesday then, two seasons previous must have felt like something from the Ice Ages. In the 2001/02 season they had reached the semi-final only to be beaten by the eventual winners. On 13 August 2003, the Owls were dumped out of the first round on penalties in front of their home supporters against a very dogged Hartlepool United. Graeme Lee had given the home side the lead in the 50th minute before United came back to level from the spot just six minutes later via Paul Robinson. The match went into extra time and this time it was the visitors who took the lead, in the 104th minute, before Richard Wood restored parity just before the end of the first period. The tie went to penalties, and it was Hartlepool who entered the second round with a 5-4 victory.

Arguably the tie of the second round took place at The Valley on Tuesday, 23 September 2003, when Charlton Athletic hosted Luton Town. The 10,905 in the ground that evening were treated to a goal-fest in 120 minutes of exhilarating cup football and penalties. Kevin Foley gave the Hatters the lead on the half-hour mark before Dave Bayliss extended it just two minutes later. Charlton pulled a goal back on 41 minutes and then Kevin Lisbie secured parity just before the hour. Luton restored their lead with just 12 minutes to go when Gary McSheffrey converted and this time it looked very much like they had done enough with the score 3-2 in their favour and just seconds remaining of injury time. However, the veteran striker Paolo Di Canio had other ideas as he scored to take the game into extra time. Charlton then took the lead for the first time when Claus Jensen scored in the 95th minute. It was now the turn of Luton to make the comeback and they did so just five minutes later. The game was finally decided by penalties, and it was the Addicks who came out victorious by 8-7, in a game that no team really deserved to lose.

The day after saw Middlesbrough take on Brighton at home. Like events at The Valley, this too went to extra time, but this is where the similarities end as it was a torrid game that Brighton were unlucky not to have taken the lead in as they outplayed their hosts. One goal settled this one, and it was scored by Malcolm Christie. The Premier League club, under the guidance of Steve McClaren, simply did not deserve it on the night, but it was a significant win for the team who had not won a major trophy in their history.

Arsenal were flying in the Premier League when they faced Rotherham United at home in the third round on 28 October 2003. They had not lost a domestic game so far in the season and sat top of the Premier League. Rotherham were experiencing contrasting fortunes as they sat 22nd in the First Division. There was only going to be one winner and it appeared to be going to plan as Arsenal had led since the 11th minute with a goal scored by Jérémie Aliadière. The game was entering its final seconds as Darren Byfield scored the equaliser for the visitors to send the away fans into rapture. There were no further goals in extra time as Rotherham stood firm in the face of the Arsenal offensive, but the Gunners won the shoot-out 9-8 to finally claim a spot in the fourth round. The match of the round took place at Ewood Park where Blackburn took on the holders, Liverpool. Just shy of 17,000 fans were treated to a seven-goal bonanza and it was the visitors who progressed 4-3. Dwight Yorke had given the home team the lead on 35 minutes before Danny Murphy equalised from the spot just six minutes later. Liverpool took the game by the scruff of the neck and with just ten minutes to play they found themselves 4-1 up thanks to Emile Heskey's brace and one from

Harry Kewell. Blackburn did reduce the deficit to just one goal in the final ten minutes through Barry Ferguson and another from Yorke, but it was too little, too late as the Reds progressed.

There were no such late dramas and scares for table-topping Arsenal in the fourth round as they romped to a 5-1 home victory against Wolverhampton Wanderers. Middlesbrough progressed 5-4 on penalties after 120 minutes where no goals were scored in their home tie against Everton.

It took another penalty shoot-out for Middlesbrough to reach the semi-finals as they knocked out Spurs at White Hart Lane, 5-4. The game had finished 1-1 after 120 minutes with Spurs taking the lead as early as the second minute and Boro equalising as late as the 86th minute. Darren Anderton put the home team in front with Michael Ricketts making the game all square. The Teessiders were joined in the semi-final by Bolton Wanderers, Aston Villa and Arsenal.

The first semi-final game took place at Highbury on 20 January 2004, and it was the first defeat for Arsenal domestically, as Middlesbrough won 1-0 with Juninho the match-winner in the 53rd minute. It was all to play for still in the second leg, but in the other tie Bolton practically made sure that they were going to Cardiff for the final the night after the game at Highbury, running out 5-2 winners at home to Aston Villa. It was basically the Jay-Jay Okocha show as the Nigerian ran the game for the Trotters from the outset, opening the scoring after just two minutes. After just 17 minutes, the home side had added a further two goals via Kevin Nolan and Stelios Giannakopoulos. Villa managed to pull a goal back just a few minutes later via their striker, Juan Pablo Ángel. The Colombian reduced the deficit to only one goal in the 56th minute to bring nerves to the Bolton party and Sam Allardyce in the dugout. However, a further two goals scored by Bruno N'Gotty in the 74th minute and the mercurial Okocha just six minutes later restored Bolton's three-goal lead once more. The return leg took place at Villa Park on Tuesday, 27 January 2004 in front of 36,883 fans, Villa winning 2-0, but it wasn't enough for them to overthrow Bolton who found themselves in the final for the second time in nine years. Joining them were Middlesbrough who inflicted the second domestic defeat on Arsenal and won 3-1 overall. Boudewijn Zenden extended Boro's lead on 69 minutes before Edu pulled a goal back in the 77th minute. Any hopes of the league leaders winning were dashed with just five minutes to go, and to make matters worse for Gunners boss Arsène Wenger it was an own goal scored by José Antonio Reyes.

The final was played in Cardiff on Sunday, 29 February 2004, and it meant that regardless who was victorious, there was a new winning team to be engraved on to the trophy and into the history books.

The game started in spectacular fashion for Middlesbrough who found themselves two goals up before the tenth minute, from Joseph-Désiré Job and a Boudewijn Zenden penalty. Incredibly, there was a third goal scored in the 21st minute when Kevin Davies got one back after a mistake made by Boro goalkeeper Mark Schwarzer. Disappointingly for the Bolton fans and the neutrals watching on the TV screens, there were no further goals in the match. The team from Teesside laid the ghost of the 1998 League Cup Final and in doing so had qualified for the 2004/05 UEFA Cup, their first entry into European competition.

Season 2004/05
The Final
27 February 2005
Liverpool 2 (Riise, Núñez) Chelsea 3 (Gerrard own goal,
Drogba, Kežman (after extra time))
Millennium Stadium, Cardiff
Attendance: 71,622
Referee: S.G. Bennett

José Mourinho had announced himself to the British public when his Porto team knocked out Manchester United in the 2003/04 Champions League. His sprint down the Old Trafford track upon celebrating the decisive goal immediately entered into football folklore. Porto went on to win the Champions League that season, to add to the UEFA Cup they had won the previous year. Therefore, his stock was as high as it could be when he took over at Chelsea in 2005. The London club had been purchased in 2003 when the Russian billionaire Roman Abramovich bought out Ken Bates, who later would own Leeds United. It quickly became very apparent that the companies that Abramovich owned were serious players with substantial financial clout that would soon see Chelsea challenge the likes of Manchester United and Real Madrid in terms of football success and a brand known all over the world.

Mourinho had cut his teeth working with some of the finest coaches in the game. Initially he was Bobby Robson's interpreter in Portugal when the ex-England manager was at the helm at Sporting CP, and then at Porto, before becoming his assistant at Barcelona. The Portuguese also worked under Louis van Gaal at the Spanish giants.

Mourinho's move to England was news all over the world and he immediately made himself the hottest ticket in town by self-proclaiming as 'the Special One'.

Middlesbrough's defence of the cup started in fine fashion in the third round with a 3-0 home win versus Coventry City, and Tottenham continued to fire in the goals with a 4-3 away win after extra time against runners-up Bolton. Chelsea and Liverpool went through without conceding goals – Chelsea winning 1-0 at home against West Ham United with Mateja Kežman scoring in the 57th minute. Liverpool cruised to a 3-0 away win at Millwall, with Salif Diao giving the Reds a half-time lead before a brace in the second half from Milan Baroš.

It was the turn of Neil Mellor to bag a couple of goals in the 83rd and 89th minutes for Liverpool in the fourth round, and as a result Middlesbrough's bid to retain the cup came to an end at Anfield. Chelsea and Manchester United were also 2-0 winners in their games,

Newcastle and Crystal Palace the teams on the receiving end respectively.

There was a south-west London derby in the quarter-finals as Fulham took on Chelsea, the Blues ensuring local bragging rights with a 2-1 victory with goals from Damien Duff and Frank Lampard, Brian McBride replying for Fulham. Liverpool joined Chelsea in the semi-finals by winning a penalty shoot-out at Tottenham after a 1-1 draw. Also through were Watford, who cruised past Portsmouth at Vicarage Road, two goals for Heiðar Helguson and one for Bruce Dyer making the difference. Manchester United made up the four semi-finalists with a 1-0 victory at Old Trafford against Arsenal in the tie of the round, David Bellion scoring the only goal in the very first minute.

The semi-final first legs saw Liverpool at home to Watford and Chelsea entertaining Manchester United. There was only one goal scored in the two matches with Steven Gerrard on target to make it advantage Liverpool. Gerrard then scored the only goal at Vicarage Road to send his team to yet another Cardiff final, their third since the turn of the century, with the aggregate score being 2-0.

Around 67,000 attended the second leg at Old Trafford and were treated to a very close, end-to-end game. Chelsea took the lead after 29 minutes and held this until the 67th minute, when Ryan Giggs equalised. United's joy was cut short in the 85th minute when Damien Duff produced the winning goal to send Mourinho and his team through to their first League Cup Final since 1998.

The showpiece in Cardiff was played on Sunday, 27 February 2005 in front of just under 72,000 fans, divided equally in blue and red – and it certainly lived up to its expectations.

It was a pulsating affair that took shape almost straight after the kick-off when Liverpool scored the quickest goal in the final to date, as Fernando Morientes crossed the ball from the right where it was met on the volley by John Arne Riise and went straight into the Chelsea goal. First blood to the Reds, but both teams came out of the blocks fighting, Riise having another chance just a couple of minutes later. Chelsea continued to attack to get back into the game with attempts by Duff and Joe Cole but to no avail. As well as being an open, attacking final, it also saw several bookings with Sami Hyypiä, Djimi Traoré shown yellow for Liverpool and Frank Lampard receiving similar treatment for Chelsea.

There were no further goals in the first half, but the match maintained its high intensity in the second period with Chelsea doing most of the pressing, and they were unlucky not to be back on level terms in the 54th minute when Liverpool goalkeeper Jerzy Dudek produced a double save, firstly, from a header from Eiður Guðjohnsen and then the rebound from William Gallas. Liverpool had chances on the break, although Gallas was close again to levelling and Gerrard and Milan Baroš came close to extending the lead. Gerrard did get on the score sheet in the 79th minute, but alas it was in his own net to give Chelsea a lifeline. Chelsea were awarded a free kick which was taken by their Portuguese right-back, Paulo Ferreira. It found the head of Gerrard, whose intentions were to clear the ball; however, it skimmed off his head and into the net. The number of first-half yellow cards indicated that there could be a second one at some point for a player. The indications were not that it was a manager though, but that was exactly what happened straight after the goal. It was Mourinho who got his marching orders from referee Steve Bennett for pressing his fingers to his lips in a gesture deemed to be aimed at the Liverpool fans.

Duff and Baroš both had chances to win it in 90 minutes, but this was a match that was destined to go into extra time. Chelsea had the first chance of the extra period when Duff's cross was met by Didier Drogba, but his header hit the post. The players were finding it hard to match the pace as the first half of extra time progressed, although both teams had chances towards the end of the half. Liverpool's Igor Bišćan put his header over the bar and Chelsea's Mateja Kežman saw his shot saved by Dudek. However, Chelsea took the lead in the first minute of the second period when a long throw-in to the near post of the Liverpool goal was missed by John Terry and Sami Hyypiä. It wasn't missed by Drogba, though, as he beat Jamie Carragher to the ball and found the back of the net, then just a few minutes later they extended their advantage. Chelsea were awarded a free kick which was taken by Lampard. The kick was punched clear by Dudek but the ball fell to Guðjohnsen who played it across the Liverpool goal for Kežman to score and make it 3-1. The drama did not stop there, and Chelsea could ill afford to rest on any laurels when Liverpool pulled a goal back. This time they were awarded a free kick which was taken by Steven Gerrard, whose pinpoint cross was met by the head of Antonio Núñez. This set up a frantic finish but Liverpool were unable to find the goal to take the game to at least a penalty shoot-out. Steve Bennett blew the final whistle and Mourinho was able to celebrate his first trophy with Chelsea. Soon he would follow this up with the Premier League championship.

The self-proclaimed 'Special One' had made it a special season for Chelsea.

Season 2005/06

The Final
26 February 2006
Manchester United 4 (Rooney 2, Saha, Ronaldo)
Wigan Athletic 0
Millennium Stadium, Cardiff
Attendance: 66,866
Referee: A.G. Wiley

The first decade of the 21st century had seen a significant amount of foreign investment with club owners now coming from the USA, Russia and China, among others. One club that bucked this new trend was Wigan Athletic. Dave Whelan had been a footballer who had played most noticeably for Blackburn Rovers in the 1950s, and was in the team that played in the 1960 FA Cup Final which was won by Wolverhampton Wanderers. During the match, Whelan suffered a broken leg after a tackle by the Wolves player Norman Deeley in the first half. Upon recovery, the left-back was sold to Crewe Alexandra. Whelan retired from the game in 1966 and set his sights on going into business. His first foray was in the grocery trade, initially setting up a stall in Wigan. Whelan then went into the retail sector by purchasing a fishing and sports shop in Wigan called JJ Bradburns. He was savvy enough to retain the name in some capacity and it was renamed JJB Sports. This was a very successful venture as stores were opened all over the UK under this new brand, as was Whelan Discount Stores which was sold to the supermarket chain Morrisons in 1978. That same year, Wigan Athletic made their bow in professional football and Whelan acquired the club in 1995. The town of Wigan was more famous for its rugby, pies and Northern Soul rather than football, but the purchase by Whelan certainly helped put it on the map. In a ten-year period, his club gained promotions that eventually led to them becoming a Premier League team for the 2005/06 season under the guidance of Paul Jewell.

Wycombe Wanderers were handed a plum second-round tie at home against Aston Villa, and a crowd of 5,365 witnessed a goal-crazy 90 minutes where the phrase 'a game of two halves' really came into play.

The home team celebrated after just six minutes when Nathan Tyson put them in front. The lead lasted just eight minutes before Villa's midfielder Steven Davis equalised. Two further goals in the first half gave the underdogs a commanding 3-1 lead with Roger Johnson and Tommy Mooney scoring. The Premier League team were still expected to turn it around, but how they did it, no one could have foreseen. Just three minutes after the break, Milan Baroš made it 3-2 and this spurred Villa into life, and it was no surprise when they made it 3-3 just after the hour when James Milner restored parity. Villa then went on to score a further five goals in 26 minutes, Davis and Milner adding to their tallies with a further brace from Gareth Barry and an own goal from Clint Easton completing an 8-3 win.

Goals were also frequent at Craven Cottage as Fulham entertained Lincoln City, and it was the home team who came out of the blocks quicker as they secured a two-goal lead going into the break – Zesh Rehman and Heiðar Helguson inflicting the damage. Lincoln took the impetus after the break and clawed two goals back in the 70th and 82nd minutes through Francis Green and an own goal by Moritz Volz, sending the match into extra time. Once again, Fulham started the first period brighter with two quick-fire goals from Liam Rosenior and Tomasz Radzinski putting their team back in control. The script had not been read by the Imps as they once again came back to make it 4-4 with the goals scored by Scott Kerr and Marvin Robinson. But their hearts were broken in the dying seconds as the game looked like it was heading towards a penalty shoot-out when Fulham's American striker, Brian McBride, netted the winning goal.

There was only one goal scored at Blundell Park, home of Grimsby Town, but it caused a bigger headline as Jean-Paul Kalala's effort in the 89th minute knocked out

Tottenham Hotspur to provide the biggest cup shock of the round, closely followed by Doncaster Rovers' penalty shoot-out win at home to Manchester City following a 1-1 draw after extra time. Wigan also went through by the same score when the only goal scored by Jason Roberts put them into the third round at the expense of Bournemouth.

Grimsby's reward for disposing of Tottenham was another potential giant-killing in front of their home fans as they entertained Newcastle United in the third round. It was to be another 1-0 scoreline, but this time in the favour of the Premier League side with the only goal scored by Alan Shearer with just ten minutes remaining. Doncaster were also at home and they progressed with a 2-0 home victory against Gillingham. There were significant wins for both Wigan and Manchester United by three-goal winning margins, Wigan winning 3-0 after extra time against Watford. Ryan Taylor had given the hosts the lead on 98 minutes before two late goals for Andreas Johansson wrapped up the win. United beat Barnet 4-1 at Old Trafford with Liam Miller, Kieran Richardson, Giuseppe Rossi and Sylvan Ebanks-Blake sharing the load and Dean Sinclair scoring the solitary goal for the London club.

The biggest shock of the round took place at Stamford Bridge where holders Chelsea took on Charlton Athletic and went out on penalties after a 1-1 draw after extra time.

Doncaster's reward for getting to the fourth round was another plum home tie against Aston Villa; however, they did not progress on penalties as they had done in the second round against much-fancied Manchester City. Rovers turned on the style to bamboozle Villa, winning 3-0 in front of a crowd just shy of 11,000, with Michael McIndoe opening the scoring with a 20th-minute penalty. Any hopes of a comeback for David O'Leary's Villa time were dashed with a further two goals in the second half in front of the TV cameras with Paul Heffernan and Sean Thornton scoring as Doncaster fully deserved the win.

Wigan deservedly beat Newcastle 1-0 with David Connolly's penalty with just minutes remaining, while Manchester United beat West Bromwich Albion 3-1 at Old Trafford, with Cristiano Ronaldo, Louis Saha and John O'Shea putting the hosts into cruise control before Nathan Ellington pulled a goal back on 77 minutes. There was only one tie that was decided by penalties, after a 2-2 draw between Millwall and Birmingham City. Julian Gray had given Birmingham the lead after just ten minutes but an equaliser by Alan Dunne just before the hour meant that the game went into extra time. Once more it was the visitors who seized the lead, through Emile Heskey, but Millwall equalised with just four minutes remaining of extra time through Marvin Elliott to send the match to a penalty shoot-out which Birmingham won 4-3.

Doncaster were drawn at home to Arsenal in the quarter-finals and it was very nearly a third Premier League scalp for them as well four days before Christmas Day, with Michael McIndoe once more on the score sheet for Rovers after just two minutes. A pulsating match went into extra time after Arsenal equalised on 63 minutes when Quincy Owusu-Abeyie levelled the tie. Once again, Rovers took the lead when Paul Green scored in the last minute of the first period, and they remained in front until the final seconds of the 120 minutes when Gilberto Silva sent the away fans into rapture and spared the blushes of Arsenal's team, and manager Arsène Wenger. This may have taken the stuffing out of Rovers as they only converted just one of their penalties while the Gunners scored their first three to win 3-1. Doncaster's road may have come to an end, but Dave Penney's team had won many admirers along the way.

There was no extra time and indeed no penalties in the other ties with Wigan beating Bolton 2-0 at home, Jason Roberts scoring a brace. Blackburn Rovers went through to the semi-finals with a 1-0 victory at Middlesbrough, Paul Dickov scoring the winner with just seconds remaining, and Manchester United were triumphant at Birmingham, winning 3-1, a Louis Saha double and a goal from Park Ji-Sung putting the match beyond the hosts, although they did pull one back in the 77th minute through Jiří Jarošík. All four goals were scored in the second half.

Wigan had not conceded a goal in the competition and this continued in their semi-final first leg at home to Arsenal, played on 10 January 2006. Most of their matches leading up to the last four had finished 1-0 and this was the case once more with Paul Scharner scoring the decisive goal with just 12 minutes remaining. It took a further 65 minutes in the second leg at Highbury for the Wigan defence to finally be breached when Thierry Henry levelled proceedings. There were no further goals in regulation play before Robin van Persie gave the home team an overall lead in the 108th minute. It looked to be the goal that took Arsenal through until Jason Roberts made it 2-1 on the night with just a minute remaining. This proved to be the crucial away goal to put Wigan into the final after the tie had finished 2-2. It was also to be the last League Cup match played at Highbury as Arsenal fans looked forward to a move to the Emirates Stadium for the 2006/07 season.

Manchester United's path to the final was also a close affair but they went through at the expense of Blackburn Rovers, 3-2 on aggregate after the first leg at Ewood Park had finished 1-1. Louis Saha had given the Red Devils the lead on the half-hour mark before Blackburn equalised five minutes later through Morten Gamst Pedersen. Ruud van Nistelrooy opened the scoring in the eighth minute of the second leg before Rovers once again hit back after 32 minutes through their Republic of Ireland midfielder, Steven Reid. However, a second-half goal by Louis Saha was a bridge too far for Rovers as United held on to their 2-1 lead on the night.

The final was played at Cardiff's Millennium Stadium on 26 February 2006. Wigan's mantra under the guidance of Paul Jewell was to play it tight in the rounds leading up to the final and as the half-time whistle blew, it had once more gone to plan, although after just three minutes their goalkeeper Mike Pollitt clutched his hamstring after innocuously fielding a ball and was clearly in trouble and he was soon to be replaced by John Filan. It was a close encounter with both teams having chances before the first goal was scored on 33 minutes, and it was very much a 'route one' goal that was aided by a mix-up in the Wigan defence. Edwin van der Sar's long kick downfield was headed on by Saha. Unfortunately for Wigan, Arjan de Zeeuw and Pascal Chimbonda collided to leave Wayne Rooney with the chance to shoot and he put the ball wide of Filan. The game remained tight and working to the plan of the underdogs until United scored three times in six minutes to effectively end the tie just after the hour with goals from Saha, Cristiano Ronaldo and a second from Rooney ending the game as a contest, United winning 4-0 and in turn claiming the biggest win in the final since the competition began. Wigan had reached their first ever final and finished tenth in their first season in top-flight football, making a mockery of those that swore their stay was a curt one.

Season 2006/07
The Final
25 February 2007
Arsenal 1 (Walcott) Chelsea 2 (Drogba 2)
Millennium Stadium, Cardiff
Attendance: 70,073
Referee: H.M. Webb

This was the last year that the final was held in Cardiff as Wembley had been rebuilt and the following season it returned to its spiritual home.

Due to European commitments, both Arsenal and Chelsea entered in the third round and recorded identical away wins as well. The Gunners won 2-0 at West Bromwich Albion with Jérémie Aliadière scoring both, while Chelsea took care of Blackburn Rovers with the goals shared between Joe Cole and Salomon Kalou. Holders Manchester United survived a scare at Crewe Alexandra. Ole Gunnar Solskjær had given them a first-half lead which was wiped out by Luke Varney in the 73rd minute. The match went into extra time and looked set to be settled by spot kicks until United grabbed the winner with just a minute to spare through Kieran Lee.

Chesterfield's fine run in the competition (they had knocked out Wolves, Manchester City and West Ham) came to an end in the fourth round as they went out in penalties to Charlton Athletic after a 3-3 draw at Saltergate on 7 November 2006. Colin Larkin, Caleb Folan and Wayne Allison all scored for the home team, but a brace from Jimmy Floyd Hasselbaink and one from Darren Bent meant that a shoot-out was required, the Addicks winning 4-3.

Chelsea progressed with a 4-0 home victory against Aston Villa with Frank Lampard, Andriy Shevchenko, Michael Essien and Didier Drogba all on the score sheet. Arsenal progressed with a slender 1-0 win at Everton, Emmanuel Adebayor settling matters with just five minutes remaining.

Three of the quarter-finals finished 1-0 with Chelsea beating Newcastle United away, Drogba scoring.

The other winners were Wycombe Wanderers against Charlton Athletic and Spurs beating a plucky Southend United in extra time.

Undoubtedly the match of the round came at Anfield as Liverpool hosted Arsenal – in fact, it turned out to be one of the greatest games in the competition's history. This is how *The Guardian* reported on the substantial amount of goals scored: 'The rout began in the 27th minute when Jérémie Aliadière, outstanding all night, capitalised on some rank defending to defy a malfunctioning offside trap and poke the ball beneath Dudek. The home side stirred. Manuel Almunia, the Arsenal goalkeeper, palmed away Fábio Aurélio's free kick and Luis García turned the ball across the six-yard area for Fowler to score. But Baptista made it 2-1 with an exquisite free kick that left Dudek rooted to the spot. Then, in first-half stoppage time, Dudek et al went awol again as Cesc Fábregas swung in a corner and Song bundled the ball in. The rumblings of dissent from the Kop grew louder a minute later when Baptista played a one-two with Aliadière and stroked in his second.

'Four-one down, the best Liverpool could hope for in the second half was to restore some dignity and at least Dudek could cite the moment, on 56 minutes, when he saved Baptista's penalty after a Sami Hyypiä foul on Aliadière. Baptista made amends, however, completing his hat-trick from 25 yards four minutes later.

'Briefly, Liverpool surged back. Gerrard volleyed a splendid goal and saw Almunia tip his free kick on to the bar. Then, after García too had been carried off, Hyypiä headed in Gabriel Paletta's cross to make it 5-3 but not even Liverpool, with their history of comebacks, could recover this time and soon afterwards Baptista scored another brilliant breakaway goal – becoming the first visiting player to score four times at Anfield since Dennis Westcott in a 5-1 win for Wolves 61 years ago. A busy night for the statisticians and an even busier one for Liverpool's defenders.'

The semi-finals had a 'southern' feel as Wycombe were drawn against the might of Chelsea with the north London derby taking place in the other as Spurs took on Arsenal. Both first legs were entertaining as Wycombe held Chelsea 1-1 and Spurs and Arsenal drew 2-2.

It was all to play for in the return legs, but it was the home teams going through to the final in Cardiff. Firstly, Chelsea made light work as they romped home 4-0 with two goals from Andriy Shevchenko in the first half and Frank Lampard doing the same in the second period to make it 5-1 over the two legs. This was no disgrace for Wycombe as they had enjoyed a great run in the competition under the guidance of Paul Lambert. Arsenal needed extra time to beat Spurs 3-1 and 5-3 on aggregate.

The game had been nip and tuck and it took until the 77th minute with the breakthrough as Emmanuel Adebayor put the home team in front on the night and 2-1 overall. However, with five minutes to play, the lead was wiped out when Mido scored for Spurs, but in extra time Aliadière and a Pascal Chimbonda own goal put paid to any hopes of Tottenham of reaching the final.

The final was played on 25 February 2007; the build-up centred around the average age of the Arsenal players being less than 21. However, by the end the match had become known for the ugly scenes on the pitch.

Theo Walcott gave Arsenal the lead after just 12 minutes after the young Englishman went past Ricardo Carvalho. Chelsea equalised when Drogba was given the benefit of the linesman's flag to slot home just six minutes later, and then with just six minutes to go he headed in a powerful winning goal to provide Chelsea with their fourth victory in the competition and the last final in Cardiff.

However, it was what happened in the 90th minute that became the main topic of conversation with the pundits in the studio and the fans when three players were sent off after Mikel John Obi clashed with Kolo Touré. This resulted in a mass brawl that involved players and managers on the bench. Referee Howard Webb dished out red cards to Obi, Touré and Adebayor, and gave yellow cards to Cesc Fàbregas and Frank Lampard.

Over 11 minutes of added-on time was played before the final whistle was blown to signal an ugly end to the first cup final meeting between these London giants. José Mourinho had now won the League Cup with Chelsea for the second time in just three seasons.

Season 2007/08

The Final

24 February 2008
Chelsea 1 (Drogba) Tottenham Hotspur 2 (Berbatov,
Woodgate) (after extra time)
Wembley Stadium, London
Attendance: 87,660
Referee: M.R. Halsey

The first League Cup tie that could lay claim to being back 'on the road to Wembley' occurred on 13 August 2007 when Peterborough United hosted Southampton in the first round. It finished in favour of the hosts as the Posh went through 2-1, with all three goals coming in the first half. Southampton striker Grzegorz Rasiak played villain and then hero, firstly putting the ball into his own net in the 21st minute before scoring at the right end on 37, after George Boyd had extended Peterborough's lead on 26 minutes. It was truly another 'game of two halves' between Milton Keynes Dons and Ipswich Town. The Dons came out of the blocks so much faster than the Tractor Boys and were three goals up in the first 22 minutes, with Leon Knight, a penalty converted by Kevin Gallen and an own goal by Alex Bruce making the difference. Ipswich were shell-shocked but managed to pull a goal back on the stroke of half-time when Alan Lee scored from the spot. This prompted them to take the game to their hosts, especially when Kieran Murphy put the ball into his own net to make it 3-2. Ipswich levelled with practically the last kick of the game when Owen Garvey scored deep into stoppage time. There were no further goals as the tie went into extra time, with the Dons going through 5-3 on penalties.

Aston Villa recorded the biggest win of the second round when they travelled to Wrexham, where Martin O'Neill's team won 5-0 with Shaun Maloney bagging two of them and Luke Moore, Nigel Reo-Coker and Marlon Harewood completing the rout.

There was an intriguing East Midlands derby when the draw pitted Nottingham Forest at home to Leicester City. Forest had been leading 1-0 at half-time when Leicester defender Clive Clarke collapsed with a cardiac arrest in the dressing room. The match was abandoned, and when it was replayed nearly a month later, Leicester allowed Forest to have that advantage, Reds goalkeeper Paul Smith dribbling straight up the field from the kick-off to score. Alan Sheehan levelled just after the half-hour mark but Forest were back in the lead after 64 minutes with what looked very much like the winner.

However, two goals in the final few minutes from Richard Stearman and Stephen Clemence meant the Foxes went through 3-2.

Leicester's reward was another away tie at Aston Villa in the third round, and once again they were victorious, with Matty Fryatt scoring the only goal, in the 76th minute. Sheffield United equalled Villa's winning margin from the previous round with a 5-0 home victory against Morecambe, with Billy Sharp and Luton Shelton both scoring twice and ex-Villa player Lee Hendrie also on the scoring sheet.

Chelsea's defence of the cup started almost as emphatically as it had done for the Blades, with a 4-0 away win at Hull City – Scott Sinclair and Steve Sidwell scoring alongside Salomon Kalou who scored the other goals for the Blues. Tottenham Hotspur eased past Middlesbrough 2-0 at White Hart Lane, with goals from Gareth Bale and Tom Huddlestone, both coming in the final 20 minutes.

It was a similar experience for Spurs in the fourth round with another home match that finished 2-0. Blackpool were the team on the losing side with Robbie Keane and Pascal Chimbonda on goalscoring duties this time around. There was a fourth consecutive away match for Leicester in the competition as they were paired with Chelsea, but it was not a fourth consecutive win as the Londoners won 4-3, although it was to be a late, late show to spare the holders' blushes. Leicester took the lead after just six minutes when Gareth McAuley converted a chance, but two goals from Frank Lampard in the first half gave the favourites the lead going into the break. DJ Campbell equalised in the 69th minute and, just five minutes later, the Foxes were back in the lead with Carl Cort scoring. Chelsea were once again level with just three minutes remaining when Andriy Shevchenko sent the home fans into a rapture that had more to do with relief than anything else. The match looked like it was going to extra time but in the dying moments Lampard scored to take the ball home and his team into the quarter-finals. Chelsea were now under the stewardship of Avram Grant after the departure of José Mourinho.

The tie of the round saw Chelsea at home to Liverpool in a repeat of the 2005 final with the Blues winning 2-0 – Lampard and Shevchenko once again on the score sheet. Spurs got their third successive 2-0 victory – the difference being that it was done away from White Hart Lane with a Jermain Defoe goal followed up by a second from Steed Malbranque enough to beat Manchester City.

There was yet another north London derby in the semi-finals with Arsenal taking on Spurs, and while Chelsea hosted Everton. Arsenal and Spurs carried out a 1-1 draw at the Emirates with Theo Walcott cancelling out an effort from Jermaine Jenas to set up an intriguing second leg at White Hart Lane. Jenas was once more on the mark for Spurs as he made the tie 2-1 in their favour after just three minutes, but by the time that Emmanuel Adebayor had scored for the Gunners, it was just a mere consolation as Spurs had run rampant with three more goals – ex-Gunner Nicklas Bendtner, Robbie Keane and Aaron Lennon inflicting the damage before Malbranque scored to make it 5-1 on the night and 6-2 on aggregate.

It was a closer affair between Chelsea and Everton, although it was two victories for the London Blues. Goals from Shaun Wright-Phillips and an own goal from Joleon Lescott were enough for Chelsea to win the first leg 2-1 with Everton on the score sheet courtesy of their Nigerian striker, Yakubu. Chelsea then won 1-0 at Goodison to go through 3-1 over the two legs, Joe Cole on target in the 69th minute.

The first final back at the newly revamped Wembley Stadium took place on 24 February 2008. Chelsea took the lead just six minutes before the break and it was attributable to another goalkeeping mistake, Didier Drogba hitting a 20-yard free kick into the net with Paul Robinson badly out of position.

Spurs could have taken the lead before going one down when Pascal Chimbonda hit the bar, much to the relief of the Chelsea defence, but there was no relief in the 70th minute when they did. Chelsea left-back Wayne Bridge handled in the box and Dimitar Berbatov coolly converted the resulting penalty.

Just nine years previously at the old Wembley, Spurs had won the competition with a goal in the dying moments of the final, and history repeated itself as they beat the hot favourites with Jonathan Woodgate winning the match (just like Steffen Freund had done in 1999) after Petr Čech had disastrously punched the ball on to his head from Jenas's free kick deep into stoppage time. This was Tottenham Hotspur's fourth victory in the competition following their wins in 1971, 1973 and 1999 and gave them their first trophy of the new century.

The 2008 success had taken them level with Nottingham Forest and just one behind Aston Villa. The win had come under Juande Ramos. The Spanish manager had taken over in October 2007, making the victory even more remarkable. Although Ramos only lasted 12 months in the hot seat and wasn't without controversy, at least the Spurs fans could seek solace that he hadn't played for and managed Arsenal, just like George Graham had done when they had last won the cup.

Season 2008/09
The Final
1 March 2009
Manchester United 0 Tottenham Hotspur 0
(after extra time)
Manchester United won 4-1 on penalties
Wembley Stadium, London
Attendance: 88,217
Referee: C.J. Foy

Tottenham's defence in the competition began with a long third-round trip to the north-east and a 2-1 victory over Newcastle United with goals from Roman Pavlyuchenko and Jamie O'Hara putting them in control before Michael Owen pulled one back in the dying minutes. Manchester United's campaign started with a 3-1 home victory over Middlesbrough – Cristiano Ronaldo, Ryan Giggs and Nani all on the score sheet for the Red Devils.

The biggest shock of the fourth round came at Stamford Bridge as Chelsea, now under the management of Brazilian World Cup manager Luiz Felipe Scolari, hosted Burnley. Didier Drogba had given Chelsea the lead on 27 minutes before Adi Akinbiyi equalised for Owen Coyle's claret and blue men in the second half. There were no further goals as the match went to penalties with the visitors winning 5-4. There were no such cup upsets for Manchester United or Spurs as United beat Queens Park Rangers 1-0 courtesy of a Carlos Tevez penalty and Spurs saw off Liverpool 4-2 in a thrilling match at White Hart Lane, with braces from Pavlyuchenko and Fraizer Campbell doing the damage while Damien Plessis and Sami Hyypiä replied for Liverpool.

Burnley continued overcoming the odds once more in the quarter-finals with a 2-0 home victory over Arsenal, and Derby County joined them in the semi-final with a 1-0 win at Stoke City. Tottenham overcame a plucky Watford team at Vicarage Road 2-1, where Pavlyuchenko was on the score sheet for the third consecutive round when he converted a penalty on the stroke of half-time to restore parity after Tamás Priskin had given the Hornets the lead. Spurs' passage was assured when Darren Bent scored with just 14 minutes remaining. By far and away the most entertaining game of the round came at Old Trafford as Manchester United entertained Blackburn Rovers and it was one that Carlos Tevez would not forget as he scored four goals in a thrilling 5-3 win, Nani once more on target. Benni McCarthy scored two goals for Rovers and the other was scored by Matt Derbyshire.

The semi-finals paired Spurs with Burnley and Derby against United. It was one foot in the final for Spurs as they beat Burnley 4-1 in the first leg – Michael Dawson, Jamie O'Hara, Pavlyuchenko (keeping up his record of scoring in every round) and a Michael Duff own goal inflicting the damage in the second half. Burnley had taken the lead on 15 minutes when Martin Paterson put the visitors in front. A sellout crowd at Pride Park witnessed the home team winning 1-0 through a goal scored by Kris Commons on the half-hour mark. United were to make amends in the return leg with a 4-2 victory to take the tie 4-3 on aggregate – Nani, John O'Shea, Tevez and Ronaldo all scoring, the Rams' replies coming from a Giles Barnes brace, one of which was from the penalty spot.

The second leg on 21 January 2009 supplied all the drama as Burnley took the game to Spurs and after 90 minutes had reduced their visitors' three-goal lead to nothing, taking the game into extra time which had looked most unlikely at the start. Robbie Blake, Chris McCann and then Jay Rodriguez in the 88th minute sent the home crowd into rapture. Spurs were shell-shocked and the match looked like it was going to be decided by penalties until Roman Pavlyuchenko (who else) and Jermain Defoe in the last minutes broke claret and blue hearts – Spurs winning 6-4 on aggregate, but there is no doubt that Owen Coyle's team won the hearts and minds in the second leg.

The final was played at Wembley on 1 March 2009. United and Spurs had played in great semi-finals where a total of 17 goals had been scored. The punters and fans were confident that the free-scoring would continue as referee Chris Foy blew his whistle to start the match at 3pm. However, at the end of 120 minutes, not a single goal had been scored and with not many chances created either. The previous year's final had seen significant goalkeeping errors that had resulted in goals being scored. This time around it was the heroics of a goalkeeper who had not been a first-choice keeper either that captured the headlines.

United's Ben Foster had been second choice to Edwin van der Sar but was given a Wembley opportunity as manager Sir Alex Ferguson decided to rest his number one with impending games in the FA Cup, Premier League and Champions League coming up. Foster was United's hero with a stunning save from Aaron Lennon in the regular 90 minutes which was the game's only real talking point in terms of excitement, as well as a chance for Ronaldo when his shot hit the upright. Foster then went on to make a crucial save in the shoot-out from Jamie O'Hara as United won 4-1 on penalties. It had been a game of two defences coming out on top and a largely disappointing final for the purists and, indeed, the punters.

Season 2009/10

The Final
28 February 2010
Aston Villa 1 (Milner) Manchester United 2
(Owen, Rooney)
Wembley Stadium, London
Attendance: 88,596
Referee: P. Dowd

A remarkable pattern of play had emerged in the final which had been achieved exactly 20 years previously. Arsenal had won the League Cup in 1987 before losing to Luton Town in 1988. Luton then went on to be runners-up in 1989 to Nottingham Forest who then retained the cup in 1990.

However, 2007 had seen Chelsea win the competition for the second time in the 21st century before succumbing to local rivals Spurs in 2008. Manchester United then beat the holders in 2009 on penalties before retaining in 2010.

The biggest win of the first round was at St James' Park where Exeter faced 1967 champions Queens Park Rangers. The Hoops won 5-0 – Wayne Routledge scoring three of them with support from Alessandro Pellicori and Hogan Ephraim.

The second-round draw saw a rematch of the 1985 final when Norwich City were drawn at home to Sunderland, and another Friendship Trophy match. Revenge was a dish best served cold this time around for the Black Cats as they ran out 4-1 winners. Winning by the same score were Portsmouth against Hereford United and Blackpool versus Wigan Athletic. The biggest victory, though, came at the Keepmoat Stadium as Doncaster hosted Spurs. The away team were looking for a third consecutive final appearance and intentions were clearly stated with a 5-1 victory.

It was déjà vu for Tottenham in the third round as they went on their travels once more and won the match by the same 5-1 scoreline – this time it was Preston North End on the receiving end. A Peter Crouch treble and goals by Jermain Defoe and Robbie Keane made the difference. Aston Villa and Manchester United went through with identical 1-0 home victories – Villa beating

Cardiff City with a goal scored by Gabby Agbonlahor in only the third minute and United progressing with Danny Welbeck's second-half goal against Wolverhampton Wanderers.

When Aston Villa won the 1994 League Cup Final, they had won 4-1 at Sunderland on the way. It was a much closer affair this time around with Villa going through 3-1 on penalties after no goals had been scored in the previous 120 minutes. Manchester United progressed with a 2-0 away win at Barnsley, Welbeck once more on the score sheet with Michael Owen adding the other. There was also a repeat of the 1987 final, not only in terms of the teams playing but also the scoreline as Arsenal beat Liverpool 2-1 at the Emirates – Fran Mérida and Nicklas Bendtner scoring for the Gunners with Emiliano Insúa replying for the Reds.

Manchester United maintained their clean-sheet record into the quarter-finals as they beat Spurs 2-0 at Old Trafford on the first day of December 2009, with a Darron Gibson brace separating the teams. Aston Villa conceded their first goals in the competition but still came away from Fratton Park with a 4-2 victory over Portsmouth in a thrilling match – Emile Heskey, James Milner, Stewart Downing and Ashley Young all on target. A Stiliyan Petrov own goal and a Kanu goal for Portsmouth completed the scoring. Joining Villa and United in the semi-finals were Manchester City, who beat Arsenal 3-0, and Blackburn Rovers, who knocked out Chelsea 4-3 on penalties after a thrilling 3-3 draw that went into extra time.

Blackburn were drawn out of the hat at home to Aston Villa and City faced United in the other first leg. Both were tight affairs, Villa winning 1-0 at Ewood Park with a goal scored by James Milner and City edging out United 2-1 (the Red Devils' first goals conceded in the tournament), Carlos Tevez inflicting damage on his previous employers with a goal in either half with Ryan Giggs on the score sheet for United.

The second leg at Old Trafford was also a very tight affair and looked to be heading into extra time with United winning 2-1. The first half was goalless but the night burst into life in the second period when Paul Scholes and Michael Carrick put United into an overall lead. However, a goal from Tevez put the cat among the pigeons until Wayne Rooney scored the decisive winner deep into stoppage time to put United back into the final 4-3 on aggregate.

The return leg at Villa Park produced one of the most thrilling matches in the competition's history, with ten goals scored and at times having the potential to go either way. Nikola Kalinić had put Rovers ahead on aggregate to shock the Villa team and crowd. However, by half-time, Villa had once again taken control as they pulled the two goals back to lead 3-2 on aggregate – Stephen Warnock and James Milner netting. Villa then took complete command by scoring three more in the opening 17 minutes of the second half. A Steven Nzonzi own goal was followed up with goals by Gabriel Agbonlahor and Emile Heskey. A minute later, back came Rovers with a goal from Martin Olsson. There was to be another twist when Rovers made it 5-4 on the night through their Australian midfielder, Brett Emerson, to set up a frantic finish before Ashley Young scored the tenth goal of the evening to make it 6-4 on the night and 7-4 overall to Villa.

It had been a season of repeat cup finals and the meeting between Aston Villa and Manchester United served to be no different as the teams took to the Wembley field on 28 February 2010. The 1994 final had seen Aston Villa take their fourth League Cup trophy as they beat United 3-1. Now it was the turn of the Red Devils to claim their fourth and also revenge as United won 2-1, although it was not without its controversy.

Villa took the lead after just five minutes when United defender Nemanja Vidić brought down Gabriel Agbonlahor. Referee Phil Dowd immediately pointed to the spot to award a penalty. James Milner converted the spot kick, but the Villa players and the bench clearly felt Dowd should have sent Vidić off after he hauled down Agbonlahor as the young striker closed in on goal, and it had been a last-man situation. The sense of injustice was heightened just seven minutes later when 11-man United equalised through Michael Owen after Richard Dunne had lost possession to Dimitar Berbatov. Owen was soon to pull up with an injury that forced Sir Alex Ferguson to make a change and it was the substitute who scored the winning goal with just 16 minutes remaining, Wayne Rooney rising high to plant a header past Brad Friedel to give United the lead which they held on to despite Heskey going close late on. It had been a disappointing end to the game for Martin O'Neill's charges who had started brightly but faded as United took control and joined Liverpool and Nottingham Forest in defending the League Cup.

6

The 2010s

Season 2010/11
The Final
27 February 2011
Arsenal 1 (Van Persie) Birmingham City 2
(Žigić, Martins)
Wembley Stadium, London
Attendance: 88,851
Referee: M.L. Dean

The first round of the competition had been split into a north and south divide. The biggest shock came at Valley Parade where Bradford City beat Nottingham Forest 2-1 after extra time, despite the two divisions that separated both clubs. Matt Thornhill had put four-time winners Forest one up in the first half before Dave Syers levelled in the 57th minute with James Hanson scoring the winner in the 100th minute.

Birmingham's campaign started with a 3-2 home win against Rochdale, with Gary Jones giving the away team the lead on 26 minutes before the Blues equalised just two minutes later via a James McFadden penalty. The Premier League hosts took control after the break and raced into a 3-1 lead with goals from David Murphy and Matt Derbyshire before Jones pulled one back with his second on the evening to make it a nervy end for Alex McLeish's men.

It was the turn of Milton Keynes Dons to be defeated by Birmingham at St Andrew's in the third round as the Blues ran out 3-1 winners. The game was effectively over after the half-hour mark with the hosts scoring three quick goals. Alexander Hleb opened the scoring after 24 minutes, and the lead was extended in the 26th minute by Nikola Žigić. Craig Gardner bagged the third in the 28th minute, rounding off a six-minute goal blitz, and Aaron Wilbraham scored a consolation with ten minutes to go. The tie of the round came at White Hart Lane where Tottenham were paired with their local rivals Arsenal in a mouthwatering clash. Henri Lansbury put the Gunners into the lead after 15 minutes before Spurs equalised just after half-time through Robbie Keane. There were no more goals as the game went into extra time and where Arsenal really tore into their north London hosts, Samir Nasri converting two penalties in just a matter of minutes in the first period and Andrey Arshavin putting the match to bed at the very end of it to make the scoreline 4-1 to the Gunners.

Birmingham were once more drawn at home in the fourth round and this time it was not such an easy ride. In fact, they were just seconds from going out to a very spirited Brentford team who took a 68th-minute lead through Sam Wood that lasted deep into stoppage time when Birmingham equalised through Kevin Phillips. It was a goal that the Blues barely deserved as the Bees had been much the better team. Birmingham settled the event with a 5-4 penalty shoot-out victory. Arsenal were once again drawn away to a Premier League club, but the geographical travelling could not contrast more than a trip to White Hart Lane (as they had done in the previous round), this time going to Newcastle United. It may have been a much larger round trip for the Gunners, but it didn't stop them scoring four more goals in the process, and bettering their previous result. A Tim Krul own goal just before half-time gave Arsenal a 1-0 lead which, by the end, had been increased to 4-0. Second-half goals by Nicklas Bendtner and a brace from Theo Walcott inflicted a heavy defeat for the Magpies.

All four quarter-finals ended with home victories. West Ham beat Manchester United 4-0 with two goals apiece for Jonathan Spector and Carlton Cole. Ipswich Town saw off West Bromwich Albion 1-0 with a second-half Grant Leadbitter penalty, Arsenal beat Wigan Athletic 2-0 with an own goal from Antolín Alcaraz in the first half and a second-half goal from Nicklas Bendtner enough to see the Gunners through. Birmingham fans had the bragging rights over their Villa counterparts in the last quarter-final, winning 2-1. Seb Larsson put the home side a goal up from the penalty spot in the 12th minute, then it was the turn of Villa's Gabriel Agbonlahor to place the ball into the net on the half-hour mark. There were no more goals scored until the 84th minute when Nikola Žigić bagged the winner on an emotionally charged night in the West Midlands.

West Ham were drawn against Birmingham and Ipswich at home to Arsenal in the semi-final first legs, and both home teams took slender leads into the second matches – West Ham winning 2-1 and the Tractor Boys 1-0. However, those scores were not enough to earn either side a victory as Birmingham and Arsenal overturned the losses – the Blues winning 3-1 and 4-3 on aggregate with second-half goals scored by Lee Bowyer, Roger Johnson and Craig Gardner deep into stoppage time. What made this comeback even more remarkable was that West Ham had taken the lead through another goal from Carlton Cole in the 31st minute and led 3-1 until the hour. Arsenal took care of business by winning 3-0 in the return leg and going through 3-1 on aggregate. Just like Birmingham had done, all three goals came in the last 30 minutes, Nicklas Bendtner, Laurent Koscielny and Cesc Fàbregas scoring them.

The final was played at Wembley on 27 February 2011. Arsenal entered it as firm favourites but nearly found themselves a goal down after just a couple of minutes when Lee Bowyer burst through before being felled by goalkeeper Wojciech Szczęsny. It looked like a certain penalty and a possible red card but Bowyer had been deemed offside, even though the TV cameras suggested he was not. Birmingham took the lead, though, in the 28th minute when a corner was sent into the Arsenal box, where Roger Johnson was the quickest to react, winning the initial header towards goal which was then flicked in off the head of Nikola Žigić and past Szczęsny into the net. The Birmingham fans were in dreamland, but just 11 minutes later Arsenal levelled when Robin van Persie volleyed an Arshavin cross in with his right foot. The rest of the match saw Arsenal dominate, but the Blues' defence stood firm, although both teams had chances to take the lead. The final was heading into extra time when Birmingham's goalkeeper Ben Foster sent a long ball into the Arsenal half. It was flicked on by Žigić and appeared to be heading safely into the hands of Szczęsny. Inexplicably, Koscielny attempted to play the ball and ended up distracting Szczęsny. The ball found its way to the feet of Obafemi Martins, who tapped it into an empty net to send his team-mates and supporters into delight. Martins had signed for Birmingham on loan from Rubin Kazan less than a month before, but this goal cemented his place in Birmingham folklore for eternity.

Season 2011/12
The Final
26 February 2012
Cardiff City 2 (Mason, Turner) Liverpool 2 (Škrtel, Kuyt)
(after extra time)
Liverpool won 3-2 on penalties
Wembley Stadium, London
Attendance: 89,044
Referee: M. Clattenburg

Cardiff City had successfully applied to participate in the Football League in 1920, and it is fair to say that the marker that they put down was noted instantaneously.

They finished as Second Division runners-up on goal average to Birmingham City in their first season and reached the semi-finals of the FA Cup. They took to top-flight football in the same way that they had done in the second tier and a few seasons later they found themselves runners-up to Herbert Chapman's Huddersfield Town. It had come down to the final game of the season, which saw them draw 0-0, with record scorer Len Davies missing a penalty that would have made the Welsh club the champions of England. The following season saw Cardiff reach the FA Cup Final, losing 1-0 to Sheffield United. However, the bridesmaids of football in the 1920s were able to grab the bouquet of flowers in 1927 to win the FA Cup against Arsenal, and be the first team outside of England to win the coveted trophy.

Now they were looking to do the same in the League Cup.

Cardiff's first match of the campaign began in the southern section of the first round away at 1986 winners Oxford United at the Kassam Stadium, the Bluebirds winning 3-1 after extra time with Craig Conway scoring their first goal after just 12 minutes before Oxford's Simon Clist equalised on the half-hour mark. Peter Whittingham and Nathan Jarvis were on target in extra time to send the away fans happy.

The second-round draw pitched Cardiff at home to Huddersfield Town and once again they needed extra time after a last-ditch goal deep into stoppage time. Cardiff found themselves ahead after just 17 minutes of the game with two goals in a minute scored by Gábor Gyepes and Jonathan Parkin. However, three second-half goals for Huddersfield looked to take the Terriers through – two from Jordan Rhodes and one from Danny Ward doing the damage. Cardiff were back in the match in the dying seconds when their Scottish midfielder Don Cowie restored parity. Craig Conway restored Cardiff's lead in the first few minutes of extra time, before Don Cowie scored his second of a pulsating match with just a few minutes remaining, Cardiff winning 5-3.

Liverpool were 2-1 winners at Brighton & Hove Albion with Craig Bellamy and Dirk Kuyt scoring in the third round. It was the third consecutive round where Cardiff participated in extra time as they hosted Leicester City, Cowie scoring his third goal in the competition for Cardiff before Steve Howard equalised in the first half. Leicester took the lead in the 66th minute through Lloyd Dyer before Rudy Gestede took it into extra time with just eight minutes remaining. The game was settled on penalties in favour of the home team. The first 13 kicks were all converted before Leicester's Gélson Fernandes failed to score in sudden death, sending Cardiff through 7-6.

There was no need for extra time and penalties in the fourth round for the Bluebirds as they squeezed past Burnley 1-0 at home, courtesy of a goal scored by Joe Mason. The following evening Liverpool came away with yet another 2-1 victory – this time Stoke City fell victim, Luis Suárez bagging the goals in each half with Kenwyne Jones scoring for the home team.

A similar pattern occurred for both teams in the quarter-finals with Cardiff being drawn at home and Liverpool once again on the road. Kenny Miller and Anthony Gerrard scored for Cardiff as they beat Blackburn Rovers 2-0. Liverpool also qualified for the semi-finals with the same score away at Chelsea – Maxi Rodríguez and Martin Kelly scoring for the team in red, sending the home fans away feeling bluer than they wanted to be.

There would be an all-second-tier clash and an all-Premier League one in the semi-finals, guaranteeing that the final would not be contested by teams in the same division.

Cardiff's first leg was away to Crystal Palace, who had put out the mighty Manchester United at Old Trafford in the previous round, and it was first blood to the Eagles as well, as a single goal from Anthony Gardner gave them a slender 1-0 victory going into the second leg. Once again the tie was settled on penalties, just as Cardiff had required in the third round, putting them into their first ever League Cup Final. Gardner had been the hero for Palace in the first leg but was soon to be a zero as his own goal in just the seventh minute restored parity. There were no further goals in regulation time or extra time, and Cardiff went through 3-1 from the spot – Palace missing three out of the first four.

The other semi-final pitched Liverpool away to Manchester City with the Reds once again victorious on the road in the first leg, earning a 1-0 win thanks to a penalty converted by talisman Steven Gerrard.

It was a much-improved game in the second leg with Manchester City taking the lead just after the half-hour through Nigel de Jong before another penalty had been converted by Gerrard in the 41st minute. There was a similar pattern in the second half with City once again getting back in the tie via Edin Džeko in the 67th minute before Craig Bellamy equalised for the second time just seven minutes later. There were no further goals and Liverpool celebrated a 3-2 aggregate win at the final whistle.

The final was played at Wembley on 26 February 2012. It was the Premier League versus the Championship, red versus blue and, most interestingly, England versus Wales.

Cardiff drew first blood when Joe Mason scored in the first half, slotting the ball home neatly, but Liverpool equalised in the 60th minute through Martin Škrtel. It went to extra time and no further goals were scored until the second period when Dirk Kuyt put the favourites into the lead for the first time. The drama was not over, though, and with minutes remaining, Cardiff equalised to make the score 2-2, courtesy of a corner that was not cleared and then was put away by Ben Turner as he was first to react. The final whistle blew soon afterwards and despite missing their first two penalties, Liverpool won the shoot-out 3-2 and claimed the trophy for a record eighth time.

It had been a valiant campaign for Malky Mackay and his Cardiff team who just fell short of becoming the first team outside of England to lift the trophy.

However, it would not be long before another Welsh team had the chance again to do so.

Season 2012/13
The Final
24 February 2013
Bradford City 0 Swansea City 5 (Dyer 2,
Michu, De Guzmán 2)
Wembley Stadium, London
Attendance: 82,597
Referee: K.A. Friend

This was the first season under new sponsorship as the competition was now under the guidance of one of the USA's largest financial corporations, Capital One.

Bradford City were formed in 1903 and were elected to play in the Second Division immediately. In their fifth season they achieved promotion as champions and they were to stay a top-flight club until the 1922/23 season where they once more represented the second tier. From the 1930s to the early 1980s they played all their football either in the third or fourth tiers. By the latter part of the decade, they were once again in the Second Division, but suffered relegation back to the third tier before gaining promotion back in the 1996/97 season. They were promoted to the promised land of the Premier League in the 1999/2000 campaign and stayed there for two seasons, where they also experienced European football in the Intertoto Cup. They stayed up on the last game of their first season with a 1-0 victory against

Liverpool thanks to David Wetherall scoring the all-important goal. They were the halcyon days for the West Yorkshire club and occurred just 15 years since the fire disaster that took the lives of 56 spectators in 1985 at their home ground, Valley Parade. Bradford once more found themselves slipping back into the fourth tier by the 2007/08 season and this was where they found themselves as their 2012/13 League Cup campaign commenced.

Bradford's journey began away in the northern section of the first round with a trip to Notts County. The only goal came in extra time through James Hanson in front of a crowd of 3,460. The attendance was significantly more by the time that Phil Parkinson's men had played their last match in the League Cup that season. Just a few days after Bradford progressed, the competition experienced its first great game when Derby County welcomed Scunthorpe United to Pride Park. Derby were three up at half-time and coasting to victory. The Rams were able to add two more in the second half; however, Scunthorpe scored five themselves during this period with the final two being scored in injury time. A wonderful and wacky match was decided on penalties with the away team winning 7-6. The Derby scorers were Richard Keogh, Jake Buxton (two), Theo Robinson and Nathan Tyson, while Scunthorpe's goals were split between Andy Barcham, Mike Grella, Bobby Grant (two) and Connor Jennings.

Bradford's reward was another away trip in the second round, this time to Vicarage Road, the home of Watford. The Bantams were once again the underdogs against their second-tier opposition. The game remained goalless until the 71st minute when it looked like everything was going to plan as Watford took the lead through Ikechi Anya. However, Bradford had other ideas and equalised with just six minutes remaining through Kyel Reid. The game was petering out but deep into stoppage time, Bradford's Garry Thompson bagged what looked like an unlikely winner just moments before.

Swansea City got off to a good start in the competition in the second round as they hosted Barnsley, winning 3-1 to ensure no cup upset for them as they had suffered in the previous season. Danny Graham and a brace from Luke Moore settled matters, although Barnsley did pull a goal back in the 69th minute through Bobby Hassell.

There was an all-fourth tier clash in the third round guaranteeing a representative in the fourth round at least when Bradford were finally awarded a home tie, against Burton Albion. Burton had raced into a two-goal lead in the first half and maintained this position going into the final ten minutes. Nahki Wells then decided to take matters into his own hands as he scored two goals in the 83rd and 90th minutes to hand a reprieve to the home team, and victory was snatched from the jaws of defeat with a winning goal scored by Stephen Darby in extra time. Swansea had been drawn away to League One outfit Crawley Town. It looked very much like this game would also go to extra time with the score evenly poised at 2-2, Swansea scoring courtesy of Michu and Graham once more with Josh Simpson and Hope Akpan replying for the hosts. However, deep into stoppage time, Garry Monk scored to send the away fans happy and avoid another gruelling half-hour for the team and their manager, Michael Laudrup.

The fourth round of the competition produced some fine matches that have stayed long in the memory of fans who were there. The only game that produced no goals came at the DW Stadium as Premier League Wigan Athletic played host to Bradford. The Bantams were truly seen as very much the underdog as for the first time they were playing a top-flight team. The game went to penalties with the first four being scored to make it 2-2 – David Jones and Ben Watson for the home team with Nathan Doyle and Gary Jones for Bradford. However, two further misses from Wigan with Shaun Maloney and Jordi Gómez guilty of the crime meant that two further conversions from Darby and Alan Connell were enough to provide an upset. Bradford were through to the quarter-finals for the third time in their history.

Swansea continued their fine run in the competition with their best result to date as they defeated holders Liverpool 3-1 at Anfield. Goals from Chico Flores and Nathan Dyer had seemingly put the Swans into the quarter-finals. However, the Reds were not in the mood to give up their trophy and pulled one back through Luis Suárez in the 74th minute to set up a great finale. There was a fourth goal, and it was Swansea who booked their place with a third and decisive strike from Jonathan de Guzmán deep into injury time.

The most mouthwatering tie of the round saw Chelsea paired at home to Manchester United, attracting the biggest crowd of the round, 41,126, and it did not disappoint as the Blues won 5-4 after extra time. However, this was not to see the most goals in a single match of the round. That had taken place the night before when Reading took on Arsenal on 30 October – the Gunners winning 7-5 after extra time. This was the BBC's opening gambit as they reported on the most thrilling of games, although it really doesn't tell the full picture: 'Theo Walcott scored a scintillating hat-trick as Arsenal produced one of the great comebacks to take their place in the last eight of the League Cup. Jason Roberts, a Laurent Koscielny own goal, Mikele Leigertwood and Noel Hunt put Reading 4-0 up after 35 minutes. Walcott found the net before the break and in injury time, while Olivier Giroud and Koscielny also struck. Marouane Chamakh scored in extra time before Pavel Pogrebnyak levelled, but Walcott and Chamakh had the final word.'

Arsenal's 7-5 victory also went into the record books as the most goals scored in one match in the history of the League Cup, and with Chelsea's victory over Manchester United the evening afterwards, both represented cup football at its finest.

Graham Bracey had been a Reading fan since 1954 and recalls the match, 'I had seen some great games at Elm Park. I was the last person ever to walk off the pitch there as I was captain of a team who played in a tournament. But nothing compared to that night at the

Madejski when we played the "Gooners". I went to the match with a work colleague who was a massive Arsenal fan. It was great watching his face every time we scored in that crazy first half, but that goal from Walcott just before the break took the edge off things and I told him that his team would win still. I should have put money on it.'

The competition took a nap for a month or so to catch its breath before the quarter-finals, which took place between 11 and 19 December. It certainly recharged its batteries.

First up was a repeat of the 1975 League Cup Final as Paul Lambert took his Aston Villa side to his old club, Norwich City. Steve Morison gave the home team the lead on 19 minutes, but this was wiped out just two minutes later through Villa's Brett Holman. There were no further goals until the last 11 minutes with three more being recorded, and all Villa – Andreas Weimann scoring two of them before Christian Benteke scored in the last minute as he had done in the previous round to make the score 4-1. On the same evening, Bradford hosted Arsenal. The Bantams had been the underdogs in every round of the competition up to this point, and this was most certainly the case as they took to the pitch to face the might of Arsenal, one of England's and Europe's elite teams, expertly managed by the mercurial Arsène Wenger. The attendance was just short of 24,000 for this eagerly anticipated match, and apart from the vast majority (and townsfolk) in the stadium, no one was giving Bradford any chance of becoming the first team from the fourth tier to make the semi-finals since Wycombe Wanderers did it in the 2006/07 season. However, on just 16 minutes it looked a distinct possibility as Garry Thompson volleyed the hosts ahead from a free kick taken by Gary Jones. This was how it stood until just two minutes from normal time when Thomas Vermaelen headed home a Santi Cazorla cross at the back post much to the relief of the north London establishment. Neither side could take the advantage in extra time and so it went to penalties with successful spot kicks taken by Nathan Doyle, Jones and Alan coupled with unsuccessful ones from Cazorla, Marouane Chamakh and Vermaelen giving the Bantams a famous win that shook the football world to its core.

Joining Bradford and Aston Villa in the semi-finals were Swansea, who defeated Middlesbrough at the Liberty Stadium 1-0 aided by an own goal scored by Seb Hines. The last team through were Chelsea, who once again scored five goals as they had done in the previous round against Manchester United. It was another United in Leeds this round at Elland Road, the Blues winning 5-1. Leeds had taken a half-time lead via Luciano Becchio before being taken apart in the second period with Chelsea having five different scorers to make this a true team effort – Juan Mata, Branislav Ivanović, Victor Moses, Eden Hazard and Fernando Torres completing the rout.

The semi-final draw saw Bradford take on Aston Villa in the first leg at home and Chelsea entertaining Swansea. Both first legs were decisive ones.

Swansea beat Chelsea 2-0 with goals from Michu and Danny Graham, while no fewer than 60 places separated Aston Villa and Bradford as the teams took to the field (it had been 67 when Bradford had defeated Arsenal in the previous round). Once again, the Bantams made the gap look significantly smaller as they took a 19th-minute lead through Nahki Wells. At that point it had been totally against the run of play as goalkeeper Matt Duke produced a string of outstanding saves to keep Villa, and Christian Benteke, at bay. That was the end of the scoring until 13 minutes from the end when defender Rory McArdle doubled Bradford's lead with a powerful header. Bradford had been putting in crosses all match and Villa never looked comfortable dealing with them, so it came as no surprise that a second goal came this way. That sprung Villa into life and they pulled a goal back from Andreas Weimann, with just eight minutes remaining. The home team kept their counsel, and it was no surprise when they once more doubled their lead through Carl McHugh with just two minutes to go.

Swansea had done the damage in the first leg and kept it very tight in the second leg. Chelsea could not breach the white wall and the game finished goalless with the Welsh club reaching Wembley 2-0 on aggregate.

In 1994, Aston Villa overturned a 3-1 deficit to march past Tranmere Rovers and reach that season's final. Now they needed to do the same at Villa Park in the return leg. It looked very much like history was going to repeat itself when Christian Benteke gave them the lead on the night after 24 minutes. The claret and blue onslaught was now expected and sure enough it came. However, no goal was forthcoming and alarm bells began to ring just ten minutes into the second half when Bradford equalised on the night to maintain their two-goal advantage. James Hanson, who previously had been employed as a shelf stacker, flashed a superb header past Shay Given from Gary Jones's corner. There was still plenty of time for the Villa faithful to believe that they could once again turn defeat into victory. What Villa really needed was a quick response, but Bradford stood firm and even had chances to score themselves. A nervy last few minutes of injury time occurred when Weimann pulled a goal back, but it was too little and too late for any further comeback. Despite losing on the night, Bradford had won the tie 4-3 on aggregate. As referee Phil Dowd blew his final whistle there were jubilant scenes in the away end as the Bradford players and management team joined them to celebrate getting to a major final for the first time since 1911, and who could blame them?

Bradford had seen off no less than three Premier League clubs in the shape of Wigan, Arsenal and now Aston Villa. They had to do it once more, this time against Swansea in the final at Wembley on the 24 February 2013.

It was the first time that either team had reached the League Cup Final, so a new name was going to be inscribed on the trophy, and it was the first final between a team from the top division and the bottom.

Rochdale had reached the final in 1962 as a member of the lowest level in professional football, but they had played Norwich who played in the second tier.

Nathan Dyer gave the Swans the lead after just 16 minutes, and it was increased just five minutes before the break when Michu put the ball in the net.

A further three goals were scored by the team in white in the second half. A brace from Jonathan de Guzmán and another from the man of the match Nathan Dyer completed the rout, while Bradford also had goalkeeper Matt Duke sent off. Swansea may have looked on while Cardiff were taking the plaudits the previous season, but they could seek solace that they went one better by lifting the trophy just 12 months on with the promise of European football to follow. They had now become the first non-English team to win the League Cup. It had been a 12-month period for Wales's biggest clubs with plenty of admirers won in both camps.

The final proved a bridge too far for Bradford as they were soundly beaten by a rampant Swansea team who were celebrating their first major trophy, in their centenary season as well. Unfortunately, Bradford saved their worst performance in the competition for the final, in front of 32,000 Bantams who sang their hearts out.

It was the first time that a winning margin of five goals had happened in the final of the competition, and despite being on the receiving end, the Bradford players had done the fans proud and put the club on the map once more. The disappointment of losing the final was not something that Phil Parkinson and his players dwelled on, however, as an amazing season was capped with promotion via the play-offs to enter League One.

Season 2013/14
The Final
2 March 2014
Manchester City 3 (Touré, Nasri, Navas)
Sunderland 1 (Borini)
Wembley Stadium, London
Attendance: 84,637
Referee: M. Atkinson

There was a first-round shock when Middlesbrough took on Accrington Stanley at the Riverside Stadium. The 1998 runners-up and 2004 winners were expected to take care of their fourth-tier opponents with some ease as the players took to the pitch. However, it was Stanley who came away with a 2-1 victory. It had started brightly for the home team as they took the lead after just nine minutes when Lukas Jutkiewicz scored, but a goal from Marcus Carver five minutes before the break brought the visitors back into the game. The winner came in the 81st minute when Piero Mingoia scored the winning goal. Newport County continued flying the flag for the fourth-tier clubs away at second-tier ones, with a 3-1 win at Brighton & Hove Albion, after extra time. In a similar fashion, Brighton took the lead on 18 minutes when Ashley Barnes scored, and the Seagulls maintained this until the 81st minute when Danny Crow levelled matters. It was the same player on the mark just a few minutes into extra time to give County the lead and this was cemented by Conor Washington just before the end of the first period.

However, there was to be no further progression for either Accrington or Newport in the second round. Both teams were awarded with ties against Premier League opposition – County were soundly beaten 3-0 at West Bromwich Albion with Stanley losing 2-0 at home to Cardiff City.

Wigan Athletic had beaten Manchester City in the FA Cup Final just a few months prior to the two teams being drawn to play each other at the Etihad in the third round, where they both entered the competition due to being involved in European matches. City extracted considerable revenge for the FA Cup loss. Edin Džeko had given them a 1-0 lead going into the break with Wigan very much still in the game. Then, four second-half goals put paid to any hopes that Wigan had; a brace from Stevan Jovetić and further goals from Yaya Touré and Jesús Navas completed the 5-0 rout.

Tottenham Hotspur almost enjoyed the same victory but a 4-0 away win at fellow Premier League club Aston Villa was equally as impressive. Jermain Defoe scored two of them deep into stoppage time in both halves, sandwiched between goals by Paulinho and Nacer Chadli. The biggest clash of the third round saw the two giants of north-west football play each other when Manchester United entertained Liverpool on 25 September 2013 at Old Trafford. It was the home team who progressed with a slender 1-0 victory courtesy of a goal scored by Javier Hernández a minute after the restart. It was also significant that this was United's first game in the competition without Sir Alex Ferguson, who had been in charge since 1986, with David Moyes now installed in the hot seat following the great man's retirement.

The first batch of fourth-round ties took place on 29 October, and it was a goal-fest as 23 were scored in just five matches – Manchester United scoring four of them without reply at home to Norwich City, and West Ham and Chelsea both winning 2-0 away from home against Burnley and Arsenal respectively.

A crowd of 17,932 at the King Power Stadium witnessed an entertaining match when Leicester City defeated Fulham 4-3, the winning goal coming in the 89th minute via Lloyd Dyer. Eight goals were shared at St Andrew's when Birmingham City took on Stoke City in an all-Midlands clash – Stoke winning the penalty shoot-out 4-2 after extra time.

The other teams progressing to the quarter-finals were Manchester City, who defeated Newcastle United at St James' Park, 2-0 after a goalless 90 minutes – Álvaro Negredo and Edin Džeko both scoring – while Spurs and Sunderland also went through.

Sunderland, under the guidance of Gus Poyet, saw off the challenge of his former club Chelsea and it was a late, late show as well. Frank Lampard had given Chelsea the lead just after the restart with the Black Cats taking the game into extra time with a goal from Fabio Borini with just minutes to spare. The winner was scored by Ki Sung-yueng with just minutes to spare in extra time, earning a 2-1 success. This was also the only home victory of the quarter-finals as Manchester City knocked out Leicester 3-1, Manchester United also beat Stoke and West Ham were victorious at Tottenham Hotspur.

There had never been a Manchester derby in any major final previously, and hopes were high that this season was the first as City and United were kept apart in the semi-final draw. City were due to take on West Ham in the first leg at home and Sunderland were at home to United. Manchester City had started the campaign at home with a comprehensive victory at home to Wigan and they went one better in the first leg to cement a place in the final without really having to play a second one. Three goals from Álvaro Negredo, two from Edin Džeko and one from Yaya Touré ensured that City fans had the chance to book hotels near Wembley early. The second leg was a mere formality and once again it was City who came out on top, 3-0, to win the tie 9-0 on aggregate – two further goals from Negredo (taking his tally to five in two matches) and an effort from Sergio Agüero completing events. The West Ham players looked shell-shocked after the two matches.

It was a much closer affair between Sunderland and Manchester United as Sunderland won the first leg 2-1. A Ryan Giggs own goal deep into first-half stoppage time separated the teams at the break before United came back to equalise through Nemanja Vidić. Sunderland were back in front in the 65th minute when Borini converted a penalty to give his team a slender 2-1 lead going into the second leg at Old Trafford. A Johnny Evans goal in the 37th minute took the match into extra time at 2-2. It looked very much like Sunderland had taken it when they equalised in the 119th minute to lead 3-2, Phil Bardsley scoring against his former employers. Sunderland fans were dreaming of Wembley once more but, with just seconds remaining, Javier Hernández restored United's lead on the night. Seconds later, the game finished with the match tied at 3-3 and so it was on to penalties to see who would be joining Manchester City. However, it was not to be the Manchester derby that many had predicted as Sunderland won the shoot-out 2-1.

The final was played at Wembley on Sunday, 2 March 2014, and it was the underdogs who drew first blood when Borini continued his fine goalscoring exploits with the opener after just 10 minutes, after he had held off a challenge from City's Vincent Kompany. It could have been 2-0 going into the break when Borini once again broke free, but this time Kompany made amends with a last-ditch tackle to deny the Sunderland player.

Sunderland were to rue this chance in the second half as City scored two quick goals in the space of a minute. Firstly, Yaya Touré curled a beautiful shot into the Sunderland net to equalise and then they went 2-1 up with Samir Nasri firing home.

Sunderland had another great chance in the 90th minute when Steven Fletcher failed to control the ball, and the match ended as a contest just moments later when Jesús Navas finished off a swift City counterattack to make it 3-1. This now meant that City had picked up all the domestic trophies having won the Premier League in 2012 and the FA Cup the previous season. They would add considerably more as the decade progressed.

Susan Chaudhry was in the crowd at Wembley that day, just like she had been at the FA Cup Final against Wigan in the previous season. Susan could feel the wind of change taking place on the blue half of her city, 'I had been supporting City since I was a child. I was too young to remember the glory days of the late '60s and '70s, but I sure do remember the disappointments of the '80s and '90s. I went to a lot of the games that we played in the third tier, and what made it even worse was that United were ruling the world. My husband is a red and he would constantly remind me of where we were compared to his club! As a City fan on the coach to Wembley that day, the defeat to Wigan in the FA Cup Final the year before was still sore. This was another game we should win but it's all about what happens on the day.

'I was sat high up in the cheap seats and the ground was a sea of blue, and one end red and white. The whole place had a friendly feel. Both sets of fans were in great voice. Sunderland started well and deservedly went ahead in less than ten minutes. Two fantastic goals in two minutes in the ten minutes after half-time sealed the deal for City – the first with the best goal I have seen at Wembley, a looping 25-yard shot from Yaya Touré. We all went mad when that went in. It was just such a great goal and so precise and so spectacular it took your breath away. Then a couple of minutes later Sami Nasri had his best moment in a City shirt with another magnificent goal. It completely took the wind out of Sunderland's sails, and they never really recovered. Even though we didn't score the third goal until the 90th minute I knew it was going to be our day.

'My overriding memory was coming out of Wembley and walking down the stairs to our buses and a group of Sunderland fans giving us a round of applause. The respect between those two sets of fans on that day was genuinely warming. It doesn't happen enough.'

Even though this was Manuel Pellegrini's first trophy for Manchester City (he would follow it up with the Premier League title at the end of that season), Susan knew that there was something in the air and that it would be the next appointment that would really take the club forward. She continues the story, 'I had now seen us win every domestic trophy in a few seasons since the takeover. We had appointed a few managers so didn't really have the stability at the top. In 2012 City had brought in a new CEO and director of football who had worked for Barcelona, and all the time Pellegrini was at City there were rumours among the fans that City were putting everything in place for another man to take the helm. That this had ALWAYS been the plan.'

For now, Susan, like a lot of City fans, could relish the day that had seen Manchester City win the League Cup for the first time since 1976. And Sunderland fans had once more shone the light.

What a comeback! Mark Lazarus turns away after scoring the winning goal in the first final held at Wembley in 1967 as QPR beat WBA, 3-2

Third time lucky as Brian Little secures Aston Villa's second League Cup in three years after a mammoth final against Everton that took in two replays in 1977

The Luton Town players parade the cup in front of their jubilant fans after beating Arsenal in 1988

The agony and the ecstasy! Birmingham City players celebrate the winning goal in the 2011 final against Arsenal, whose players can only look on, dejected

Five alive! Robbie Fowler congratulates Steve McManaman after his two wonder goals beat Bolton Wanderers in the 1995 final to give Liverpool a fifth victory in the competition — one more than Aston Villa and Nottingham Forest

Walking up Wembley Way! Fans of both Swansea City and Bradford City make their way together before the 2013 final, Bradford becoming only the second team from tier four to make it to the final after Rochdale in 1962

You saw me sitting alone! Manchester City fans watching Tottenham Hotspur players warming up before the 2021 final. Only a few thousand fans were allowed in from both teams because of the Covid pandemic that had swept throughout the world. City won the game 1-0 equalling Liverpool's haul of four consecutive victories in the competition

41 years apart! – Swindon fan Trevor Byron Jones with his football hero – Don Rogers, in 1969 and 2010

It's come home! – Wolves fan Darren Wootton (left) with the League Cup in 1980 that he was allowed to take home for the night

Potteries proud! – Stoke fan Mark Sutcliffe with some great memories hanging on his wall from 1972

You wear it well! – West Brom fan Cliff Crancher with his 1967 rosette

1977 and all that! – The author (in the middle) with John Deehan (left) who played a major part in the marathon finals for Aston Villa alongside one of the new signings, Jimmy Rimmer (right). The cup was just out of sight and the picture was taken at school in the same year

Just the ticket! Thomas Dunlop's actual ticket from the decisive second-leg final clash in the inaugural final of the competition in 1961

No. 1326
ASTON VILLA FOOTBALL CLUB LIMITED
The Football League Cup Final (2nd Leg)
VILLA PARK . BIRMINGHAM
TUESDAY, 5th SEPTEMBER, 1961
Kick-off 7-15 p.m.
Aston Villa
v.
Rotherham United
RESERVED SEAT
8/6
This Portion to be retained
Secretary
Aston Villa F.C. Ltd.
If postponed, this ticket will be valid for the date on which the match is re-arranged. This ticket is subject to the By-laws and Regulations of the Football Association

Entrance :
TRINITY ROAD
DOOR
D
Row G
Seat No.
39

Just the ticket! P. Morgan's actual ticket from the 1969 final. Complete with the match score scribble!

THE EMPIRE STADIUM — WEMBLEY

THE FOOTBALL LEAGUE

Swindon 3
Arsenal 1.

CUP
FINAL

3 – 1
after extra time

SAT., MARCH 15, 1969

KICK-OFF 3.30 p.m.

YOU ARE ADVISED TO TAKE UP
YOUR POSITION BY 3 p.m.

TURNSTILES

B
ENTRANCE

1131

19

EAST
STANDING
ENCLOSURE

CHAIRMAN:
WEMBLEY STADIUM LTD

STANDING
10/-

TO BE RETAINED   (SEE PLAN AND CONDITIONS ON BACK)

Heading for the cup! Zlatan Ibrahimović scores the winning goal for Manchester United v Southampton in 2017

Season 2014/15

The Final

1 March 2015

Chelsea 2 (Terry, Costa) Tottenham Hotspur 0

Wembley Stadium, London

Attendance: 89,294

Referee: A. Taylor

The tie of the first round undoubtedly took place in the southern section when Dagenham & Redbridge played Brentford. Twelve goals were shared and it was the first time the competition had seen a match finish 6-6. Brentford's Stuart Dallas had put his side two up before the tenth minute had been played. The lead was halved on 17 minutes when George Porter scored but it was once more extended when Nick Proschwitz made it 3-1 to the Bees just after the half-hour. Dagenham were back in it, though, on the stroke of half-time through Ashley Chambers. Andre Boucaud levelled after 55 minutes only to see Brentford regain the lead via Andre Gray with just seven minutes remaining. Then, just as they had done in the first period, Dagenham scored deep into stoppage time through Ashley Hemmings. The drama continued in extra time when Brentford took the lead once more through Montell Moore, before Dagenham responded yet again with a goal scored by Jamie Cureton. The home fans must have thought that they had won it when Hemmings scored his second goal to make it 6-5 in the 113th minute of a pulsating match. However, it was to be decided on penalties after Harlee Dean levelled. The tie was finally settled in a shoot-out which was won 4-2 by Brentford. The 12 goals scored matched the record set in one game that had been held for a couple of seasons when Arsenal beat Reading 7-5.

If a game that finished 6-6 had not been enough to whet the appetite in the first round and become a great talking point, then what happened in the second round at the home of Milton Keynes Dons positively lit up social media on 26 August 2014 when Manchester United, now under the management of Louis van Gaal, came to town.

This was the first time since 1995 that United had appeared in the second round, and by the end of the match the mighty Red Devils could have been forgiven for wishing that they hadn't. A careless mistake from Johnny Evans in the 25th minute allowed Will Grigg to open the scoring for the Dons with the only goal of the half. No one could have predicted what would happen in the second half as the home team ran United ragged with a further three goals to win 4-0. Grigg scored his second in the 63rd minute, chesting the ball past a hapless David de Gea. Two further goals from Benik Afobe completed the rout and shook the football world to its core as a result.

Milton Keynes Dons were not the only third-tier team taking on and defeating top-flight opponents. Leyton Orient beat Aston Villa 1-0 at Villa Park, 24 hours after the Manchester massacre. The shock winning goal came with just three minutes remaining from Romain Vincelot.

The third round saw an amazing game at Anfield between Liverpool and Middlesbrough, which finished

14-13 on penalties in favour of the home team after a 2-2 draw following extra time. Chelsea and Spurs progressed with home victories – Chelsea beating Bolton Wanderers 2-1 at Stamford Bridge and Spurs taking care of Nottingham Forest, 3-1. There was further progression for Milton Keynes Dons as they beat Bradford City 2-0, but it was goodbye to Leyton Orient who went out 1-0 at home to Sheffield United.

It was then the turn of the Dons to fall at the hands of the Blades in the fourth round when United won 2-1 in Milton Keynes. Tottenham continued with a fine 2-0 home win against Brighton & Hove Albion, and Chelsea avoided a potential banana skin with a 2-1 victory at fourth-tier side Shrewsbury Town.

Newcastle United had surprisingly knocked out the holders, Manchester City, in the fourth round on their travels, so another trip away to Tottenham Hotspur in the quarter-final would not have overly bothered them. However, Spurs had other ideas and another successful home win was negotiated with a convincing 4-0 result. Chelsea were victorious on the road once more, winning 3-1 at Derby County.

The semi-finals paired Liverpool at home to Chelsea and Spurs at home to Sheffield United in the first legs, and both were tight affairs. Eden Hazard had given Chelsea a 1-0 first-half lead before Liverpool made it 1-1 via Raheem Sterling. Tottenham kept up their perfect home form in the competition with a 1-0 victory, a penalty converted by Andros Townsend separating the two teams.

Chelsea won their second leg 1-0 with a goal from Branislav Ivanović in extra time to secure a 2-1 aggregate win against Liverpool, while it was late heartbreak for Sheffield United as they took on Spurs in the return leg at Bramall Lane in front of a bumper crowd of 30,000. Christian Eriksen had stretched Spurs' lead with the only goal in the first half but two goals in as many minutes changed the whole trajectory of the tie with just 13 minutes remaining via a brace from United's Ché Adams.

Just as it looked like the match was heading into extra time, Eriksen netted his second to put his team 3-2 ahead and into another Wembley final, a repeat of the 2008 occasion.

Seven years previously, Spurs had run out 2-1 winners. This time, it was Chelsea who took the honours with a 2-0 victory – goals in either half from John Terry and Diego Costa making the difference and José Mourinho's love affair with the League Cup continuing in his second spell in charge of the Blues.

Season 2015/16

The Final
28 February 2016
Liverpool 1 (Coutinho) Manchester City 1 (Fernandinho)
(after extra time)
Manchester City won 3-1 on penalties
Wembley Stadium, London
Attendance: 86,206
Referee: M. Oliver

This was to be the last season that the competition was known as the Football League Cup, with its various sponsorship deals over the years, as from 2016/17 season there was a rebrand and it would be known as the EFL Cup, with the governing body now renamed the English Football League, to be referred to as the EFL.

The first round brought together two of the giant-killing clubs of the previous season when Milton Keynes Dons hosted Leyton Orient. The Dons had put out Manchester United and Leyton Orient had eliminated Aston Villa. It was the Red Devil slayers that came out on top with a 2-1 victory, although it had been mightily close. Orient had taken the lead when Dean Lewington put the ball into his own net after 36 minutes. It was a lead that lasted until the very last moments of the match, when Orient's Mathieu Baudry emulated Lewington by scoring an own goal, and then the Dons scored with just seconds remaining when Carl Baker sealed the win.

The last time that Aston Villa and Birmingham City met in the League Cup had been in the 2010/11 season, but it was Villa's turn to win this time in the third round, with Rudy Gestede scoring the crucial goal on 62 minutes. Given what Milton Keynes Dons had done to Manchester United in the previous season, Southampton could have been forgiven for feeling a little apprehensive of making the trip to Buckinghamshire. However, there was no such worries of any further shocks as the Saints ran out 6-0 winners, Jay Rodriguez, Sadio Mané and Shane Long all netting two goals apiece.

Liverpool survived a scare of their own as they overcame Carlisle United at Anfield on penalties, after a 1-1 draw over 120 minutes – the Reds going through 3-2 on a shoot-out.

It also proved to be a close affair for Liverpool in the fourth round when they edged out newly promoted Bournemouth, 1-0 at Anfield, with Nathaniel Clyne scoring the only goal. There was a straightforward victory for Manchester City as they hosted Crystal Palace, winning 5-1 – Wilfried Bony, Kevin De Bruyne, Kelechi Iheanacho, Yaya Touré and Manu García all on the score sheet.

Sheffield Wednesday had lost to Arsenal in the finals of the League Cup and FA Cup in 1993, so a 3-0 home victory on 27 October was a bit of revenge with Ross Wallace, Lucas João and Sam Hutchinson all scoring.

If Liverpool's route thus far had been one of trepidation, then in the quarter-finals the shackles came off as they travelled down to the south coast and trounced Southampton 6-1, Divock Origi scoring three of them supported by a brace from Daniel Sturridge and another from Jordon Ibe, although it had been future Reds star Sadio Mané who had opened the scoring for the Saints with a goal in the first minute. Manchester City's rich form continued with a 4-1 home victory against Hull City at home. Wilfried Bony had opened the scoring in the 12th minute and it remained 1-0 until the last minutes when four more were added – Kelechi Iheanacho and two from Kevin De Bruyne for Manchester City with Hull's Andrew Robertson scoring a consolation deep into injury time.

The semi-finals paired Stoke City at home to Liverpool and Everton at home to Manchester City. It looked very much like an all-Merseyside final was on the cards after the first legs. Ibe's goal for Liverpool in the first half was enough to give them victory while Everton beat Manchester City 2-1 in a thrilling game at Goodison Park. Ramiro Funes Mori had given the Toffees the lead on the stroke of half-time before City equalised with 14 minutes remaining when Jesús Navas netted. However, just two minutes later Goodison Park once more erupted when Romelu Lukaku gave Everton the lead which they were able to maintain.

Liverpool's route to the final had begun by winning a penalty shoot-out and it was to be this way for them again in the semi-final second leg after Stoke had secured a 1-0 away win after extra time, the only goal scored by Marko Arnautović on the stroke of half-time. The shoot-out was a close affair with both teams matching each other in terms of kicks scored and missed until the second sudden-death one taken by Stoke's Marc Muniesa which was missed – Liverpool winning 6-5.

There was also a close affair at the Etihad. Ross Barkley had doubled Everton's overall advantage when he put his team 1-0 up on the night, and 3-1 overall. However, that lead was decreased once more in the 24th minute when Fernandinho scored for City. Two goals in the last 20 minutes were enough to give City the victory goals required to go through to the final with

De Bruyne and Sergio Agüero on target to ensure their second final appearance in three years, winning 4-3 on aggregate.

The final was played at Wembley on 28 February 2016, and it was a victory to Manchester City in the manner that Liverpool had got through on a couple of previous rounds – on penalties.

It was a case of the old and the new in terms of management on the benches for the clubs on the day. It had been common knowledge that Manuel Pellegrini was vacating the managerial hot seat at City and his faith in keeping his second-choice keeper in goal was justified as Willy Caballero made crucial saves in the shoot-out from Lucas Leiva, Philippe Coutinho and Adam Lallana. City won 3-1 on penalties after successful conversions from Jesús Navas, Sergio Agüero and Yaya Touré.

In regulation play, it had been first blood to the team in sky blue when Fernandinho kept up his fine scoring record in the competition by putting his team in the lead in the 49th minute.

City should really have put the game to bed when former Liverpool player Raheem Sterling missed a couple of great opportunities, which allowed the Reds to capitalise in the 83rd minute when Coutinho scored to level the final at 1-1.

For new Liverpool boss Jürgen Klopp, it had signalled a disappointing start to his first season in charge. It did not last as he went head-to-head in seasons to come with Manchester City's new manager following Pellegrini's exit.

Season 2016/17
The Final
26 February 2017
Manchester United 3 (Ibrahimović 2, Lingard)
Southampton 2 (Gabbiadini 2)
Wembley Stadium, London
Attendance: 85,264
Referee: A.M. Marriner

The campaign took on a whole 'retro' feel in the 2016/17 season as it was the first time since the 1981 final that there was to be no actual sponsorship of the competition, following the withdrawal of Capital One.

The second round saw an amazing penalty shoot-out at Pride Park between Derby County and Carlisle United. Darren Bent had given the Rams the lead on 56 minutes but a last-gasp equaliser from Mike Jones ensured extra time was needed. There were no further goals, Derby winning 14-13 on penalties – both teams taking 16 kicks each and Carlisle's Joe McKee missing his one to ensure the Rams were in the third round on a mammoth night of drama.

Due to European participation, Manchester United and Southampton did not enter the competition until the third round. A Charlie Austin penalty in the 33rd minute and a second-half strike from Jake Hesketh were enough for Southampton to see off the challenge of fellow Premier League team Crystal Palace at St Mary's Stadium. On the same night, United avoided a potential banana skin with a 3-1 victory over Northampton at Sixfields. Michael Carrick gave the Red Devils the lead on 17 minutes. Northampton's hopes of an upset increased when they were awarded a penalty minutes before half-time that was converted by Alex Revell. However, there was to be no romance for the Cobblers as second-half goals from Ander Herrera and a young Marcus Rashford put paid to their hopes.

The Red Devils and the Saints both then recorded 1-0 wins in the fourth round at home and against fellow Premier League opponents. Sunderland were the victims at St Mary's with the only goal scored by Sofiane Boufal. A huge crowd of 74,196 were at Old Trafford with Juan Mata putting United a goal up against local rivals Manchester City in the 54th minute. There were no further goals with the bragging rights firmly on the red side of the city.

The result of the quarter-finals came at the Emirates as Arsenal entertained Southampton with most people's betting slips firmly in favour of the home team. However, it was the south coast side that left with a semi-final berth. It was a convincing performance from the Saints even though the Gunners were under par with a few players missing. Goals from Jordy Clasie and Ryan Bertrand secured victory for a Southampton side which inflicted a first defeat on the Gunners since the opening day of the season. On the same evening, Manchester United also progressed with a convincing 4-1 home victory against West Ham United, who had beaten Chelsea in the previous round. José Mourinho was now in the hot seat at Old Trafford, but he was not there to watch the match from his usual spot in the dugout as he was serving a one-match ban. Nevertheless, he was happy to see a brace each for Zlatan Ibrahimović and Anthony Martial with Ashley Fletcher on target for the East Enders. United and Southampton were joined by Liverpool who saw off the challenge of Leeds United with a 2-0 home victory, two goals from Divock Origi and Ben Woodburn in the last 14 minutes making the difference. Hull City also progressed with a 3-1 penalty shoot-out victory at home to Newcastle after a 1-1 draw after extra time – Mohamed Diamé putting the Magpies ahead in the 98th minute before Robert Snodgrass levelled matters just 60 seconds later.

There was home advantage for United and Southampton in the semi-final first legs, the Red Devils against Hull and the Saints versus Liverpool. Both teams took advantage to build leads that were taken into the second legs. Second-half goals by Juan Mata and Marouane Fellaini without reply gave United a 2-0 victory and Southampton beat Liverpool 1-0 with Nathan Redmond scoring the only goal in the 20th minute. The consensus was that Liverpool were expected to right the wrongs in the first leg, but this was not to be as Southampton reached the EFL Cup Final at Wembley with a fully deserved victory crowned by Shane Long's late winner at Anfield.

Claude Puel's side, defending a 1-0 lead from the first leg, should have put the tie out of Liverpool's reach inside the first 45 minutes but Dušan Tadić's close-range shot was blocked by keeper Loris Karius and captain Steven Davis blazed another great chance wildly over.

Liverpool raised the tempo in front of the Kop in the second half, but Daniel Sturridge wasted their two best chances. Fraser Forster acrobatically hooked an Emre Can shot off the line and the hosts also had a late penalty appeal turned down when substitute Divock Origi tumbled under Jack Stephens's challenge. Southampton broke clear in the closing moments and Long finished convincingly from Josh Sims's pass to send them into their first final in this competition since 1979, winning 2-0 over the two legs.

Hull gave Manchester United a fright in their return leg, leading at half-time by a single goal courtesy of Tom Huddlestone's penalty in the 35th minute to set up an intriguing second half with United 2-1 up on aggregate. In the 66th minute, Hull's dreams were dashed as Paul Pogba equalised on the night to restore United's two-goal advantage. An 85th-minute goal from Oumar Niasse put Hull back in front in the leg but no further goals ensured that United progressed to the final with a 3-2 aggregate win.

It was to be a repeat of the 1976 FA Cup Final when Southampton had shocked United with a 1-0 victory. Could history repeat itself?

Before the final, Southampton fans had gotten themselves in trouble with Royal Mail. They had decreed that red pillar boxes in Hampshire would benefit from a stripe or two of white paint to commemorate the final and Southampton's participation in it. The rationale from certain sections of the fanbase was that if it was good enough for the 2012 London Olympics, then it was good enough for the EFL Cup Final of 2017. Unfortunately, Royal Mail itself did not share the same evaluation, instead likening it to 'vandalism' and immediately restored them to originality.

The FA Cup Final of 1976 had not lived up to expectations as a spectacle but the EFL Cup Final 41 years later most certainly did, and it was not shy of controversy either in the way that it was officiated.

Manolo Gabbiadini thought he had scored the game's first goal but it was controversially disallowed for offside. Southampton were to rue the decision further when Zlatan Ibrahimović opened the scoring in the 19th minute.

Jesse Lingard doubled the lead in the 38th minute and Southampton looked lost. Their heads did not drop, though, and Gabbiadini brought them back into the game on the stroke of half-time to make it 2-1 and somewhat atone for the goal that many believed should have stood earlier.

Amazingly, Southampton were level when Gabbiadini equalised for the Saints when he flicked the ball low into the net with his left foot shortly after half-time. Now it was the time for Southampton to keep up the pressure with Tadić, James Ward-Prowse and Oriol Romeu coming close with shots saved or hitting the post. This came back to haunt Southampton when, with just three minutes remaining, Ibrahimović scored his second with a close-range header to break the Saints' hearts and provide José Mourinho with yet another medal in the competition.

Season 2017/18

The Final

25 February 2018

Arsenal 0 Manchester City 3 (Agüero,
Kompany, D. Silva)

Wembley Stadium, London

Attendance: 85,671

Referee: C.L. Pawson

The lack of sponsorship in the previous season was short-lived as it was announced that the Carabao Dang Energy Drink company would become the latest backer of the competition.

Pep Guardiola's first foray in club management had been with the team that he had played for with distinction and style for well over a decade, Barcelona, firstly in the youth setup before making his first-team debut in 1990. The Spanish playmaker also played for his country as well. Guardiola's playing career later took him to Italy, Qatar and Mexico. His management career echoed his playing one as he took the reins of Barcelona's B team before making the step into full management with the Catalan club in 2008. This is where the world would sit up and take notice as, under his tenure, Barcelona were crowned champions of Europe on two separate occasions after beating Manchester United in both finals. The first one came in the 2008/09 season when Barcelona won the treble of La Liga, Copa del Rey and Champions League, Guardiola becoming the youngest manager to lift the famous European trophy – he was just 37 at the time. Before taking over at Manchester City, Guardiola also managed Bayern Munich. His pedigree was as high as it could be when he arrived in the blue half of Manchester as he put pen to paper on an initial three-year contract in February 2016. Guardiola's credentials when it came to top-flight football could not be questioned and it was easy to understand why City wanted him.

The last time that Bristol City had played any top-flight football themselves had been in the 1979/80 season. Since then, the south-west club nicknamed the Robins had spent time in each of the three divisions below it. As the world waited with bated breath to see what Guardiola was going to do at Manchester City, Bristol City were playing in the Championship and had been since getting promoted as League One champions at the end of the 2014/15 campaign. In the same month that Guardiola signed up, Bristol City were busy obtaining the services of Lee Johnson who became manager in February 2016, the difference being that their appointment was immediate as opposed to Guardiola, who took over at the end of the current season.

Manchester City and Arsenal took their bow in the third round with both winning by slender margins – Arsenal 1-0 at the Emirates against third-tier Doncaster Rovers with Theo Walcott scoring the only goal after 25 minutes, and City 2-1 at fellow Premier League team West Bromwich Albion, Leroy Sané scoring both goals with Claudio Yacob replying for the Baggies.

It was even closer for the pair in the fourth round as their matches went to extra time at the very least. There was a stalemate at the Etihad Stadium where City hosted

Wolverhampton Wanderers with no goals scored in 120 minutes and Guardiola's men winning the shoot-out 4-1, while Arsenal progressed with a 2-1 victory in extra time against a very stern Norwich City team. It looked as if the Championship club would hold on to a 34th-minute lead that had been given to them via Joshua Murphy. However, goals in the 85th and 96th minutes put paid to any such cup shock with both scored by Eddie Nketiah.

All quarter-finals were close affairs with Manchester City once again going through via a penalty shoot-out victory away at Leicester City. Bernardo Silva gave them the lead on 26 minutes, and this lasted deep into injury time when a penalty was converted by Leicester's Jamie Vardy. There were no more goals as the game finished all square. Vardy had been the hero in normal time but his penalty miss, along with Riyad Mahrez's, put the away team through 4-3. Danny Welbeck's goal for Arsenal in the 42nd minute was the difference in their home tie against West Ham United as the north London team once more progressed by a slender margin. The following night saw both hosts progress 2-1 to make up the semi-final numbers. Chelsea beat Bournemouth 2-1 at the Bridge with Willian giving them the lead on 13 minutes, which lasted until the 90th minute when Bournemouth equalised via Dan Gosling. However, any hopes that the Cherries had of taking the game into extra time were dashed just seconds later when Álvaro Morata restored Chelsea's lead and this time they were able to hold on to it. The other game took place at Ashton Gate as Bristol City took on holders Manchester United. The home team's chances were slim according to the bookies and perhaps the rest of the country as the players took to the field. And like the games at Chelsea and Leicester City, the drama went right down to the final seconds. This is how Sky Sports reported on the match: 'Manchester United crashed out of the Carabao Cup in a 2-1 defeat to Bristol City as Korey Smith scored a dramatic stoppage-time winner to send the Championship side into the last four. Despite naming a strong line-up that included Paul Pogba, José Mourinho saw his team fall behind to a spectacular opening goal by Joe Bryan before Zlatan Ibrahimović fired home an equaliser. Substitute Romelu Lukaku had chances to win it for United but with extra time looming, Smith struck the decisive blow with the last kick of the game to land them a semi-final tie with Manchester City.'

United became the fourth top-flight team that had fallen at the hands of Bristol City in the campaign. After disposing of Plymouth Argyle 5-0 in the first round at home, the Robins had beaten Watford 3-2 at Vicarage Road, Stoke City 2-0 at Ashton Gate and then Crystal Palace 4-1, also at home. No one could have begrudged their success and they had earned their semi-final place, where they would play Manchester City over two legs with Chelsea facing Arsenal in the other. Manchester's City would play host to the City of Bristol in the first leg on 9 January 2018. It was a very tight affair with Bristol City taking the lead on the stroke of half-time when they were awarded a penalty which was duly tucked away by Bobby Decordova-Reid. The lead lasted until ten minutes into the second half when Manchester City equalised through their midfield maestro, Kevin De Bruyne. As had been the norm in the last round there was a goal in the closing seconds when Sergio Agüero put the home team in front to take a slender 2-1 advantage back to Ashton Gate. It was all to play for as 'cup fever' gripped Bristol. In the other semi-final, the first leg ended in stalemate at Stamford Bridge where no goals were scored.

Just over 26,000 packed into Ashton Gate with the vast majority baying for Premier League blood for the fifth time where they witnessed a great game that once again saw goals scored at the death. Leroy Sané and Sergio Agüero had seemingly broken Bristol hearts with a goal apiece either side of half-time to give the team from Manchester a 4-1 lead. However, the spirit from Lee Johnson's men once again came to the fore when Marlon Pack gave them some hope in the 64th minute to set up a storming finish. The red onset materialised but they were unable to find the net until deep into stoppage time when defender Aden Flint scored. There were still a couple of minutes to go, but almost immediately Agüero went up the other end to put his team back in the lead, 3-2 on the evening and 5-3 overall. It had been a valiant effort by Bristol City, but Manchester City were just a step too far for the Championship outfit.

Pep Guardiola's first opponents in an English final were Arsenal after they beat Chelsea 2-1 at the Emirates in their second leg. Eden Hazard gave Chelsea the lead on just seven minutes before the Gunners pulled the tie back just five minutes later when Antonio Rüdiger put through his own net. Matters were settled on the hour when Arsenal's Granit Xhaka scored to set up a Manchester v London final which would be played on 25 February 2018.

Goals from Agüero after 18 minutes and Vincent Kompany and David Silva after the break gave City their fifth win in the competition, equalling the haul of Aston Villa and, more importantly, Manchester United.

Guardiola had now collected his first trophy for City, the EFL Cup, just like José Mourinho had done in 2005 when he first came to manage in England. He was the manager that the City fans had waited for.

And just like the Portuguese maestro, this was just the start.

Season 2018/19
The Final
24 February 2019
Chelsea 0 Manchester City 0 (after extra time)
Manchester City won 4-3 on penalties
Wembley Stadium, London
Attendance: 81,775
Referee: J. Moss

There were major changes to the format of the competition announced in June 2018 after the EFL summer conference in Portugal. The most significant was that extra time was scrapped in favour of going straight to penalties in all rounds except for the final itself. The rationale was that it would reduce 'additional fatigue' issues. The 'ABBA' penalty format, which had been introduced in 2017, was also taken off the menu. The decision to revert to the traditional approach of teams alternating proved to be a popular one among the football purists. Other changes included deleting seedings for the first two rounds but retaining north and south sections for those stages, which had been in place for a couple of seasons. Finally, the Video Assistant Referee (VAR) system was also introduced for ties taking place at Premier League grounds.

Burton Albion were formed in 1950. The Staffordshire club started life playing in the Birmingham & District League, before switching to the Southern League eight years later. During the 1970s they were promoted and faced relegation at regular intervals. The club plied their trade in the Southern League and then the Northern Premier League for the next decade before being promoted to the Football Conference in the 2001/02 season, under the tenure of player-manager Nigel Clough, the son of the legendary Brian Clough. They were promoted to League Two in the 2008/09 season where they spent several seasons before gaining promotion to League One. This was followed up by another promotion to the Championship which they spent a further two seasons playing in, but by the time of the 2018/19 season they were back in League One.

The Brewers were drawn away at Shrewsbury Town in the first round and came away with a 2-1 victory, but it was in the second round where people sat up and took notice of them as they entertained Aston Villa at the

Pirelli Stadium on 28 August. A Liam Boyce goal after 52 minutes earned them a famous victory and a notable scalp for Clough, who was once more at the helm as manager having left in 2009 for Derby County and later led Sheffield United to the League Cup semi-finals in 2015 before returning later that year.

Burton's reward in the third round was home time against another team playing in claret and blue; this time it was Burnley. A Kevin Long goal just before the break gave the visitors the lead. However, two second-half goals from the hero of the last round, Liam Boyce, and Jamie Allen ensured a safe passage to the next round for the home team.

Burton were once again drawn at home in the fourth round and faced another intriguing match against Nottingham Forest, the four-time winners. Clough had played for the East Midlands club under his father before making the switch to Liverpool. Once more, Albion claimed a famous scalp, winning 3-2. The game came to light in the second half and just after the hour Albion found themselves two up, an own goal from Saidy Janko and one scored by Scott Fraser doing the damage. Forest were back in it through Lewis Grabban in the 70th minute before Albion's two-goal lead was maintained in the 82nd minute when Jake Hesketh sent the fans wild. Forest ensured a nervy ending when they pulled a goal back in the 91st minute but Albion held on and now were in the quarter-final draw, which took them to face yet another previous winner, Middlesbrough. The only goal of that game came in the 48th minute and was scored by Hesketh once more. Burton Albion had made it to the semi-finals and could start dreaming of playing at Wembley.

The first semi-final took place on 8 January 2019 when Tottenham took on Chelsea at White Hart Lane in the first leg with Spurs taking a slender 1-0 lead thanks to a Harry Kane penalty in the 26th minute. It was all to play for in the second leg.

In complete contrast was the other semi-final, the first leg of which took place a day later when Manchester City hosted Burton Albion. West Ham may have been forgiven for thinking that their 8-0 victory in a previous round was the biggest winning margin in the competition during the season, but City had other ideas as they won 9-0 – Gabriel Jesus scoring four with the others shared between Kevin De Bruyne, Oleksandr Zinchenko, Phil Foden, Kyle Walker and Riyad Mahrez. It may have been a scourging of the highest order, but Pep Guardiola had paid Burton respect by fielding a very strong starting line-up. The return leg was devoid of any serious action except for a goal for Sergio Agüero just before the half-hour mark. The 10-0 semi-final aggregate win set a new record for the biggest margin, overtaking City's own score from a few seasons earlier when they had defeated West Ham 9-0.

The second leg between Chelsea and Spurs did not set any scoring records but was still a fascinating match with Chelsea racing into a two-goal lead in the first half through N'Golo Kanté and Eden Hazard. However, a second-half goal from Fernando Llorente meant that the tie was decided by penalties, which Chelsea won 4-2.

The final took place on 24 February 2019. Manchester City had beaten Chelsea 6-0 in the league just a few weeks before and the Londoners, now being managed by Maurizio Sarri, had a game plan to stifle City's play which worked during a 90 minutes where no goals were scored. However, it was an incident that occurred in the closing minutes of extra time that the final will always be remembered for. Kepa Arrizabalaga had been Chelsea's number one choice in goal and indeed had been a record signing for the club as well. Sarri had noticed that his keeper had been struggling with cramp and therefore made the decision to bring on substitute Willy Caballero, who saved three penalties in a shoot-out to help Manchester City win this trophy against Liverpool in 2016. Kepa simply refused to leave the field and the match was held up for several minutes as it became a battle of wits between the manager and his goalkeeper. It ended with Kepa staying on and Sarri storming off down the tunnel.

The BBC reported on those final moments: 'İlkay Gündoğan, Sergio Agüero and Bernardo Silva scored from the spot for City and even though Kepa saved from Leroy Sané, it was to no avail. Jorginho's spot kick was saved by Ederson and David Luiz hit the post as Chelsea were sunk, despite César Azpilicueta, Emerson and Eden Hazard converting their penalties.

'City retained the trophy, but Kepa's insubordination is the headline story.'

It proved to be an ugly end to an ugly final and the match had not lived up to any expectations at all. Sarri had been undermined by one of his players and something had to give. Chelsea went on to win the Europa League under Sarri when they defeated Arsenal 4-1 in the final, but at the end of the season, it was announced that he was heading back to Italy to be closer to his elderly parents and to also manage Juventus. Kepa continued to man the goal for Chelsea.

Season 2019/20

The Final
1 March 2020
Aston Villa 1 (Samatta) Manchester City 2
(Agüero, Rodri)
Wembley Stadium, London
Attendance: 82,145
Referee: L.S. Mason

Bury had been very unlucky to lose a mammoth penalty shoot-out with Nottingham Forest in the previous season's first round, and in this year's northern section matches they found themselves in a precarious position after they could not fulfil their tie against Sheffield Wednesday. The match was eventually awarded to the Owls, following Bury's failure to provide clarity or evidence to the EFL pertaining to their ability to fulfil their financial obligations. Bury were soon expelled from the EFL.

Dean Smith was now the manager of the team that he had supported as a boy, Aston Villa, and they were drawn away at Crewe Alexandra on 27 August 2019. There was no repeat of the shock exit as they had experienced against Burton in the previous season as they trashed the hosts 6-1, with Ezri Konsa, Keinan Davis, Frédéric Guilbert, Jack Grealish and a brace from Conor Hourihane doing the damage. Ryan Wintle scored the consolation for the home team. There was a shock in the southern section when Premier League outfit Crystal Palace hosted Colchester United, who played three divisions below. The game finished goalless with Colchester winning 5-4 in the shoot-out.

The Essex club's reward was a plum home tie with Tottenham Hotspur in the third round, and history repeated itself with United once more winning on penalties after another goalless stalemate, this time 4-3 in the shoot-out.

Manchester United fared slightly better than Spurs when they won a penalty shoot-out against Rochdale after a 1-1 draw at Old Trafford. West Ham United were on the receiving end of a 4-0 defeat at Oxford United with all four goals coming in the second half with Elliott Moore, Matty Taylor, Tarique Fosu and Shandon Baptiste all on the score sheet to provide a memorable night for the home fans at the Kassam Stadium

There were resounding wins for Arsenal, Manchester City, Leicester City, Southampton and Chelsea to restore top-flight superiority. Villa went through to the fourth round with a 3-1 away win against fellow Premier League side Brighton & Hove Albion.

Colchester United were vying to take the romance baton from Burton Albion after their run in the previous campaign and recorded a 3-1 win at Crawley Town in the fourth round. Burton also had the chance to emulate themselves but fell at the fourth-round hurdle, losing 3-1 at home to Leicester City. Aston Villa and Manchester City progressed with home wins against Premier League opposition, Villa beating Wolves 2-1 and City defeating Southampton 3-1.

The tie of the round occurred at Anfield on Wednesday, 30 October 2019. It also proved to be one of the greatest games in the history of the competition, as reported by the BBC on the same evening as Liverpool beat Arsenal on penalties following a 5-5 draw: 'Liverpool beat Arsenal on penalties to secure their place in the quarter-finals of the Carabao Cup after ten goals were scored in a thrilling contest at Anfield. Celebrations broke out in front of the Kop after 20-year-old Liverpool goalkeeper Caoimhín Kelleher saved Dani Ceballos' penalty to set up a 5-4 shoot-out win. Teenager Curtis Jones coolly thumped the final penalty in off the post to make it five from five for the home side. Divock Origi's 94th-minute scissor kick had sent the game to penalties after Liverpool had twice come from behind to draw level.

'Arsenal's Joe Willock thought he had given his side a memorable victory with a sensational long-range strike in the second half but there was more to come on an unforgettable night at Anfield. The Gunners were minutes away from victory after Willock's stunning long-range effort put them 5-4 up, before Origi struck. Liverpool led just once during normal time – after just five minutes, when Shkodran Mustafi slid in and diverted the ball into his own net.'

The issue facing Liverpool now was how could they fulfil their quarter-final with Aston Villa? They had won the previous season's Champions League and were due to play in the Club World Cup in Qatar. The result was that Liverpool fielded a line-up of relative unknowns with under-23 boss Neil Critchley managing the team. It was Liverpool's youngest ever side and Villa took full advantage to progress to the semi-finals with a 5-0 win. Four of the goals were scored in the first half through Conor Hourihane, an own goal from Morgan Boyes and two goals from Jonathan Kodjia. Wesley completed the scoring deep into stoppage time. Joining Villa in the semi-finals were Leicester City, who beat Everton on penalties after a 2-2 draw, and the two Manchester clubs who saw off the hopes of the lower-division teams – City beating Oxford away 3-1 and United winning 3-0 at home to Colchester.

It was an all-Midlands and an all-Manchester affair in the semi-final draw with Leicester taking on Aston Villa and United at home to City.

Once more, City put themselves into a strong first-leg position with a 3-1 win at Old Trafford on 7 January 2020. Bernardo Silva, Riyad Mahrez and an own goal by Andreas Pereira inflicted the first-half damage and even though United pulled a goal back with 20 minutes remaining through Marcus Rashford, it still looked very ominous for the red half of the city. There was only one further goal in the second leg and, to their credit, it was United who won it 1-0 with Nemanja Matić scoring. City held firm to take the tie 3-2 on aggregate and move into their third consecutive final.

The aggregate score of 3-2 also occurred in the other semi-final. Leicester and Villa drew 1-1 at the King Power Stadium with Frédéric Guilbert giving the visitors the lead on 28 minutes, Kelechi Iheanacho cancelling it out in the second half. There followed a similar pattern in the return leg with Iheanacho equalising once more in the second half after Matt Targett had given the hosts a half-time lead. However, a last-minute winner from Villa's Trézéguet ensured victory and with that his club's ninth appearance in the final since 1961.

The final was played on 1 March 2020 and was won once more by Manchester City, who had made it three victories on the trot and were just one behind equalling the record of four set by Liverpool. City dominated the first half an hour and found themselves two up. Young starlet Phil Foden headed a chipped ball from Rodri in the 20th minute across goal into the path of Sergio Agüero for the first goal, the Argentine's shot coming off Tyrone Mings and into the net. Ten minutes later City were two up when they scored from a corner via the head of Rodri. Replays showed that the goal was one of fortune as it appeared that the ball had gone out off a City player and that the corner was wrongly awarded. City continued to dominate, but Villa were back in it just moments from half-time when Mbwana Samatta powered a header home that almost broke the net. There were no further goals in the second half as City won 2-1, although Villa did come close to equalising when Björn Engels had a powerful header pushed on to the post by Claudio Bravo.

The final was to be one of the last major sporting events that took place in England, and indeed elsewhere, for several months as the world found itself in the grip of one of the worst pandemics ever recorded and everything shut down. It took some time to get back to normal.

7

The 2020s

Season 2020/21
The Final
25 April 2021
Manchester City 1 (Laporte) Tottenham Hotspur 0
Wembley Stadium, London
Attendance: 7,773
Referee: P. Tierney

The first case of what was known as COVID-19 (or coronavirus) occurred in China in November 2019. The novel virus was first identified in an outbreak in the Chinese city of Wuhan in December 2019. By the turn of 2020 it had started to spread to other countries and slowly the world started to shut down. The pandemic affected all aspects of everyday life with sport being a large part of it. By the end of May 2020, there were only three top-flight national leagues not suspended due to the pandemic. Bizarrely, these were the Turkmenistan Higher League, Belarusian Premier League and the Liga Primera de Nicaragua.

Despite all league and FA Cup games having to be rescheduled during the 2019/20 season, resulting in matches not being concluded until July 2020, the EFL Cup

– sponsored by Carabao – was still able to start in August 2020, albeit in the latter part of the month. The format remained the same with strict Covid restrictions taking place for players, staff, officials and reporters. The one thing missing was the fans and there was no representation until the actual final itself. Two previous winners of the competition met in the southern section of the first round, when Luton Town hosted Norwich City. It was a memorable game for Luton's James Collins who scored a hat-trick in the final 11 minutes as his team won 3-1.

Aston Villa had the chance to gain revenge in the second round when they were drawn away once more at Burton Albion. Burton had knocked Villa out of the competition just a few seasons earlier, but it wasn't to be the case this time, despite the Brewers taking the lead after just two minutes when Colin Daniel netted. Villa drew level with a few minutes left of first-half action through their new £28m striker, Ollie Watkins. The score stayed at 1-1 until the last few minutes when the Premier League team took control and the match with two sucker-punch goals through Jack Grealish and Keinan Davis. Bournemouth and Crystal Palace could not score against each other in the southern section as the game went to penalties, with the first ten for each side skilfully put away. Both teams missed the 11th before David Brooks converted for Bournemouth and Luka Milivojević missed his, resulting in the south coast club progressing 11-10 overall.

There were emphatic wins for Chelsea and Newcastle in the third round – the London club beating Barnsley

6-0 with Kai Havertz scoring three of them. Newcastle went one better with a 7-0 away win at Morecambe. Liverpool were also in the goals after a 7-2 victory at Lincoln City. Manchester City were aiming for their fourth consecutive final and progressed with a 2-1 home win against Bournemouth. Tottenham were given a bye into the next round. They were due to play Leyton Orient away, but the game had to be postponed due to the number of Orient players who had tested positive for Covid. The tie was due to be rescheduled but just a few days after the original date, Orient confirmed that they could not fulfil the fixture.

Newcastle were once more drawn away to play fourth-tier opposition in the fourth round and survived a mighty scare to go through on penalties. This time they were up against Newport County who took the lead after just five minutes when Tristan Abrahams scored. This lead was held until just three minutes from time when Jonjo Shelvey equalised. The game was then decided on penalties with the Magpies winning it 5-4. Tottenham replicated exactly what Newcastle had done with a 1-1 draw against Chelsea and winning the shoot-out 5-4 themselves. There was excitement when Liverpool were drawn to play Arsenal at home once more. It had only been the previous season when they had drawn the match 5-5 before winning on penalties. That excitement was somewhat cooled as this time around, after a 0-0 draw, it was the Gunners who went through 5-4 in the shoot-out. Manchester United, Manchester City, Everton, Stoke and Brentford all went through to the quarter-finals without the necessity of penalties.

The only team that went through from the quarter-finals after being drawn at home were Brentford, who beat Newcastle 1-0, with Josh Dasilva scoring the only goal. There were away wins for Spurs at Stoke, Manchester City at Arsenal and Manchester United at Everton.

For the first time, the semi-finals were played over just one leg. This was to ease the congestion caused by Covid delaying the start of the season.

Tottenham Hotspur faced Brentford and once more Manchester United faced Manchester City. Both games ended 2-0 with Spurs and City going through to meet in the final. Goals from Moussa Sissoko and Son Heung-min made the difference at the new Tottenham Hotspur Stadium, while John Stones and Fernandinho scored to take City through. It is not often that a manager is relieved of his duties just days before a cup final, but this was exactly what happened to Spurs' José Mourinho, who was vying to win the trophy with his third club. Ryan Mason was given the caretaker role.

The final was played in front of a crowd of just 7,773 socially distanced fans on 25 April 2021. There were 2,000 supporters from each club making up this number, and while it was just a fraction of the normal crowd, it was still a good sight to see and hear fans in the stadium.

The match was settled in the 82nd minute when Aymeric Laporte scored the only goal. A free kick from Kevin De Bruyne on the left was met by Laporte as he rose higher than Sissoko to flick his header on and past Hugo Lloris.

The 1-0 win for Manchester City had equalled Liverpool's four consecutive League Cup wins, which had been set in the early part of the 1980s. The difference being that City had won them all with the same manager in Pep Guardiola and Liverpool had done it with Bob Paisley and Joe Fagan, who had achieved theirs in front of capacity crowds as well.

Season 2021/22

The Final
27 February 2022
Chelsea 0 Liverpool 0 (after extra time)
Liverpool won 11-10 on penalties
Wembley Stadium, London
Attendance: 85,512
Referee: S.B. Attwell

COVID-19 was still playing a part in proceedings, despite the fact that fans were now allowed back into stadiums, when Harrogate Town were due to take on Rochdale in the northern section as Harrogate were unable to fulfil the fixtures with players testing positive. Rochdale were given a bye into the second round.

There were three victorious teams in the second round who enjoyed significant winning margins of 6-0 in their ties. Aston Villa, Arsenal and Norwich saw off Barrow, West Bromwich Albion and Bournemouth respectively. However, it was not to be the biggest winning margin with that award going to Southampton who came away from Newport County with an 8-0 victory. Mohamed Elyounoussi took the match ball home with support from Armando Broja (two goals), Nathan Tella, Kyle Walker-Peters and Nathan Redmond.

Manchester City's first game in the competition came in the third round and once more it looked ominous for the rest when they defeated Wycombe Wanderers 6-1 at the Etihad. It was not the biggest win, though, as Brentford beat Oldham Athletic 7-0 at the Brentford Community Stadium, with Marcus Forss scoring four. Liverpool also got off to a winning start with a 3-0 success at Norwich City thanks to two goals from Takumi Minamino and one by Divock Origi.

Chelsea had knocked out Aston Villa in the third round, 4-3 on penalties after a 1-1 draw at Stamford Bridge, and they won in exactly the same way against Southampton in the fourth round. Kai Havertz had given Chelsea the lead just before half-time with Ché Adams equalising just after the break. The last time that Manchester City had been knocked out of the competition had been at Old Trafford on 26 October 2016 when they had lost to a solitary Juan Mata goal. Five years and one day later, they fell to another United – West Ham. The game finished without any goals being scored before it moved to a penalty shoot-out. West Ham's five penalties were precise and consistent, but by and large City's were the same except for Phil Foden's effort, and the Hammers won 5-3 without the need for City to take their fifth spot kick. Liverpool's run of winning away without conceding a goal continued as they beat Preston North End 2-0 – Minamino and Origi once again on target.

West Ham's reward for knocking out the perennial winners was a short away trip to the previous season's other team in the final, Tottenham Hotspur, in the quarter-finals – the home team winning 2-1 with all three goals scored in the first half. Steven Bergwijn and Lucas Moura scored for Spurs with Jarrod Bowen replying for the Hammers.

Liverpool were drawn at home to Leicester City and produced a remarkable comeback in the 90 minutes before winning 5-4 on penalties. Leicester had raced into a 3-1 lead at half-time with a goal from James Maddison and a double from Jamie Vardy. Liverpool were back in it when Diogo Jota reduced the deficit before Minamino kept up his record of scoring in every round with a last-gasp equaliser. Arsenal were convincing winners, 5-1 at home against Sunderland, and Chelsea overcame Brentford 2-0 away from home.

The semi-final first legs took place on 5 and 13 January 2022. The first match was at Stamford Bridge where Chelsea beat Spurs 2-0, Kai Havertz scoring after just five minutes, with an own goal from Ben Davies stretching the lead on 34.

A week later it was the turn of Liverpool to take on Arsenal at Anfield with it all to play for in the second leg after a goalless draw.

Chelsea and Liverpool won their respective away legs to reach the final, the Blues succeeding 1-0 (and 3-0 overall) with the only goal scored by Antonio Rüdiger. Liverpool progressed with a 2-0 victory over Arsenal – Diogo Jota scoring goals in each half.

The final was played on 27 February 2022. Liverpool were in the hunt for four major trophies, and this was the first one that they took, winning on penalties after a 0-0 draw.

Despite the lack of goals, it had been an entertaining match with Chelsea putting the ball into the net three times and each time they were judged to be offside – Romelu Lukaku's the most contentious, and Mason Mount guilty of missing chances also. It was not all one-way traffic, though, goalkeeper Édouard Mendy producing a string of fine saves to deny the Reds. Liverpool also had the ball in the net, but a chance for Joël Matip was also judged offside.

Kepa Arrizabalaga had been the villain of the piece in the 2019 final when he had refused to be substituted in the dying minutes of the final before penalties, and now irony was in full voice on stage with him now being brought on in Chelsea's goal for the impending spot kicks. It was to have a major impact on the outcome. The decision had been an understandable one by Thomas Tuchel as he had done something similar in the European Super Cup Final at the start of the season against Villarreal, bringing on Kepa for the shoot-out, in which he saved two penalties and the Blues lifted the trophy.

The penalties themselves were as dramatic as the match itself with a total of 22 taken. As the 20th had been successfully converted, it had made the score 10-10.

Each penalty taken from both teams had been scored. It had now come down to goalkeeper v goalkeeper. First up was Kepa who put the ball high and wide to give advantage to the team in red. Now it was the turn of Caoimhín Kelleher to become the taker and he duly slotted the ball into Kepa's goal. The gamble had not paid off for Chelsea and for the second time in three years they had lost the final on penalties.

Jürgen Klopp had now won his first domestic cup competition for Liverpool, following their successes in the Champions League of 2019 and becoming champions of England for the first time in 30 years in 2020. He soon added the FA Cup just a few months later. Again, it was against Chelsea and won on penalties after another 0-0 draw. This was the first time since 1993 that the same two teams contested the League Cup and FA Cup finals, with Arsenal beating Sheffield Wednesday on both occasions back then. Manchester City went on to claim the league title at the expense of Liverpool and the amazing feat of winning the quadruple was also dashed when Real Madrid beat the Anfield giants in the Champions League Final.

It may have been a disappointing end to the season for Liverpool, but their ninth League Cup victory put them out on their own once more and one ahead of Manchester City.

What made this even more remarkable is that it had taken them 21 years to finally win their first trophy, in 1981. Liverpool had certainly made up for lost time since.

Season 2022/23

The Final
26 February 2023
Manchester United 2 (Casemiro, Rashford)
Newcastle United 0
Wembley Stadium, London
Attendance: 87,306
Referee: D. Coote

There was another mammoth penalty shoot-out in the northern section first round when Tranmere travelled to Accrington Stanley on 9 August 2022. The match finished all square at 2-2. Accrington had raced into a two-goal half-time lead through Korede Adedoyin and Ryan Astley before being pegged back in the second half with the goals scored by Josh Hawkes and a last-gasp equaliser own goal from the unfortunate Astley, who had the dubious honour of scoring at both ends. An incredible 13 penalties were taken by both teams with only three missed, Shaun Whalley missing the decisive 13th for Stanley before Hawkes scored to make it 12-11 to send the away fans home happy. The standout result in the southern section came at Whaddon Road, the home of Cheltenham Town, as they entertained Exeter City. Just like at Accrington, it was the away fans who left the happiest.

It was not a mammoth penalty shoot-out either as they thrashed the home team 7-0. A brace from Sam Nombe and one each for Archie Collins, Matt Jay, Jack Sparkes, Harry Kite and Josh Coley made it a very happy journey for Exeter supporters.

Tranmere's reward for their victory was a home tie with Newcastle United. Eddie Howe had been appointed as Newcastle's manager in October 2021 after the Middle Eastern takeover of the club and with the Magpies perilously close to the relegation trapdoor. The momentum with the takeover, coupled with astute new signings and improvements in the squad, had seen them move up the table to finish in a very respectable 11th place. What made this even more remarkable was the fact that Newcastle had not registered a win in any of their first 14 games of the season. It was first blood to Tranmere on 24 August 2022 with a goal scored by Elliott Nevitt in the 21st minute. Parity was secured with five minutes of the first half remaining when Jamaal Lascelles levelled. The tie was settled just seven minutes after the restart when Chris Wood put the Premier League sleeping giants into the third round.

Newcastle's next match in the competition was at home against Premier League opposition in Crystal Palace. The match did not live up to its premier billing with clear-cut chances few and far between with the game scoreless after 120 minutes. It was the turn of Newcastle's shot-stopper, Nick Pope, to be the hero who put his team through to the fourth round, saving from Luka Milivojević, Jean-Philippe Mateta and Malcolm Ebiowei as Newcastle went through 3-2 on penalties. Chris Wood, Kieran Trippier and Joelinton all scored for the home team.

Manchester United's involvement in the competition began in the third round due to having European commitments, and they played host to Steven Gerrard's

Aston Villa. No goals were scored in the first half, but the match certainly came to life in the second period with six goals being recorded. Aston Villa's Ollie Watkins opened the scoring on 48 minutes before United equalised just a minute later through Anthony Martial. Villa were back in front on 61 when United's Portuguese defender Diogo Dalot scored into his own net. The away team's inability to hold on to the lead once more came to bear when Marcus Rashford restored parity. At this stage, the match could have gone either way, but it was United who had the killer edge when they took the lead with just 12 minutes to go, Bruno Fernandes putting his team in front for the first time in a frantic second half before the game was put out of Villa's reach when Scott McTominay stretched the lead in injury time, wrapping up a 4-2 win.

Southampton and Liverpool progressed with victories at home to third-tier teams. However, it certainly wasn't plain sailing as both matches were decided by penalties. Southampton hosted Sheffield Wednesday and went through 6-5 in the shoot-out after a 1-1 draw at St Mary's. Josh Windass had given the Owls the lead on 24 minutes before the Saints equalised on the stroke of half-time via a James Ward-Prowse penalty. Liverpool hosted Derby County and there were no goals scored in 120 minutes, Lewis Dobbin missing the vital fifth penalty for the Rams. There was to be over a month's break in between the third and fourth rounds due to the World Cup finals being held in Qatar in November and December 2022, with Premier League and Championship matches also frozen for the period.

Newcastle and Manchester United were both at home again in the fourth round. An Adam Smith own goal was enough for the Magpies to progress at the expense of Bournemouth, while the Red Devils were 2-0 victors against Championship leaders Burnley. The tie of the round took place on 22 November when Manchester City entertained the holders, Liverpool. Goal machine Erling Haaland gave City the lead on ten minutes before Fábio Carvalho put the Reds back in the game ten minutes later. City were back in front just two minutes into the second half when Riyad Mahrez scored, but just a minute later Liverpool once more picked up the pace and they made it 2-2 via the ever-reliable Mohamed Salah. The currency of the past few seasons for both clubs had been fast-paced, entertaining football that had seen them both neck-and-neck for the league title, and this match was living up to its billing. It was settled in the favour of City when Nathan Aké netted to put his team through 3-2.

Both finalists also had home victories in the quarter-finals. Manchester United played host to Charlton Athletic on 10 January 2023. Charlton had put out Brighton & Hove Albion in the previous round and could not be taken lightly by United, but three goals without reply saw them prosper into the semi-final draw. Brazilian winger Antony opened the scoring after 21 minutes, before two late goals deep into stoppage time from Marcus Rashford put paid to any chance of an upset. Newcastle went through with a 2-0 victory over Leicester City, with Dan Burn and Joelinton scoring in the second half. Joining the two Uniteds in the semi-final were Nottingham Forest, who put fellow Midlanders Wolverhampton Wanderers out on penalties following a 1-1 draw after extra time. Southampton played host to Manchester City who were firm favourites to go through. However, a brilliant display by the Saints saw them win 2-0 with both goals scored in the first half, through Sékou Mara and Moussa Djenepo.

The semi-final draw pitted Nottingham Forest at home to Manchester United in the first leg and Southampton at home to Newcastle. The Red Devils left the opening encounter with practically one foot in the final as they ran out 3-0 winners, Rashford and Wout Weghorst putting the away team two up at half-time. Weghorst had been a United player for just a few days as he was signed on loan from Burnley. United sealed victory in the 89th minute with fans already booking hotels in London when Bruno Fernandes finished proceedings.

It was a much closer affair in the other semi-final as Newcastle ran out 1-0 winners with a goal scored by Joelinton. The advantage was a slim one but certainly gave the Magpies a springboard just a week later at St James' Park, to which they duly capitalised – Sean Longstaff scoring both goals. It was the stuff of dreams for the local hero, who was born in North Shields and had come through the ranks. Ché Adams pulled a goal back for the Saints to set up an intriguing second half, but there were no further goals as Newcastle reached their first Wembley final in 24 years, 3-1 on aggregate.

There was to be no such intrigue at Old Trafford as Manchester United continued where they had left off in Nottingham in the first leg with a further two goals to win the tie 5-0 on aggregate. Second-half goals from Anthony Martial and Fred confirmed those hotel bookings.

This was the first time that two Uniteds had contested the final of the League Cup. The only other time that it had happened in another competition was in the FA Cup of 1999, when the same teams met at Wembley. The stakes could not have been higher this time. Newcastle were looking to pick up their first domestic trophy since 1955; while for Manchester United it had only been a six-year gap, but for a club that had won many trophies in the previous couple of decades it seemed as long.

And just like the last time that both clubs had met in a final, the game ended 2-0 to the Red Devils, with goals coming from Casemiro and Marcus Rashford in a six-minute spell towards the end of the first half. United moved one ahead of Aston Villa and Chelsea, with six wins in the competition.

Season 2023/24

The Final
25 February 2024
Chelsea 0 Liverpool 1 (Van Dijk) (after extra time)
Wembley Stadium, London
Attendance: 88,376
Referee: C. Kavanagh

There was a touch of Hollywood in the first-round southern section, as newly promoted Wrexham took their place back in the EFL Cup for the first time in 16 years when they hosted Wigan Athletic on 8 August 2023. Wrexham, co-owned by actors Ryan Reynolds and Rob McElhenney, progressed to the second round, winning 4-2 on penalties after a goalless 90 minutes. There was a meeting of two previous winners in the northern section when Stoke City took on West Bromwich Albion on the same evening. It was the red and white stripes coming out on top as Stoke went through 2-1.

The second round was notable for having Spurs and Chelsea being in the draw, due to lack of European competitions for both sides. For Spurs, it was the first time since the 2009/10 season and it was a quick exit for them as well as they lost 5-3 on penalties at Fulham, after a 1-1 draw in normal time. Chelsea were drawn to play AFC Wimbledon at Stamford Bridge – the Premier League outfit progressing with a slender 2-1 victory.

Middlesbrough and Leicester enjoyed wins against teams that they had beaten in previous finals – Boro beating Bolton Wanderers 3-1 away, and Leicester also winning on their travels, 2-0 at Tranmere Rovers.

The theme of teams paired together from previous finals continued in the third round with repeats of the 1976 and 1977 finals when Newcastle were drawn at home to Manchester City and Aston Villa hosted Everton. This time, though, Everton and Newcastle progressed – the Toffeemen with a 2-1 win at Villa Park and the Magpies with a 1-0 victory at St James' Park. The tie of the round came at Portman Road as a plucky Ipswich came from two goals down in the first 15 minutes to win 3-2 against Wolverhampton Wanderers. The Premier League team were ahead through efforts from Hwang Hee-chan and Toti Gomes. However, Ipswich were back in the game and level at the break with goals from Omari Hutchinson and Freddie Lapado. A wonder strike from Jack Taylor put the Tractor Boys into the lead in the 58th minute, and also into the fourth-round draw.

There was a repeat of the previous season's final when Manchester United were paired at home to Newcastle United and it was the Magpies who gained revenge with a convincing 3-0 win at Old Trafford – Miguel Almirón, Lewis Hall and Joe Willock all converting.

There were two clubs in the quarter-finals that didn't represent the Premier League, and they were drawn against each other when Port Vale of League One hosted Middlesbrough of the Championship, ensuring at least a semi-final berth for an EFL team. This had been the furthest that Port Vale had been in the history of the competition, but it was the Championship club who ran out worthy winners by scoring three goals before the hour from Johnny Howson, Morgan Rogers and Matt Crooks. The other ties played on 19 December 2023 featured all-Premier League clashes that went to penalties after 1-1 draws in regular time, following late equalisers from the home teams. Newcastle had taken the lead at Chelsea in the 16th minute when a mixture of tenacity and bad defending allowed Callum Wilson to smartly poke the ball home. The lead lasted well into injury time but

Mykhailo Mudryk scored as the home crowd breathed a huge sigh of relief. That relief turned to celebrations in the shoot-out, with Chelsea progressing 4-2.

A Michael Keane own goal had given Fulham the lead at Everton just before half-time. This was eventually wiped out with just seven minutes remaining, Beto heading in from a loose ball. There were 16 penalties taken with only three missed. Unfortunately for Everton, two of them came from their players as Fulham wrapped up a 7-6 win.

There was no such ambiguity in the final all-Premier League clash the following evening, which was once more played in Merseyside as Liverpool hosted West Ham United. Despite being up against one-way traffic and not having any shots on target, the Hammers found themselves just 1-0 down at the break after Dominik Szoboszlai netted. The pattern of play continued in the second half and this time Liverpool made the Londoners pay. Two goals from Curtis Jones and one apiece from Cody Gakpo and Mohamed Salah completed the rout. West Ham's goal in the 77th minute from Jared Bowen was their first shot on target. The two teams had fiercely contested the 1981 final, but the quarter-final tie in 2023 had been completely dominated by Liverpool who registered a total of 29 shots to the visitors' two.

There was a stark contrast in semi-final appearances when Liverpool and Fulham were drawn together with the first leg at Anfield. This was Liverpool's 19th time at this stage of the competition, a record, while Fulham were making their bow. Middlesbrough hosted

Chelsea in their first leg and was a repeat of the 1998 final. Newcastle and Everton had exacted revenge in previous rounds against the teams who had beaten them in the finals. The question was – could Middlesbrough follow suit?

It was home advantages that reaped first-leg leads with Middlesbrough taking a slender 1-0 win against Chelsea at the Riverside, local boy Hayden Hackney coolly converting after 37 minutes. Liverpool came from behind in the other semi-final to register a 2-1 victory over a plucky Fulham side. The London club took the lead on 19 minutes at Anfield through Willian and remained in front until the 68th minute when Jones continued his scoring form with the equaliser before Gakpo turned the match on its head with the winning goal just three minutes later. Fulham were to rue a golden chance just moments before Liverpool got themselves back in the match when Bobby Decordova-Reid failed to convert to put his team two up at a crucial stage.

If Middlesbrough harboured any hopes of exacting revenge for the 1998 final, then they were cruelly taken away in a blistering first half at Stamford Bridge in the return leg, with Chelsea leading 4-0 at the break and virtually ending the match as a contest. Raheem Sterling had a hand in the first three of these and an unfortunate own goal from Johnny Howson started the rout before Enzo Fernández, Axel Disasi and Cole Palmer added to the score sheet. Palmer was back in the goals in the 77th minute before Noni Madueke made it 6-0 moments later. A neat curling shot from Boro's Morgan Rogers with just minutes to go reduced the aggregate score to 6-2 in the favour of the Blues.

Liverpool's route to the final was not as convincing, but a goal from Luis Díaz put the Reds in control as early as the 11th minute at Craven Cottage. A beautiful long diagonal pass from Jarell Quansah found the Colombian who brilliantly trapped the ball with his chest before running into the Fulham penalty area to fire a deflected shot past Bernd Leno. Fulham got themselves back in the tie with just 13 minutes remaining when Issa Diop finished from close range after some nifty footwork from ex-Liverpool player Harry Wilson. There were no further goals, though, with Liverpool marching on with a 3-2 aggregate victory.

It had been a campaign that saw several ties played that had been previous finals in the competition, but it was left to the actual final to highlight the most significant. This was the third time that Chelsea and Liverpool had met in the final, setting a new record in the process, with both teams claiming a victory each.

The final was played on Sunday, 25 February 2024. The first real chance fell to Chelsea in the 20th minute when Cole Palmer's close-range shot was superbly saved by Liverpool's regular League Cup keeper Caoimhín Kelleher. Liverpool were forced into an early substitution when Ryan Gravenberch went off with an injury and was replaced by Joe Gomez. Raheem Sterling had the ball in the net 12 minutes later for Chelsea, but the goal was disallowed by VAR due to an offside in the build-up.

Liverpool's first real chance arrived five minutes before the break when a Cody Gakpo header hit the post. Once again, the teams went into half-time without a goal being scored but the first half had been an eventful affair. It was Liverpool's turn to have a goal chalked off for offside just before the hour when Virgil van Dijk powered a header into the Chelsea net, VAR once again overturning the original decision. It was then Chelsea who hit the post after a beautiful ball from Palmer found Connor Gallagher in the 74th minute but his flick hit the left-side post. Chelsea had their chances to win the match in the last ten minutes of normal time, but for the second consecutive final featuring these teams, the match went into extra time – and without a goal being scored.

Chelsea had finished as the strongest team, but it was the Merseyside club who dictated the play in the first period of extra time with Harvey Elliott coming close with a half-volley. Van Dijk had been unlucky with the goal that was disallowed in the first half of the 90 minutes, but all this changed with three minutes to go of extra time when his header from a corner crossed the line to put Liverpool in front. It was a well-deserved goal and victory for Liverpool as moments later the game ended; the Reds became the first team to reach double figures in the competition when they were crowned winners for a record 10th time.

Epilogue

On 10 August 1999, *The Guardian* published the following story in its sports section. It centred around comments made by Gianluca Vialli. His Chelsea team qualified for the Champions League for the first time in their history as they finished third in the 1998/99 season: 'The League Cup had been won under the sponsorship of the brewing company, Worthington. The 1998/99 season had brought no further silverware for Chelsea, but that third-place finish had brought them new recognition, a newly found respect and meant that Chelsea would be plying their trade among Europe's elite.

'Gianluca Vialli issued a thinly veiled criticism of the Worthington Cup yesterday as his multinational Chelsea team stood on the threshold of playing in Europe's most coveted competition. Vialli did not call for the Worthington Cup to be scrapped and he has previously insisted he will be aiming to win the trophy this season, even if he again fields weakened teams. Chelsea's manager argued, "In England you probably have too many cups with the Champions League as it is now. You have the FA Cup and another cup; what's the point in that? Probably one cup should be more than enough."'

Manchester United's love affair with the League Cup in the 20th century had been hit and miss. They reached the final for the first time in 1983 and won their first trophy in 1992. At the time it had enhanced their reputation as one of England's finest cup teams. They were soon to become champions of England once more and on regular occasions. As a result, the focus for Alex Ferguson and his team was on now becoming European champions via the new UEFA Champions League. Since the European Cup's inception in 1955 the teams that participated in the competition had won their relevant league title. Most seasons saw the winners and runners-up play in nine matches: the preliminary round (later known as first round), the first round (later known as the second round), quarter-finals, semi-finals and the final. These were played on a home and away basis with the final being just one game on neutral territory. Nine became 11 matches in the 1991/92 season. The reason for two more games was that the eight winners in the second round were split into two groups of four with the winners of each group going through to the final. This was exactly the same format for the 1992/93 season when the competition became known as the Champions League. At that time, there was still one team from each country involved. Over the years since, some of the more prominent leagues now have up to four clubs involved, including England.

The revamp of the European Cup into the Champions League brought with it more prestige and greater financial rewards as a result of the prize monies afforded to the winners and best-placed clubs. This was not lost on the people in the Manchester United boardroom and its shareholders. Winning cup finals had saved Alex Ferguson and breathed new life into the club. And now they were winning league titles, so the obvious progression was once more to conquer Europe as they had done in 1968 when they were last crowned champions of the continent. There is no doubt that Ferguson continued to add real quality to his squad, but was this enough to compete for four major trophies in the season?

Perhaps the first signs of the League Cup being sacrificed and not taken as seriously occurred during the 1995/96 season when United played York City in the second round over two legs. The first leg was played at Old Trafford where Ferguson put out a team of relatively unknown youngsters. United lost 3-0, and while they brought back some of the big guns for the second leg, the damage had been done and they crashed out. This in no way diminishes the achievement of York, but one wonders if it would have gone their way with a full-strength United team. The irony being that United were not even in the Champions League that season. However, it shows the start of the upward trajectory of United not fielding strong sides in the competition in the coming seasons where they were involved in the Champions League, as was the case with Arsenal as they started to win major competitions and compete in Europe's premier competition.

Another reason for the decline of the League Cup was its sponsorship deals. The reputations of the companies that did sponsor were indeed robust and reputable ones. How could it not be with one of the world's leading brands in the shape of Coca-Cola? One could argue that it changed hands too often, notwithstanding the shape of the trophy at times. But perhaps a significant downturn occurred when the competition began being sponsored by Worthington and known as the Worthington Cup in 1998. It was cruelly dubbed on the terraces as 'The Worthless Cup'. One can imagine that this 'term of endearment' was also afforded to some within the clubs as well.

It was not uncommon for lower-division clubs who were chasing promotion to even put out weakened teams in the competition, à la Manchester United, Arsenal and others from the top flight. The strangest thing that occurred at the turn of the 21st century was for this to happen to teams who were not in Europe and firmly in mid-table. The financial awards for going from 12th in the Premier League to the higher echelons was greater than the money on offer for winning the League Cup. This may have prompted board members to push this agenda, but it was the opposite on the terraces where fans were often perplexed that a 'golden opportunity' had been missed by their team for a day out at Wembley at the very least, let alone the chance of seeing silverware lifted.

And yet the competition has still provided some memorable matches in the finals, when David has once more come up against Goliath. It still turned up shocks in early rounds and provided cup final sanctuary for the likes of Birmingham City, Wigan Athletic, Swansea City,

Blackburn Rovers, Middlesbrough, Bolton Wanderers and Cardiff City.

Despite the blatant altruistic nature of premium football in the earlier days of the 21st century, the engravers of the League Cup have been busy with prodigious and familiar football institutions.Chelsea, Liverpool, Manchester United and Manchester City have won it on numerous occasions between them. Dynasties were built by the likes of José Mourinho and Pep Guardiola from winning the League Cup.

If the League Cup truly is the 'poor relation' then it resides on a council estate. It's surrounded by burnt-out cars stripped of engines (or the other way round) on either side of it. Yet it ensures that its garden is well kept and pristine. There is always a friendly face that greets you at the door and welcomes you in and there is always milk, tea and coffee.

It may have fallen early on in this new century, but it is not the case any more.

Looking back at the last 64 years that the League Cup has been in existence, it is most evident that its well-trodden road has been anything but linear. It started, it has risen, it has flatlined and it has fallen out of favour.

Yet the future of the competition continues to be open for debate in football's most important corridors. Prior to the 2023 final, talks were ongoing regarding the format as European competitions evolve both in terms of process and finances. This was how Paul MacInnes from *The Guardian* reported the situation on 20 February 2023: 'The future of the League Cup has come into question after changes to European competition meant top sides will soon play more Champions League fixtures in the autumn and winter. The EFL's chair, Rick Parry, says ticket sales and viewing figures prove the Carabao Cup is "immensely popular" and a financial lifeline for the football pyramid. But the structure of the cup remains up for negotiation, he says, if it unblocks talks that were supposed to have been resolved a year ago.

"'Last year [2022/23], we had a record audience for the Carabao Cup, with four million watching the final," Parry said. "This year attendances have been up and are pretty much at record levels. It's a competition that's immensely popular.'"

Rick Parry makes a most salient point about how 'immensely popular' and how important the EFL Cup is for football's pyramid structure in 2024. Alan Hardaker and the Football League would have been very proud of that back in 1960.

The League Cup Finals in Stats and Sponsorship

Finals:

1961 Aston Villa won 3-2 on aggregate
First leg: Rotherham 2 Aston Villa 0
Second leg: Aston Villa 3 Rotherham United 0

1962 Norwich City won 4-0 on aggregate
First leg: Rochdale 0 Norwich City 3
Second leg: Norwich City 1 Rochdale 0

1963 Birmingham City won 3-1 on aggregate
First leg: Birmingham City 3 Aston Villa 1
Second leg: Aston Villa 0 Birmingham City 0

1964 Leicester City won 4-3 on aggregate
First leg: Stoke City 1-1 Leicester City
Second leg: Leicester City 3-2 Stoke City

1965 Chelsea won 3-2 on aggregate
First leg: Chelsea 3-2 Leicester City
Second leg: Leicester City 0-0 Chelsea

1966 West Bromwich Albion won 5-3 on aggregate
First leg: West Ham United 2-1 West Bromwich Albion
Second leg: West Bromwich Albion 4-1 West Ham United

1967 Queens Park Rangers 3 West Bromwich Albion 2

1968 Leeds United 1 Arsenal 0

1969 Swindon Town 3 Arsenal 1 (AET)

1970 Manchester City 2 West Bromwich Albion 1 (AET)

1971 Tottenham Hotspur 2 Aston Villa 0

1972 Stoke City 2 Chelsea 1

1973 Tottenham Hotspur 1 Norwich City 0

1974 Wolverhampton Wanderers 2 Manchester City 1

1975 Aston Villa 1 Norwich City 0

1976 Manchester City 2 Newcastle United 1

1977 Aston Villa 0 Everton 0

1977 replay Aston Villa 1 Everton 1 (AET)

1977 second replay Aston Villa 3 Everton 2 (AET)

1978 Nottingham Forest 0 Liverpool 0 (AET)

1978 replay Nottingham Forest 1 Liverpool 0

1979 Nottingham Forest 3 Southampton 2

1980 Wolverhampton Wanderers 1 Nottingham Forest 0

1981 Liverpool 1 West Ham United 1 (AET)

1981 replay Liverpool 2 West Ham United 1

1982 Liverpool 3 Tottenham Hotspur 1 (AET)

1983 Liverpool 2 Manchester United 1 (AET)

1984 Liverpool 0 Everton 0 (AET)

1984 replay Liverpool 1 Everton 0

1985 Norwich City 1 Sunderland 0

1986 Oxford United 3 Queens Park Rangers 0

1987 Arsenal 2 Liverpool 1

1988 Luton Town 3 Arsenal 2

1989 Nottingham Forest 3 Luton Town 1

1990 Nottingham Forest 1 Oldham Athletic 0

1991 Sheffield Wednesday 1 Manchester United 0

1992 Manchester United 1 Nottingham Forest 0

1993 Arsenal 2 Sheffield Wednesday 1

1994 Aston Villa 3 Manchester United 1
1995 Liverpool 2 Bolton Wanderers 1
1996 Aston Villa 3 Leeds United 0
1997 Leicester City 1 Middlesbrough 1 (AET)
1997 replay Leicester City 1 Middlesbrough 0 (AET)
1998 Chelsea 2 Middlesbrough 0 (AET)
1999 Tottenham Hotspur 1 Leicester City 0
2000 Leicester City 2 Tranmere Rovers 1
2001 Liverpool 1 Birmingham City 1 (AET, Liverpool won 5-4 on penalties)
2002 Blackburn Rovers 2 Tottenham Hotspur 1
2003 Liverpool 2 Manchester United 0
2004 Middlesbrough 2 Bolton Wanderers 1
2005 Chelsea 3 Liverpool 2 (AET)
2006 Manchester United 4 Wigan Athletic 0
2007 Chelsea 2 Arsenal 1
2008 Tottenham Hotspur 2 Chelsea 1
2009 Manchester United 0 Tottenham Hotspur 0 (AET, Manchester United won 4-1 on penalties)
2010 Manchester United 2 Aston Villa 1
2011 Birmingham City 2 Arsenal 1
2012 Liverpool 2 Cardiff City 2 (AET, Liverpool won 3-2 on penalties)
2013 Swansea City 5 Bradford City 0
2014 Manchester City 3 Sunderland 1
2015 Chelsea 2 Tottenham Hotspur 0
2016 Manchester City 1 Liverpool 1 (AET, Manchester City won 3-1 on penalties)
2017 Manchester United 3 Southampton 2
2018 Manchester City 3 Arsenal 0

2019 Manchester City 0 Chelsea 0 (AET, Manchester
   City won 4-3 on penalties)
2020 Manchester City 2 Aston Villa 1
2021 Manchester City 1 Tottenham Hotspur 0
2022 Liverpool 0 Chelsea 0 (AET, Liverpool won 11-10 on
   penalties)
2023 Manchester United 2 Newcastle United 0
2024 Liverpool 1 Chelsea 0 (AET)

Winners by club:

Club	Wins	Years won
Liverpool	10	1981, 1982, 1983, 1984, 1995, 2001, 2003, 2012, 2022, 2024
Manchester City	8	1970, 1976, 2014, 2016, 2018, 2019, 2020, 2021
Manchester United	6	1992, 2006, 2009, 2010, 2017, 2023
Aston Villa	5	1961, 1975, 1977, 1994, 1996
Chelsea	5	1965, 1998, 2005, 2007, 2015
Tottenham Hotspur	4	1971, 1973, 1999, 2008
Nottingham Forest	4	1978, 1979, 1989, 1990
Leicester City	3	1964, 1997, 2000
Arsenal	2	1987, 1993
Norwich City	2	1962, 1985
Birmingham City	2	1963, 2011
Wolverhampton Wanderers	2	1974, 1980
West Bromwich Albion	1	1966
Middlesbrough	1	2004

Queens Park Rangers	1	1967
Leeds United	1	1968
Stoke City	1	1972
Luton Town	1	1988
Sheffield Wednesday	1	1991
Swindon Town	1	1969
Oxford United	1	1986
Blackburn Rovers	1	2002
Swansea City	1	2013

Sponsors:

1960/61 to 1980/81: No sponsor
1981/82 to 1985/86: Milk Marketing Board*
1986/87 to 1989/90: Littlewoods*
1990/91 to 1991/92: Rumbelows
1992/93 to 1997/98: Coca-Cola
1998/99 to 2002/03: Worthington
2003/04 to 2011/12: Carling
2012/13 to 2015/16: Capital One
2016/17: No sponsor
2017/18 to present: Carabao

* The trophy was sponsor-designed and not the original one as used since and before

Acknowledgements

I would like to thank all the ex-footballers and managers who helped me put this book together – their insight has been most valuable. I spent some lovely time with Jane and Don Rogers at his sports shop in Swindon. I also had many hours chewing the fat with Alan Hudson, and Kenny Hibbitt was very helpful with his memoirs from 1974 and 1980. The same can be said for people like Keith Hackett who provided wonderful stories about officiating the 1986 final and the chance meeting at breakfast with the legend that is Sir Stanley Matthews. I loved talking to the fans just as much as well. The stories made me laugh and cry almost at the same time.

My agent, Simon Goodyear, has also played a major part. This is no shock to me as he always does – and he does it with style. Cheers, Si.

To Jane Camillin, who has also been first-class, offering some great advice during the process of writing this book. A big thanks to everyone else at Pitch Publishing as well for welcoming me into the family.

As always I have to thank my family and friends for being there. I love you all.

My first ever Wembley trips were League Cup Finals. It has played a massive part in my football life, and I will always be eternally grateful to Sir Stanley Rous for coming up with the idea and for Alan Hardaker for implementing it. I sincerely hope that they would have approved.

And finally, thank you for taking the time to purchase the book. I do hope you enjoy reading it as much as I did in writing it.

Bibliography

Books:
Goodyear, S., *Memories Made in Aston: A Book for the Fans Written by the Fans* (Derby: DB Publishing, 2013)

Websites:
bbc.co.uk
theguardian.com
enfa.co.uk
theathletic.com
wikipedia.org
premierleague.com
youtube.com
manchestereveningnews.co.uk
fourfourtwo.com
birminghammail.co.uk
dailymail.co.uk
skysports.com
twitter.com
facebook.com
mirror.co.uk
thetimes.co.uk

Podcasts and YouTube channels:
The EFL
Sky Sports Football
Liverpool FC
British Pathé